Historians and Theologians in Dialogue

John Munsey Turner

Church in the Market Place Publications

2011

ISBN 978.1.899147.84.7

The Revd John Munsey Turner was born in Wolverhampton. He read History at St Catharine's College, Cambridge and trained for the Methodist ministry at Didsbury College and Bristol University. Circuit appointments followed in Colchester, Burton upon Trent, Sheffield and Leeds, where he was University Chaplain. From 1970-1981 he was a tutor in Church History at Queen's College, Birmingham before becoming Superintendent Minister at Halifax (1981-1989) and Bolton (1989-1994). From 1994-2005 he was a part-time lecturer at Hartley Victoria College, Manchester. He is the author of several books including:

Conflict and Reconciliation, Studies in Methodism and Ecumenism in England 1740-1982

John Wesley: the Evangelical Revival and The Rise of Methodism in England.

He now lives in Horwich, near Bolton, and continues to exercise his gifts as a writer and preacher.

Drouks
8 april 2013
from Rosemary

Preface

Sir Herbert Butterfield once spoke of a 'bright Empire of the theologians, and the rather more mundane domain of the historians'. This book of recent chapters and articles seeks to make a bridge between these two worlds.

Several very different historians are featured – Sir Herbert himself, Gordon Rupp, the 'guru' of so many. Both these Cambridge professors were very different from the St Catharine's College don who became a monk of the Community of the Resurrection J N Figgis, and his theologian contemporary PT Forsyth. The latter was probably the most significant Free Church theologian of the twentieth century. He certainly strayed into the historians' territory on matters of church and state. Then there is the almost forgotten figure of Henry Bett, at home in Methodism and the Middle Ages, a strange polymath, and, very different again, R F Wearmouth, a product of the Primitive Methodism of the North East.

John Wesley, inevitably, comes into the picture. I seek to analyse the way in which Methodist scholarship on both sides of the Atlantic, has given us a picture, largely free from caricature and mythology, of how 'many Methodisms' have developed. Again, the 'Empires' merge in some of these recent writers such as the late Albert Outler and Professor David Hempton. I hope these chapters will show that church history is very much alive, and as Professor Norman Sykes always asserted is part of the academic study of history rather than dominated by 'the bright Empire'.

The chapters on the Reformation and views of the Middle Ages, I hope, underline this. The life of the Methodist Church in its spirituality and effect on politics is opened up in the last three chapters. I hope they may induce a debate or two.

I am most grateful to the Reverend Robert Davies for publishing this series of articles.

John M Turner March 2010, Bolton

Chapter 1

Salvation and Church History: Insights into the Reformation

A recent ecumenical commission representing Roman Catholics and Anglicans agreed on a definition of salvation. 'The will of God, Father, Son and Holy Spirit, is to reconcile to himself all that he has created and sustains, to set free the creation from its bondage to decay and to draw all humanity into communion with himself... Through Christ's life, death and resurrection the mystery of God's love is revealed, we are saved from the powers of evil, sin and death and we receive a share in the life of God. All this is pure unmerited gift. The Spirit of God is poured into the hearts of believers – the spirit of adoption, who makes us sons and daughters of God.'[1] The Church historian has to ask what difference such an offer has made to people, the glory and the scandal of the institutional Church. He or she, too, can be committed both to the profession of the faith and to the profession of presenting as accurate a picture as possible of its consequences.

Reformation studies have changed a good deal since the notable renaissance of Luther and Calvin studies in the 1930s. 'Perhaps the most striking change of the last twenty years has been the decline of interest in the doctrinal disputes of the sixteenth century.'[2] Clearly we dare not dodge what Professor Kent has called 'the unacceptable face of the Church' that followed the schism in Western Christianity in the sixteenth century (which led to the emergence of the Protestant Churches, beginning with Lutheran and Reformed groups). Nevertheless the analysis of contrasting spiritualities might enable us to explore how we can think of salvation in contemporary terms. An 'ecumenism in time' can be enriching and challenging still.

We are all heirs of both the Middle Ages and the Enlightenment. It is not the case that Martin Luther (1483-1546) was the first of the moderns. We have to take him as he was, a man between God and the devil, as his latest interpreter, the Dutch historian Heiko Oberman, calls him. Nevertheless we can still talk about the Reformation of the Church and new ways of looking at the relationship of God and humanity, even if many of Luther's ideas stem from the thinking of St Augustine, St Bernard of Clairvaux and the so-called 'Via Moderna' of the late Middle Ages, which stressed God as the sovereign, personal God who had revealed and displayed his will to redeem mankind.[3]

Let us go back to the year 1515, to the little town of Wittenberg in Saxony. The young Augustinian friar, Martin Luther, was Professor of Theology at the university. Despite all its faults and the need for 'reform in head and members', medieval Christianity was producing religious renewal again.[4] Luther was desperately concerned about salvation: 'If ever a monk could get into heaven by monkish devotion, then I was that monk.' Penances, fastings, prayers, sacraments – he tried them all, as did many of his generation. For him and others like him, there was a growing level of expectancy and yet no peace of mind. The search for salvation, for rest for his 'bruised conscience', was illusive. His mentor, von Staupitz, pushing back to a medieval and Augustinian tradition of a theology of the cross, bade him begin with atonement, with the 'wounds of Christ'. Here is still a matter where Protestant and Catholic are one. I remember as a sixth former being fascinated by Luther's quest and his exploring of Paul's letters. It was the preaching of the cross in an ordinary Methodist church that enabled me to see the heart of the matter and I recall the Good Friday, after what was a real conversion experience, when the words of Isaac Watts sung in Malvern parish church (shades of Piers the ploughman!) rang in my soul/;

His dying crimson, like a robe
Spreads o'er his body on the tree;
Then I am dead to all the globe
And all the globe is dead to me. (HP 180)

So Luther was able to read the Psalms and the letters of Paul with a new eye.[5] Theologically, instead of beginning with human striving for God, which he perhaps harshly called a 'theology of glory', the 'modern way' which had influenced his early theology, Luther picked up the other end of the stick and began with God's gracious initiative. God comes to us in grace and love, we respond to his gift in trust and faith. This is the 'theology of the cross'. 'I greatly longed to understand Paul's *Letter to the Romans* and nothing stood in the way but that one expression "the justice of God", because I took it to mean that justice, whereby God is just and deals justly in punishing the unjust … I did not love a just and angry God but rather I hated and murmured against him … night and day I pondered until I saw the connection between the justice of God and the statement that "the just shall live by his faith". Then I grasped that the justice of God is that righteousness by which through grace and sheer mercy, God justifies us through faith. Therefore I felt myself to be reborn and to have gone through open doors into paradise.' This so-called 'tower experience'[6] was not sudden like those of Paul on the Damascus Road or John Wesley on 24th May 1738, yet here was a theological revolution which had an impact as great as that of Copernicus or Kepler in astronomy, though much of Luther's thought is found in Augustine[7] (with some profound differences) and elements of it in medieval thought, often as concerned with humankind's justification as he was. This was clearly true of Gabriel Biel and the Augustinian Gregory of Rimini who wrestled with the problem of human free will. Put in simple terms, Luther saw the depths of human degradation, human being 'curved in' on itself. He has no illusion about human pride[8] but he also points to the height and depths of the freedom of the Christian, despite the constant battle with an omnipresent devil, a feature of Luther often forgotten.[9] The Christian is 'always a sinner, always penitent, always put right with God … at the same time right with God and a sinner'. We shall see the drawbacks of this view of salvation later, but its merits are great.

The order of salvation begins with grace – free, undeserved love. Grace is always linked by Luther not with merit of any kind but with faith. Clearly most human relationships are based on merit. Arsenal picks its goalkeeper on merit and he is dropped for lack of it! That is quite proper. Your car breaks down, so you call the AA. The repairer comes, the job is done, and that's that. Again, quite right. Or there's attraction: a man is attracted to a woman because of her appeal to him. The chemistry works. So the world goes round. The relationship of grace is unlike merit or need or appeal in that it is based solely on the outgoing love of God.[10] 'Sinners are lovely because they are loved, they are not loved because they are lovely.' This is the love of the cross. Here for Luther is the very basis of human behaviour. It is an ethic not of law or guilt but an ethic of gratitude. Some modern Protestants find it all hard to realise, as did Luther's contemporaries, but it is surely at the heart of the matter, a key to the scriptures, to our preaching and to our life-style.

If Luther stresses grace – God's freely given love – he also stresses God's gift of faith, of trust. It is a matter of gift and response – 'Gabe und Aufgabe'. 'Faith is a living, daring confidence in God's grace, so sure and certain that one would stake life on it a thousand times. This confidence in God's grace and knowledge of it makes us glad and bold and happy in dealing with God and all his creatures and this is the work of the Holy Spirit in faith. Hence we are ready and glad without compulsion, to do good to everyone, to serve everyone, to suffer everything in love and praise to God who has shown in him this grace.'[11] The thrust is clear. Out of faith comes love. 'Good works do not make a good man but a good man right with God will do good works.' As Oberman puts it, 'Luther horizontalized Christian ethics; he transferred its goal from Heaven to earth. Good works are not required for salvation but crucial for surviving in a threatened world ... the gift of justification releases man from his greed for rewards and enables the believer to be truly pious "for nothing" – not from fear of punishment and Hell but to the greater glory of God and to the benefit of one's neighbour.'[12]

This is that 'faith working through love', being 'Christ to our neighbour', which gave Luther much more of a sense of Christian growth in love than John Wesley or those who still seem to blame him or his followers for Hitler, thought to be the case! Yet Wesley added to Luther. He preached 'love formed by faith', holiness flowing out of justification, for holiness implies accepting sinners with a view to making them saints in the fullest sense of the word. By accepting the Wesleyan insistence on *imparted* as well as the Lutheran stress on *imputed* righteousness we have the bedrock of Protestantism: by grace alone, by faith alone and at the heart of it the love of the cross. 'Love to the loveless shown, That they might lovely be.' (HP 173)

Now we must ask three questions. Is Luther's conception of salvation scriptural? Can it be stated in present-day styles? How does it relate to later Catholic and Protestant thinking? We shall highlight the Council of Trent, John Wesley, John Henry Newman and the ARCIC conversations between Anglicans and Roman Catholics. Recent Pauline studies[13] have rejected the classic

Protestant picture of Judaism as a works-oriented religion to be compared with late medieval spirituality. Paul's concern is not with his 'bruised conscience' or guilt but with how the Gentiles can be part of the people of God. But he also had to wrestle with the Messiahship or blasphemous claim of Jesus and his followers. Crisis enough surely!

John Ziesler has recently shown that Paul propounded his view of justification not only to answer the question, 'How can I find a gracious God?' but to answer the more immediate question, 'How can Jews and Gentiles live together in one community?' Nevertheless Paul's concept implies first the priority of God's vindication of his covenant through Christ and the restoration of relationship with himself. It comes close to forgiveness with which it is indeed equated in Romans 4:6-8.[14] This is not as remote from Luther as E P Sanders and other recent interpreters appear to think when they affirm that Paul did not have the kind of guilt feelings they attribute to Luther.[15] Ziesler also points to the possibility that when Paul uses righteousness in a verbal sense, i.e. to be made right or just, he is talking in terms of relationships and acceptance by God, but when he is talking of righteousness as a noun he is thinking of moral change in the life of the individual person concerned.[16]

Paul certainly uses three images from his age – the Temple and its sacrifices, the slave market and its transactions, the law court and its judgements. Is he saying, 'Look, it's like a slave being set free in the market place. My chains fell off literally – My heart was free!'? Think of a king declaring an amnesty and it is, as Benjamin Drewery puts it, 'the prerogative of a king to declare an amnesty without prejudice to his sovereignty. It is the prerogative of the all-righteous God to restore without prejudice to his awful purity, a lost standing to a corrupt creature.' It is declaring right relationships again. 'The one who is put right by faith shall live.'

If we find Paul a little abstract, look at the story of the waiting father and the two sons (Luke 15:11ff.). The scapegrace son has made a hash of life. He thinks up a speech to persuade his father to take him back as a slave, but his father receives the son, though we might anticipate the problems when they get tired of cold veal! There is forgiveness, so reconciliation can follow. And the elder brother? He had to learn the same truth, that all is of grace not merit; all was his from the start. There is a parallel in Charles Dickens' *David Copperfield*. 'Little Em'ly' has made a ruin of life with Steerforth. Her uncle scours land and sea to find her.[17] When he tracks her down there is forgiveness and freedom, but Rosa Dartle, the frustrated lover, can only shriek, 'Such people should be whipped to death'. Here is the elder sister – and she takes many forms and is frequently a church member!

It is no longer fashionable to point to an 'evangelical succession' of Paul, Augustine, Luther and John Wesley. Their religious pilgrimages were too dissimilar for the conventional statement that each, like Wesley, had to move from the 'faith of a servant' to the 'faith of a son'. Perhaps it is better to see justification as the anticipation of the last judgement. The end has been anticipated now, that is the kingdom of heaven when we are at one with God is not just a matter of new life after death (though it is clearly that) but new life here and now. Again and again the parables of Jesus show it: the Pharisee and the publican (Luke 18:9ff.); the cleansing of the leper (Mark 1:40ff.); the labourers in the vineyard (Matthew 20:1-16); and the two debtors (Luke 7:41ff.).

Can we summarise? We begin with the initiative of God; he takes the initiative in Jesus. 'Him who knew no sin, he made to be sin on our behalf' (2 Corinthians 5:21). If the doctrine of justification represents God as starting with human being as it is, dealing with it as it is, then this is the drive of the ministry of Jesus. Many hated him for it. This is not just acceptance, it leads to change. 'Go and sin no more' were the words to the woman taken in adultery, whom they were about to stone until Jesus said, 'Let him that is without sin cast the first stone' (John 8:1-11 manuscript uncertain). The possible danger in Luther's conception and in modern humanitarianism is to forget the element of moral change.

This initiative of God is seen in terms of grace, which is not some kind of spiritual electricity but love in action. But the grace wants to change humanity; God is not ultimately permissive, so the role of faith is vital. Faith is not far from trust. You trust the maker of a cable car as you swing across an Alpine valley. You must trust folk to mend your car and not make it a death trap. A wife trusts her husband. Faith is not believing 'six impossible things before breakfast' nor is it primarily intellectual assent; it is trust. Christian faith is trusting Christ. 'Faith in the Christian vocabulary means sure trust in God through Jesus Christ – a trust which involves the whole man, because it is a total commitment, the truth enshrined in the phrase, "Justified by grace through faith" may be calamitously misconceived. This happens if faith is thought of as a human achievement by which God's forgiveness and favour are earned.'[18] Justification means being in touch with a personal God in Christ and that relationship means eternal life beginning now. The ultimate comes into the penultimate. The person put right by faith can be a 'Christ to his neighbour'.

What of the argument that the Lutheran interpretation can lead to antinomianism – spiritual anarchy? 'If grace abounds and we are still sinners at the same time, put right *and* a sinner, why bother to be moral? Every crook will argue,' said W H Auden, 'I like committing crimes, God likes forgiving them, really the world is admirably arranged.' *That* argument was, in different forms, flung at Paul, Luther and Wesley alike. Justification by faith undermines morals! The answer is that if a sinner estranged from God can believe that God is for him or her, the battle against sin is half over. This is the psychological value of Luther's doctrine of justification. Maybe John Betjeman has it when he looks into the Bath teashop:[19]

Let us not speak, for the love we bear one another –
Let us hold hands and look.

She, such a very ordinary woman;
He, such a thumping crook;
But both, for a moment, little lower than angels
In the teashop's ingle-nook.

We may recall the story of the Frog Prince or Max Beerbohm's tale of Lord George Hell who had a mask to make him attractive to a woman and then found that her love had transformed his face into a thing of beauty.

Not dissimilar is St Catherine of Siena saying to God, 'I am not worthy' and receiving the answer, 'But I am worthy'. The English poet George Herbert, perhaps unconsciously, is along the same lines:[20]

Love bade me welcome; yet my soul drew back,
Guilt of dust and sin;
But quick-ey'd Love, observing me grow slack
From my first entrance in,
Drew nearer to me, sweetly questioning
If I lack'd anything.

'A guest', I answer'd, 'worthy to be here.'
Love said, 'You shall be he.'
'I the unkind, ungrateful? Ah my dear,
I cannot look on thee.'
Love took my hand and smiling did reply,
'Who made the eyes but I?'

'Truth Lord, but I have marr'd them; let my shame
Go where it doth deserve.'
'And know you not', says Love, 'who bore the blame?'
'My dear, then I will serve.'
'You must sit down', says love, 'and taste my meat.'
So I did sit and eat.

When we see the gracious face of God, the cost of love, we can only wonder. A whole system of ethics and morals can flow from it. If God sets us right, we set others right. If God vindicates us, we vindicate others. Maybe this, after all, is where (despite Sanders) Luther and Paul are at one. In the Epistle to the Romans eleven chapters are about wrath, grace, faith, the place of the Gentiles. Then comes the crucial 'Therefore' – the Christian life-style follows. 'Luther is a reminder to Catholic and Protestant alike that the strength of Christianity is its refusal to turn away from the central and unpalatable facts of human self-destructiveness, that it is there, in the bitterest places of alienation, that the depth and scope of Christ's victory can be tasted and the secret joy which transforms all experience from within can come to birth, the hidden but all-pervading liberation.'[21]

Yet did Lutheranism, rejecting the style of spirituality which suggested that the 'religious' could seek 'counsels of perfection' while common or garden Christians would make do with 'evangelical precepts', tend to produce a religion more for the urban sparrow than for eagles? Later, Pietism, deploring the rather frigid style of the Lutheran state churches, spawned a spirituality of Bible study, small groups, concern for education and mission which also characterised Moravianism and greatly influenced Methodism. Modern styles also take up the old Lutheran emphases. Paul Tillich, a German chaplain in the First World War, who spent most of his academic life in the USA, stresses forgiveness. 'Sometimes at that moment, a wave of light breaks out into our darkness and it is as though a voice were saying, "You are accepted, *you are accepted*, accepted by that which is greater than you and the name of which you do not know. Do not ask for a name now; perhaps you will find it later. Do not try to do anything now; perhaps later you will do much. Do not speak for anything, do not perform anything, do not intend anything. *Simply accept the fact that you are accepted*." ' That is certainly part of the truth though it seems strangely quietist now and exposed to the dangers already indicated, as Tillich's odd lifestyle showed.

Another modern Lutheran was Rudolf Bultmann, the New Testament scholar who was so anxious to preach the cross without the impediments of outmoded world views. Roger Garaudy, a Marxist who espoused Christianity, summarises Bultmann's view of faith. 'Faith frees us by elevating us to the authentic existence by which we love with the freely given love with which God loves us. Man becomes a person by his decision to go out of himself and answer the summons of love served on him by his neighbour.'[22] This is very much Luther's *Freedom of the Christian.* The person 'put right by faith' really lives authentically by giving herself to her neighbours. A final modern example is the late Gonvilleffrench-Beytag, former Dean of Johannesburg.[23] Awaiting trial for opposition to apartheid, he regarded himself as a miracle of grace. 'Salvation I believe is knowing that by myself I am hopeless and helpless and yet if I want to be accepted, God accepts me.' Maybe only in the situation of a man like that does the doctrine which was the foundation of Reformation Christianity come alive again.

A positive aspect of justification by faith is that it can save us from the constant guilt-ridden 'frantic philanthropy' which can be a substitute for genuine gospel. So often Christian thinking about the problems of industry, of economic justice, of racial equality produces only a paralysing sense of guilt or impotence or the blind fanaticism of the crusader who can see no moral issue in the world except the one he or she has chosen to concentrate on. The result is what Luther would have called a preaching of the law. But if we pick up Luther's end of the stick, we begin with people who know only too well their sin and cupidity and the sinfulness of all human institutions, including the Church. Luther's concept of the two kingdoms – the kingdom of God and the earthly kingdom of political reality – can be put in modern terms, as by the English philosopher F H Bradley who wrote of the 'realm of grace' and the realm of 'my station and its duties', which are separate yet intertwined and both under God's sovereignty. The Christian sees no hope of utopia, nor does he or she espouse the false idea that one more little revolution will do the trick and all will be well. How incredible in the 1990s so much of 1970s Christian thought seems! Knowing himself or herself to be a sinner, the Christian goes out as Christ to his or her neighbour with flexibility. Colin Morris, who was a Christian political activist in what is now Zambia and certainly not a Lutheran in his political style, nevertheless expressed the political consequences of the doctrine of justification be faith, which is very much an update of Luther: 'It is justified man that engages in the struggle for justice, it is reconciled man who seeks to end conflict, it is reborn man who works to bring to birth a new society.' The Catholic poet Gerard Manley Hopkins is sometimes strangely Lutheran. He puts the idea of our being Christ to our neighbour, Christ working through us, like this:

…the just man justices;
Keeps grace, that keeps all his goings graces
Acts in God's eye what in God's eye he is –
Christ. For Christ plays in ten thousand places
Lovely in limbs and lovely in eyes not his
To the Father through the features of men's faces.[24]

There is, of course, another side to the whole question, another way of picking up the stick. If Luther's theology stems from Augustine as well as scripture and medieval sources and his own fertile mind, there were other similar yet contradicting elements in Catholic spirituality parallel with and arising out of Luther's challenge which we must not dodge. Protestants too easily conceive the Counter Reformation[25] as a defensive, totalitarian style of religion typified by Cardinal Caraffa and the Inquisition. But here is one of the great positive religious renewals, which was a sign of new life stemming from deep roots. The whole idea of salvation was on the agenda of the Catholic Church. Attempts were made at the mediation with the Protestants at Ratisbon in 1541, when Philip Melanchthon – who was largely responsible for the Confession of Augsburg (1530) – and the Catholic Contarini struggled with a way of stressing growth in grace as well as imputed righteousness, but these ended in failure. This was the last real attempt by Catholic moderates who recognised that the Protestantism represented by Melanchthon was aware of the need to be sanctified as well as to be put right with God. Later, the Council of Trent – not without stormy disagreements – came down on Lutheran views in 1547 with a heavy hand.

Vital definitions were made in sixteen substantial chapters and thirty-three canons. Luther's views appear to be ruled out – that human beings lack free will, that nothing except faith is needed for justification, that a person once justified cannot sin or fall from grace (*Did* Luther say precisely that?), but the positive definition needs careful consideration. The German historian von Pastor called it a 'masterpiece of theology' formulating with clearness of precision the standards of Catholic truth as distinguished from Pelagian error or Protestantism. Von Pastor summarises the canons, 'Starting from the axiom that neither the heathen by their natural powers, nor the Jews by the Mosaic law are capable of participation i.e. of reaching a state of grace and of adoption as children of God, the decree first of all insists that Christ alone is the salvation of the world through the communication of the merits of his sufferings and that only for those who believe in him and have been born again in him by baptism. In adults justification has its beginnings in the calling of God through prevenient grace without any supernatural merit on the part of man. The latter can resist grace or co-operate with it. In both cases there is the exercise of free will but the co-operation is also conditioned by grace.

'With justification man receives not merely the forgiveness of sins but is also inwardly sanctified. This renewal also is not merely imputed as something adhering to man from without, but is a deep inward process fundamentally transforming the soul. Faith, however, is not alone sufficient for justification, it must be accompanied by hope and love and as the Scriptures say faith certainly must work by love since faith without works is dead. Faith working by love in a constant state of grace through the following of the commandments of God and the church results in a continual advance from virtue to virtue. In opposition to the Protestant assertion of an absolute assurance of salvation it was laid down as Catholic doctrine that no one in this life can fathom the secret of predestination by God and apart from a special revelation, know of a certainty that he is of the number of the elect.'[26]

The crucial thirty-three canons and the vital Chapter 7 with its clear-cut Aristotelian argument about the causes of justification may seem poles apart from Luther and even more from John Calvin's order of salvation. In the eighteenth century, John Wesley would shuffle the theological pack of cards again and, while disagreeing with the Council's definition of justification, his stress on sanctification in his theology has always formed a link (often not realised) between Roman Catholicism and Methodism at this point. He separated imputed and imparted righteousness. The letter is not pertinent to being accepted by God. The Tridentine thinking, well styled by H O Evenett as 'activism in grace', is not far from that 'optimism of grace' which characterised Wesley's Methodism. The opportunity for mission, too, coincided with the theology hammered out by Ignatius Loyola and others in the lands across the Atlantic granted by the Pope to Spanish and Portuguese colonisers. What could be more Lutheran or Wesleyan than this hymn?

My God I love thee...

Then why O blessed Jesus Christ
Should I not love thee well?
Not for the sake of winning heaven
Nor of escaping hell;

Not with the hope of gaining aught
Nor seeking a reward

But as thyself hast loved me
O everlasting Lord! (HP 171)

In the 1930s the American scholar George Croft Cell, who explored the Calvinist element in Wesley said, somewhat confusedly, that Wesley provided 'a synthesis of the Protestant ethic of grace with the Catholic ethic of holiness'. Wesley, in fact, was very near to Luther and Calvin[27] in his doctrine of justification, but stresses the growth in grace through the Holy Spirit and the means of grace – Bible, prayer, sacraments and other 'prudential means' like the class meeting – in a way which owed much to both eastern and Catholic sources.[28]

The Church historian dare not dodge or underestimate the fearful harm done to the European Christian tradition by the Wars of Religion.[29] The Church, said Gordon Rupp, lost its hold tragically both on great traditions of letters, science and human thought and also on the search for justice and liberty.
There was ecclesiastical introversion, failure of nerve, failure in compassion. This was the terrible legacy of the European conflicts that followed the Protestant and Catholic Reformations, the most important factor in the making of European unbelief. Here are the roots of the estrangement of masses of modern people from religion. Spirituality became fragmented into the mystics (like William Law), the moralists (like Joseph Butler) and the rationalists in that period of European history which Sir Herbert Butterfield and Paul Hazard saw as so crucial, between Bossuet believing and Voltaire disbelieving. This was the price of division, yet in the eighteenth century renewal and revival characterised both Catholic and Protestants in Europe.[30]

For Luther the home, the school, the workshop were all places where God could be glorified; this was one of Luther's great contributions to Christian thought, a perception of sacredness of all human callings, however humble. 'In the early sixteenth century they were bold and truly epoch making departures. Within them lay ideals of family life and social relations which both attracted and moulded the townsman, the professional people, the lesser landowner, the middle orders who were simultaneously laying hold upon the economic, social and intellectual activities of Europe.'[31] In an age of chronic unemployment it needs drastic reminting.

The renewal of the eighteenth century enabled the new, growing urban or semi-urban populations of Europe to search for and find a religion which could give them vocation, purpose and a stake in a religious society when they had no stake in anything else. Nobodies can become somebodies in God's sight. A way of salvation was offered for ordinary laymen and laywomen. Methodism had great appeal to the artisan and the domestic servant. Pietism, or Evangelicalism, used in the widest sense,[32] always carried the danger – pointed out endlessly by high church Anglican and Catholic critics – of overstressing emotion, but the key features were clearly the centrality of scriptures, the cruciality of the cross (to use P T Forsyth's phrase), conversionism, a belief that lives need to be and can be changed, and activism, the expression of the gospel in action – often enough political action, as with William Wilberforce and the 'Clapham Saints' in their battles for the bodies of slaves as well as their souls. There came into this style of preaching of salvation an 'optimism of grace' which Roger Anstey[33] has shown to be characteristic of the Enlightenment and which had a great indirect influence on Evangelicalism. John Wesley's 'Arminianism of the heart' fits in at this point. While solidly reformed in his doctrine of justification, as we have seen, he insisted on the centrality of the new birth, the assurance of that adoption and, in more Catholic vein, the transformation by grace of the reborn sinner. His brother's hymns at times suggest that 'theosis' or deification which is much more characteristic of orthodoxy.

Made perfect first in love
And sanctified by grace,
We shall from earth remove
And see his glorious face;
His love shall then be fully showed
And man shall all be lost in God. (HP 109)

One of the subsequent tragedies of Church history is the way in which the Wesleyan theology and the theology of the Oxford Movement in the Church of England never really entered into any meaningful dialogue.[34] Newman (who began as an Anglo-Calvinist) and Pusey tended to see Methodism as a sub-species of revivalism, yet in fact Newman's *Lectures on Justification* (1838),[35] written before his break with Anglicanism, are nearer to the Wesleyan emphasis than meets the eye. Unfortunately Newman has the limitation, typical of many Anglicans of his day, of ignorance of Luther in the original. He shares this with the fathers of the Council of Trent and he assumes the very scholastic arguments about cause and effect in the statement about grace in the definitions of that Council. This makes his argument at times very difficult to grasp. But on the main issue Newman is quite clear. 'Christ is acknowledged on all hands to be the sole meritorious cause of our justification … all of us are dependent on the uncovenanted mercies of God.' He combines what Luther would have called justification with what Wesley called sanctification with a subtle doctrine of the Holy Spirit as the link. 'Justification comes *through* the sacraments, is received *by* faith, *consists* in God's inward presence and *lives* in obedience.' On justification all agreed on its meritorious cause – the atonement wrought by Christ. The differences, Newman knew well, were over the formal cause – imputed or imparted – and the instrumental cause – baptism or saving faith? 'It seems that whereas Faith on our part fitly corresponds or is a corrective as it is called, to grace on God's part, Sacraments are but the manifestation of grace and good works are but the manifestation of faith; so that whether we say we are justified by faith or by works or by sacrament, all these but mean this one doctrine that we are justified by grace which is given through sacraments, impetrated (i.e. asked for) by faith, manifested in works.' Here indeed is 'faith working through love' (Galatians 5:6), the gift of the indwelling spirit. We might ask whether Newman's 'Second Journey' to creative holiness was more akin to

John Wesley and the Wesleyan theologian William Burt Pope than has been supposed.

Our century has seen further reconciliation of views. Hans Küng[36] claimed in an early book that this view of justification was very near that of Karl Barth. More recently the Catholic-Lutheran and Anglican-Roman Catholic Conversations (ARCIC II) show a remarkable synthesis of views.[37]

Several points we have already made are brought out. The danger in these bland but eirenic statements is in underestimating the cost of the division in the past and presenting a somewhat bloodless picture of what tore men and women apart. It may be true that 'We are agreed that this is not an area where any remaining differences of theological interpretation or ecclesiological emphases either within or between our communions can justify our continuing separation', but if so why are we still apart? What prevents common Eucharistic life?

The Church historian is bound always to ask – What did the spirituality of the pioneers like Luther and Wesley do for 'the sparrows'? What is the attraction? Looking at the Early Church in his classic book *Conversion*, A D Nock claims that the 'success of Christianity is the success of an institution which united the sacramentalism and the philosophy of the time. It satisfied the enquiring turn of mind, the desire for escape from Fate, the desire for security in the hereafter. Like Stoicism it gave a way of life and made man at home in the universe but unlike Stoicism it did this for the ignorant as well as for the lettered, it satisfied also social needs as it secured men against loneliness. It was not easy; it made uncompromising demands on those who would enter and would continue to live in the brotherhood, but to those who did fail it offered an equally uncompromising assurance.'[38] At the Reformation likewise the city dwellers who were swept into the Lutheran and Calvinist reform found a faith for their times combining new styles of vernacular worship in all stations of society. Some missed the medieval styles of prayer, penances and symbol, which still prevailed in the areas renewed or reclaimed by the Catholic Reformation. The opportunity for 'the eagles' still to soar in the mystical tradition is a legacy we can now all thankfully share, even if Kierkegaard's 'knight of faith' is more typical of Protestantism, the conscientious bureaucrat!

The Evangelical Revival again swept many into the orbit of faith, even if J H Plumb is astute in his claim that Methodism was more a religion *for* the poor than *of* the poor.[39] This was not the case with the later Primitive Methodism, pioneered in the Potteries, not by Oxford dons but by a carpenter and a potter. The way in which Primitive Methodism produced a self-disciplined, self-respecting, self-educated, self-reliant person is a story of how religion and social cohesion and purposeful living can go together.[40] The liberty given in conversion led to the liberty of the Christian in politics and social life, as Martin Luther had hoped it would. The dangers of smugness and complacency are clear also. What now?

Are the models of salvation we have outlined too existential and individual? Do contemporary men and women seek a gracious God or a gracious neighbour? With the demise of the devil (in the west!) and the 'abolition' of hell in the more liberal forms of Protestantism, is salvation now something even more existential than in Luther's scheme, with an affinity with psychological concern for self-fulfilment and wholeness? The stress in salvation thinking on justice in the politico-economic sense is needed to redeem this, so long as there is no substitution of political solutions for the need for relationship with God, which transcends all politics. For the Church, Richard Holloway's warning takes us back to Luther. 'Gradually the order of the Gospel is reversed by the institution that claims to enshrine it, and we end not with acceptance leading to holiness but with holiness as the price we pay for acceptance. Perhaps the most gruesome reversal of all is that we end by demanding health as a qualification for entrance into the sanatorium which was established for the sick. And the representatives of the one who came to call the sick end by demanding a clean bill of health from those who would partake of the medicine of salvation'.[41] Luther would surely say, 'Alas, yes' to that and point us to the freedom of the Christian.

References

1   ARCIC, Salvation and the Church (Anglican Consultative Council, 1987) p 9

2   J Kent, The Unacceptable Face (SCM, 1987) p 44

3   H A Oberman, Luther – Between God and Devil (Fontana, 1993) p 123

4   For recent introductions see: E Cameron, The European Reformation (Oxford University Press, 1991); S Ozment, Protestants, the Birth of a Reformation (Fontana, 1993); A E McGrath, Reformation Thought – An Introduction (Blackwell 1988); J Bossy, Christianity in the West. 1400-1700 (Oxford University Press, 1985); E Duffy, The Stripping of The Altars (New Haven, Connecticut: Yale University Press, 1993).
Older studies of Luther are still valuable, e.g. P S Watson, Let God be God (Epworth, 1947); E G Rupp, The Righteousness of God (Hodder, 1953); B Drewery in H Cunliffe-Jones (Ed), A History of Christian Doctrine, T and T Clark (1978), pp 311 ff.

5   NB McGrath, op. cit., pp 87-119. Cf H A Oberman, Masters of the Reformation (Cambridge University Press, 1981); A E McGrath, Luther's Theology of the Cross (Blackwell, 1985) and Iustitia Dei. A History of the Christian Doctrine of Justification, 2 vols (Cambridge University Press, 1989-1993)

6   Cf. McGrath, Theology of the Cross, pp 95-8; E G Rupp and B Drewery, Martin Luther (Documents) (Arnold, 1970), pp 5ff; M A Noll, Confessions and Catechisms of the Reformation (Apollos, 1991), p 94: WJ Cargill Thompson, Studies in the Reformation (London, 1980), pp 60ff

7   H Chadwick, Augustine (Oxford University Press, 1986), pp 107ff; H A Oberman, The Harvest of Medieval Theology (Cambridge, Massachusetts, 1963), Forerunners of the Reformation (London 1967), Masters of the Reformation (op. cit.), The Dawn of the Reformation (T & T Clark, 1986)

8   For a modern classic see R Niebuhr, The Nature and Destiny of Man, 2 vols (Nisbet, 1943)

9   Oberman, Luther, op cit pp 155ff

10   A Classic account is A Nygren, Agape and Eros, 3 vols (English translation, SPCK, 1939); cf R M Brown, The Spirit of Protestantism (oxford University Press, 1965) p 55

11   Preface to the Letter to the Romans. This passage was probably read at the meeting in Aldersgate Street on 24th May 1738. I have tried to remove the exclusive language! Cf P S Watson, The Message of the Wesleys (Epworth, 1964) p 8; H Bett, The Spirit of Methodism (Epworth, 1937) pp 27 ff

12   Oberman, Luther, op cit p 80 p 206

13   K Stendahl, Paul Among Jews and Gentiles (SCM, 1976); E P Sanders, Paul and Palestinian Judaism (SCM, 1977) and Paul (Oxford University Press, 1991) pp 33-76; J A Ziesler, Pauline Christianity (Oxford University Press, 1972), The Meaning of Righteousness in Paul (Cambridge University Press, 1972); Commentaries on Galatians (Epworth) and Romans (SCM)

14   Ziesler, Pauline Christianity, op cit pp 84-7

15   Sanders, Paul, op cit p 49

16   Ziesler, Righteousness, op cit, p 163, p 212. Cf V Taylor Forgiveness and Reconciliation (Macmillan, 1941); B Drewery in Cunliffe-Jones, op cit p 324

17   Cf R N Flew, The Forgiveness of Sins (Epworth, undated) p 69

18   F Greeves, Theology and the Cure of Souls (Epworth, 1960) p 23

19   John Betjeman, Collected Poems (Murray, 1979) p 105

20   D Davie (Ed) The New Oxford Book of Christian Verse (Oxford University Press, 1981) p 81

21   Rowan Williams, The Wound of Knowledge (Darton, Longman & Todd, 1979) p 158

22   P Tillich, The Shaking of the Foundations (Penguin, 1962); R Garaudy, From Anathema to Dialogue (Collins, 1966) p 36; cf R Bultmann, Kerygma and Myth (Collins, 1953) vol. 1 p 32

23   Gonville ffrench-Beytagh, Encountering Darkness (London, 1973) p 254

24   J M Turner, 'John Wesley – Theologian for the People' in URC Historical Journal (May 1986); A D Lindsay, The Two Moralities. Our Duty to God and Society (Eyre and Spottiswoode, 1940); L Newbigin, International Review of Missions (July 1979(pp 301-312; W D J Cargill Thompson, The Political Thought of Martin Luther (Harvester Press, 1984); Colin Morris, Address to the Methodist Conference 1976; D Davie (Ed) op cit p 250

25   For the Counter Reformation: A G Dickens, The Counter Reformation (Thames & Hudson, 1968); H O Evenett, The Spirit of the Counter

Reformation (Cambridge University Press, 1968); J Hurstfield (Ed), The Reformation Crisis (Arnold, 1965), Ch V 'The Counter Reformation' by H O Evenett; Noll, Confessions, op cit pp 165ff (includes the 33 canons on Justification)

26   Cited in N Sykes, The Crisis of the Reformation (Bles, 1938), pp 162-3

27   G C Cell, The Rediscovery of John Wesley (USA: Henry Holt, 1935) p 361; G Wainwright, On Wesley and Calvin (Melbourne: Uniting Church Press, 1987)

28   Cf A M Allchin, The Kingdom of Love and Knowledge (Darton, Longman and Todd, 1979), Ch 3 'Symeon and the New Theologian' and Participation in God (Darton, Longman and Todd, 1988).   Another Anglican who seems unconsciously 'Wesleyan' is Richard Holloway: cf Beyond Belief (Mawbray, 1981), Ch 9; Signs of Glory (Darton, Longman and Todd, 1982), Ch 5; Anger, Sex, Doubt and Death (SPCK, 1992), chapter on 'Anger'

29   H Butterfield, Origins of Modern Science 1300-1800 (Bell, 1949); P Hazard, The European Mind 1680-1715 (English translation, Penguin, 1964) and European Thought in the Eighteenth Century (English translation, Penguin, 1965); P Gay, The Enlightenment, 2 vols (Weidenfield & Nicholson, 1970); E G Rupp, Worldmanship and Churchmanship (Epworth, 1958), pp 14ff, 'Protestantism and Catholicism after 400 years' in D Pailin (Ed), Seventy Five Years of Theology in Manchester (Manchester University Press, 1980) pp 102ff and Religion in England 1688-1791 (Oxford University Press) pp 217ff

30   O Chadwick, The Popes and European Revolution (Oxford University Press), pp 159ff; W R Ward, The Protestant Evangelical Awakening (Cambridge University Press, 1992) and Faith and Faction (Epworth, 1993)

31   A G Dickens, Martin Luther and the Reformation (The English Universities Press, 1967) p 173

32   D W Bebbington, Evangelicalism in Modern Britain (Unwin, Hyman, 1989) p3

33   R Anstey, The Atlantic Slave and British Abolition, 1760-1810 (Macmillan, 1975); G F Nuttall, The Puritan Tradition (Epworth, 1967), Ch 8 'The Influence of Arminianism in England'

34   J M Turner, Conflict and Reconciliation (Epworth, 1985) Ch 8, 'Methodism and the Oxford Movement'

35   E Sullivan, Things Old and New (St Paul's, 1993), especially pp 154ff; J H Newman, Lectures on the Doctrine of Justification (Rivingtons, 3rd edition, 1874) pp 303, 320, 365; W B Pope, Compendium of Christian Theology (London, 1880) Vol. 3, pp 27-100

36   H Küng, Justification.   The Doctrine of Karl Barth and a Catholic Reflection (Burns, Oates, 1981); K J Kuschel and H Häring (Eds), Hans Küng – New Horizons in Faith and Thought (SCM, 1993), pp 138 ff

37   M E Brinkman, 'Justification' in N Lossky, et al, Dictionary of the Ecumenical Movement (Geneva: WCC, 1991) pp 560ff; ARCIC II, op cit

38   A D Nock, Conversion (Oxford University Press, 1931) p 211

39   J H Plumb, England in the Eighteenth Century (Penguin, 1950) p 94

40   Turner, op cit, pp 82-8; R Colls, The Pitmen of the Northern Coalfield. Work Culture and Protest 1790-1850 (Manchester University Press, 1987)

41   Holloway, Beyond Belief, op cit p 163

Since I wrote this, J D G Dunn and A M Suggate, The Justice of God. A Fresh Look at the Old Doctrine of Justification by Faith (Paternoster, 1993) has appeared. Dunn gives a brilliant summary of the biblical view of God's grace freely given, the Covenant relationship and Paul's conversion to the view that Gentiles can fully share it. He sees Luther as the 'discoverer' of justification, which ignores late medieval debate. Suggate shows rightly the relationship (as did Luther!) between justification and justice, and ends with a knock-about anti-Thatcherite polemic which seems simplistic.

Quotations from hymns are taken from Hymns and Psalms (Methodist Publishing House, 1983)

Chapter 2

John Neville Figgis (1866 – 1919) – Historian, Preacher and Prophet

1996 marked the centenary of the publication of *The Divine Right of Kings* by a young Cambridge historian, lecturer at St Catharine's College. The book was put into paperback in 1965, with a preface by Sir Geoffrey Elton, and is still authoritative on its subject, a matter by no means dead and buried. The writer was one of the more creative historians and theologians of his period, worthy of comparison with Peter Taylor Forsyth (1848-1921), his contemporary.

John Neville Figgis was a son of John Bradley Figgis, a notable minister of the Countess of Huntingdon's Connexion, that communion founded by Selina, Countess of Huntingdon. Its mode of worship could be called 'high chapel', to use a term coined by Geoffrey Wainwright, using a form of the Book of Common Prayer. Theologically, they were moderate Calvinists, not unlike the Presbyterian Church of Wales with many common links with that wing of the Evangelical Revival whose 'charismatic' leader was George Whitefield, a style of spirituality rather neglected by Methodists and others of Arminian style.[1]

John B Figgis wrote several notable books including one on holiness. He had a large and prestigious congregation in Brighton. So young Neville was born into a cultured and evangelical, but not fundamentalist, home. Like Austin Farrer and Michael Ramsey in the next generation, the Nonconformists style never entirely left him. Neville was always on good terms with his father, who followed his career and that of his brother, who became a notable doctor, with great support, though Figgis père was never happy with his son becoming a monk. The older Figgis outlived his brilliant son, who inherited his mother's rather delicate mental health. At Brighton College he was a promising scholar, in 1885 going up with an open scholarship to St Catharine's College, Cambridge. At that time the college was at a rather low ebb in its fortunes. Its Master, C K Robinson, had caused scandal by voting for himself at his election and remained Master for nearly fifty years! Figgis began as a mathematician, switched to History, gaining a brilliant First in 1889. He became the life and soul of his small college of sixty men, surrounding himself with a host of friends, remaining at college after graduation, winning the Lightfoot scholarship in 1890, the Junior Whewell Scholarship in 1891 and the Prince Consort Prize in 1892 for a scintillating essay on the *Divine Right of Kings*. That essay evolved into the book of 1896[2] revised and enlarged in 1914.

Becoming editor of the *Cambridge Review*, he made a living by coaching, teaching history at his college and lecturing at the Clergy Training School. The great influence on him was Mandell Creighton,[3] notable later as Bishop of

Peterborough and London, but earlier the first Dixie Professor of Ecclesiastical History (1884) and the first editor of the *English Historical Review*. Creighton saw church history as a branch of historical studies to be tackled with the utmost vigour, not to be 'hijacked' by the theologians, so his chair was in the History not Divinity Faculty. It was Creighton who said, 'Christianity is Christ', a phrase taken up by Figgis. There was also the influence of the great lawyer-historian, F W Maitland,[4] and towering over them all Lord Acton[5] (1834-1902), Regius Professor of History, who never wrote the great history of freedom he promised. 'His theory of liberty', says Figgis, 'was at the bottom the same as that of Creighton and was based politically upon Burke and the great theorists of Whiggism'. If Figgis followed Acton on freedom he would also agree with the famous, much misquoted, dictum in a letter to Creighton that 'power tends to corrupt and absolute power corrupts absolutely'. It was Maitland, an agnostic in religion, who pulled Figgis away from an easy faith. He never subsequently found faith easy. Like P T Forsyth, he was never conservative, did not dodge the consequence of either biblical scholarship or Darwinian theories of evolution. But it was Creighton who influenced Figgis in an Anglican direction. He was confirmed at a time when religion was sneered at by many of his friends and ordained after a short spell at Wells Theological College in 1894. After a curacy in Kettering, he was back at St Catharine's from 1897 to 1902 continuing his work in history and acting as chaplain. He assisted at St Mary's and gave the prestigious Birkbeck Lectures at Trinity College, subsequently published. The ball seemed to be at his feet.

But he was now thirty six and was advised on health grounds to give up academic work for a time. Figgis became Rector of Marnhull, a college living in North Dorset. Parishioners spoke years afterwards of their affection for their absent-minded priest stirring jam instead of tea, not knowing a bull from a cow. His father rejoiced at his willingness to help 'chapel' as well as 'church', rare then. Figgis was near a crisis of faith and career. It was almost a classic case of the 'second journey'.[6] Clues are sown in several of his books but he was not prone to write much about himself. It was this 'second conversion' which led him to Mirfield to join the Community of the Resurrection founded by Charles Gore, and at that time presided over by Walter Frere.[7] Figgis became a member of a community which gives considerable freedom to its members within a discipline of devotion. 'I have come to see that if Christians are to convince the world of their seriousness they must be prepared to live as though they meant the creed which they profess'. Figgis, whose life was a 'combination of private disaster and public acclaim' had freedom from worry about money, space for prayer, for worship, for work, for preaching. The fellowship of sacramental life meant much to him. J N F was an odd monk – he could never light his fire, he got annoyed when the bell rang and he was writing. He once lost the papers for Part II of the Cambridge Historical Tripos until one of the community found them under his bedclothes! He genuinely purred with satisfaction when St Catharine's made him an Honorary Fellow in 1909 and Cambridge University granted him a D Litt. He lectured widely in Britain and the USA, becoming a notable and popular preacher especially with students. The First World War deeply depressed him, though in its early stages (like Forsyth) he believed it to be a righteous conflict. He was then writing a definitive book on Bossuet, the French Catholic writer and preacher which he took with him to America in January 1918. The ship was torpedoed; Figgis was in an open boat for a time. The manuscript on Bossuet went to the bottom! Already suffering from rheumatoid arthritis, he was broken in health. His mind gave way and the end came mercifully on Palm Sunday 1919.

Why concern ourselves with him now? If we look at Figgis as historian, preacher and Christian prophet, we shall see that of the writers of the 1900-1920 period, Figgis must rank with P T Forsyth and the Roman Catholics Baron Von Hügel and George Tyrrell as the most enduring and readable. So let us see how an historian, Anglo-Catholic and 'twice-born' man looks at the period around the First World War.

1. The Historian

In 1935 George Dangerfield called the period before 1914, 'the strange death of liberal England' and it is easy to forget F W Maitland's dictum that: 'It is hard to think away out of our minds a history that has long lain in a remote past but which once lay in the future'. We too easily see our own dilemmas and the beginnings of the barbarism that has characterised the world since 1914. But there were symptoms of deep social malaise including pressure on parliamentary institutions. Trade Unions were becoming increasingly militant and unwilling to compromise as in the late 1970s and early 1980s. Violence in Northern Ireland, the movement for women's suffrage and (for some) an alarming breakdown in moral norms appear to us as pointers to a grim future. Christians like Gore and Figgis typified by the Christian Social Union saw the dark side of capitalism ('Each for himself and God for us all as an elephant said when he danced among the chickens'). They might agree with R H Tawney that 'Compromise is as impossible between the Church of Christ and the idolatry of wealth which is the practical religion of capitalist societies as it was between the church and the state idolatry of the Roman Empire', but the political solution was not obvious.[8] There was certainly, too, at this time a growth of xenophobia which provoked the cheering of crowds in the streets when war was declared in August 1914 – a phenomenon not repeated in 1939, we just went on digging air raid shelters. Theologically, the controversy which centred upon R J Campbell's *New Theology* of 1907 could be compared with the furore over *Honest to God* in 1963 or the *Myth of God Incarnate* in 1977.[9] Campbell, whom Forsyth called a 'theological quack', was simply the charming and popular mouthpiece of a liberal protestant approach to theology which seemed to Charles Gore to cut at the very heart of faith.

Underlying the controversy were the incompatible christologies of Harnack and Schweitzer – though *Von Reimarus Zu Wrede* which we know as *Quest of the Historical Jesus* was not known much in England until 1910 – and the idealist philosophy was then in vogue. Figgis was well aware of the trends in theology and philosophy and was almost torn apart by them. As a historian he first approached the matter from the angle of political philosophy. Where does authority lie in Church and State? *The Divine Right of Kings* analyses an idea which whatever its power at the time of the Reformation, when Luther's 'Godly prince' in the days of Henry VIII and Elizabeth I could shape 'Reformation from above', had by 1700 receded so much that when William III was asked to 'touch' for the 'king's evil' he could say 'stuff and nonsense'. But the next year Samuel and Susanna Wesley quarrelled bitterly over the legitimacy of William III's rule. Indeed only his death and the accession of Queen Anne restored them to the marital bed which produced a son, John Wesley, nine months later! The Divine Right of Kings was debated often enough in the eighteenth century, not least by Wesley himself.

From Gerson to Grotius (1907, 2nd Ed 1916), Figgis' Birkbeck Lectures, traces the transition from medievalism to the modern state. Gerson active in the Conciliar Movement desired reform 'in head and members'; Grotius, hard-headed Dutch lawyer, wrote still pertinent material on sovereignty, justice and the just war. Figgis is superseded now by Quentin Skinner[10] but his following in the wake of his mentor, Creighton, who dealt judiciously with Renaissance Popes much to Acton's disgust – still yields some important insights on the Reformation and the close parallels between Calvinist rebels and Catholic rebels. The posthumous study of the *Political Aspects of St Augustine's City of God* (Longmans 1921) is still a useful way into an interpretation of the great theologian who brooded over the Middle Ages, not least with the idea of the two kingdoms which so influenced Luther and is still grossly misunderstood.[11] The debate continues as to whether it is false to set the 'realm of grace' in opposition to the realm of 'my station and its duties' (a phrase of F H Bradley) which sees the state as not attempting to do what the church exists to do. That debate is as alive as ever when Prime Ministers in the 1980s told bishops to stick to morals, and bishops tell chancellors how to balance the budget. Figgis, in *Churches in the Modern State* (Longmans 1913) still has a relevant position. Influenced by Gierke and Maitland, he writes of the need for 'pluralism' in society, not using the word in our contemporary sense of cultural and religious plurality, but in terms of plurality of organizations between the machinery of the state and the natural institution of the family, what Burke called 'the little platoons'. Churches, trades unions, schools, universities, charitable bodies of all kinds, legal institutions, the medical establishments need autonomy and what we would now call 'subsidiarity'.[12] Figgis wanted safeguards against what he called 'The New Leviathan' typified by Bismarck's 'Kulturkampf' or educational struggle against Roman Catholic schools in Germany and the educational policy of Emile Combes in France, who espoused not only total separation of church and state (which came in 1905) but total secularization of education.[13] Figgis disagreed violently with Free Church stances against Balfour's Education Act of 1902, when the cry went up 'Rome on the rates'. Figgis saw the Free Church case for an undenominational style of religious education as a dislike of the fact that denominationalism means the recognition of the religious society as such in education. What Free Church men like John Clifford the Baptist and even P T Forsyth, demanded is that there shall be no intermediary between the state and the child and, said Figgis, 'it springs quite naturally from the passion for state absolutism which is the child of Renaissance and Reform and the grandchild of the pagan state'. There could have been few harder attacks on the radical Free Church position than that of Figgis. His pluralism led him to the assertion that the 'real world is composed of several communities large and small, that a community is something more than the sum of the persons comprising it, in other words it is a real personality not a fictitious one.[14] That debate is still wide open and is an issue of vital importance, involving church schools, Islamic schools and private institutions. The weakness of Figgis' view is that it is not clear how his state would actually work. He assumes too, as R W Dale did from quite a different standpoint, a strong and virile church, even if it were disestablished.

Figgis' fears about 'the great Leviathan' were more than justified with the breakdown of social order in Germany in the Weimar Republic, and today we need to watch the way the state in the name of freedom undermines the institutions which are the backbone of society, not least local government. Figgis as a historian assisted Lord Acton in the great enterprise of the *Cambridge Modern History*, although the ultimate production was somewhat disappointing, and with R Vere Lawrence he edited a selection of Acton's *Historical Essays and Studies*, the *History of Freedom, Lecture on Modern History* (all in 1907), the *French Revolution* (1910) and the *Letters* in 1917. He also wrote an interesting short book on *Christianity and History* (Finch 1905). Creighton-like, he states that the treatment of Church History as a thing apart is an evil. It plays into the hands of the fanatic and strengthens the bias of the partisan. Against some trends he asserts that 'the object of history is to help us to understand the present by tracing its roots in the past. History seeks to solve the problem: How human society in its existing form has come to be'. Sir Herbert Butterfield debates that concept in the *Whig Interpretation of History* (1931) – Figgis seems Whig! – and takes up Figgis's title in his more famous book after World War Two, *Christianity and History* (1949).

All this was worthy of his honorary Fellowship at St Catharine's and only a foretaste of what he could have produced had the don won over the monk.

2. The Preacher

Some of the greatest Anglican preachers have been Anglo-Catholics, often more pungent and prophetic than evangelicals. E B Pusey, at his greatest, set forth Christ crucified. Charles Gore was a prophet to his age and expected his monks to be preachers and Christian apologists. Figgis was worthy of that call. In technique he was equal to most of his day. Sharp pungent sentences, terse quotations and if rather literary, well placed illustrations and memorable beginnings and endings. I am surprised that none of the homiletical text books have discovered Figgis. 'Get them in the first sentence,' says Ken Dodd! Text Jer. 8:11. 'Peace, Peace where there is no peace'. 'The Church of England at the close of the nineteenth century was the most respectable institution ever known in the annals of the human race.' Text. Matt. 21:9. 'Hosanna to the Son of David'. Palm Sunday. 'It was a poor little pageant. A rabble of peasants from a province of a province, a few of the humbler class in its insignificant capital, a place that was to Rome what Hyderabad is to London; the central figure a wandering peasant seated on a donkey; boys and girls shouting. That is all – *that* is the triumphal beginning of a universal empire.'

He began his great series of Hulsean Lectures the *Gospel and Human Needs* (1908-9). Luke 1:68 'Blessed be the Lord God of Israel, for he hath visited and redeemed his people'. 'Has he? That is the question we are asking.' Figgis could begin a University sermon at Gt St Mary's, Cambridge – 'Ye are my friends'. 'Friendship with Jesus – that's the central fact of our life as Christians.' He could end another at Yale University, 'Someone said: A Highway robber asked "Your money or your life" but Christ asks both. May God grant you to give both.' Another at Glasgow, ends for all the world like W E Sangster or James S Stewart, even the poem! 'We cannot find even ourselves except through him – No faith in God worthy of the name, no hope of man that will not vanish except in 'that strange man upon the Cross' – who speaks peace to them that are far off and to them that are nigh; and tells us of his Father in heaven whose love stooped so far as to give his only begotten Son that all who believe in him should not perish but have everlasting life. 'Christ is the end, as Christ was the beginning, Christ the beginning for the end is Christ'.

Figgis could comfort the troubled and also trouble the comfortable. 'What I do say is that the state of our cities, the lives of the masses among the workers are a disgrace to any civilization and that in so far as this civilization calls itself Christian it is a lie. And all our comfortable piety and religious books and church circles but make the evil more glaring and are in part an excuse for the way in which the church is regarded by the working classes'.[15] If P T Forsyth was 'Catholic evangelical', Figgis is 'Evangelical Catholic'. What this means we explore as finally we ask what a prophet might be.

3. Prophet

Figgis, as we have seen, underwent a crisis of his unbelief and a conversion back to Christianity in its Anglo-Catholic form, but at the heart of his Sacramentalism was a personal sense of commitment to him, who (echoing Tyrrell and Forsyth), he called often 'the strange man on the Cross'. 'I think we can say that so far as Creed goes a man is a Christian or a non-Christian so far as he can enter into the spirit of the hymn 'When I survey the wondrous Cross'. For Figgis only a full blooded orthodox Christology with a stress on atonement could meet the real needs of the world. 'Either this thing is a delusion, the most gigantic the world has known, or else it is a revelation from beyond, a gift of grace, something that we could not have done for ourselves. Either it is what it claims, the power of God able to save the uttermost and giving peace and freedom, or it is a quack medicine'.[16] 'Saved to the uttermost' – a phrase surely from his father or the school of Samuel Chadwick! This is a far less fragile position than the 'Either God or mad or not a good man' Christology which even C S Lewis fell for, and on which A N Wilson rightly pounces.[17]

Is Figgis then a kind of Tertullian of the early twentieth century, running full tilt against those like R J Campbell (and even Tyrrell) who appeared to make thought of their day the yard stick by which to shape Christian apologetic? Figgis had soaked himself in modern thought; he knew Athens as well as Jerusalem – but his point of attack was to direct attention to what was distinctive and final in Christianity, against the 'benumbing influence of pantheism' or the 'reduced christology' which he saw as a half way house to atheism or to the fullness of the faith, which indeed Campbell came to see under Gore's influence. His position was what he would call a Christian agnosticism, a realization that logic is not the whole of reality. 'The intellect itself is incapable of embracing reality with the corollary that all our knowledge of God is figurative and provisional'.[18] There is the danger here of obscurantism – to speak of 'Mystery' to some is to speak of the obscure rather than the unfashionable, but clearly Figgis foreshadows a Christian style of existentialism and would not have been surprised by modernism or post-modernism. Figgis' prophetic stance can be summarized under four heads.

i. Western civilization was under judgement for its avarice, typified by Belgian policy in the Congo and the appalling conditions of poverty (outlined by Rowntree and William Booth) of thirty per cent of the population of Britain. Catastrophe was threatening. 'We can almost hear the thunder of the avalanche of war. War on a scale unkown'.[19] This was said when Winston Churchill, rising hope of the Liberals, was saying, 'We live in a period of superficial alarms when it is thought prophetic and statesmanlike, far seeing, clever and Bismarckian to present hideous and dreadful wars as imminent … happily for the world, war is not coming'.[20] But for Figgis there was 'death in the pot of civilization and it is not like to heal itself'. In the midst of war itself Figgis brought nought for anyone's comfort – prophetically, the proofs of *Civilization at the Cross Roads* had gone to the bottom with the *Titanic*! Talbot thought Figgis had descended to 'holy water or you frizzle'. 'For the scientific barbarism of Prussia might win in the way that the hard barbarians of the West broke into the peace lapped Roman Empire in the fifth century. God forfend this. Yet it might be'. Figgis tore the mask off the façade of Edwardian culture and saw the breakdown of ideals with on the one hand the appeal of mysticism and theosophy – the parallels today are ominous! – and on the other the 'transvaluation of values' of Nietzsche which he saw as leading to the Superman 'the great blonde beast', the reversal of the humble Christ figure. The Methodist J H Moulton uttered similar warnings and like Figgis was torpedoed for his pains! Few men saw the importance of the thinking of Nietzsche more than Figgis, for whom he had the attraction of Milton's Satan. Science, with all its importance, is not the answer to human need as some think. Figgis was Amos-like in almost masochistic denunciations of his age. Perhaps like Gore he was little heard by those to whom his message applied. Practical solutions, too, are not given. 'We live in an age of unparalleled anarchism both moral and intellectual. The confusion of tongues is worse than any Babel of old'.[21] This is certainly reminiscent of Tertullian. At a more profound level, he foresaw what emerged after the false peace, in Nazism. I know few more prophetic historians though I recall Sir Herbert Butterfield in 1956[22] saying that secularism would not last and would be followed by dark pagan mythologies and astrologies and a conflict between religions. He was more prophetic in the futurist sense than Cantwell Smith and John Hick with their 'Copernican revolution' which only seems to appeal to a white liberal fringe.[23] Religion may indeed again become a substitute for God. It is striking that the leading Marxist historian of our day, E J Hobsbawm, looks back on the 'Short Twentieth Century' – 1914-1990 – with deep gloom and sorrow. Figgis proved prophetic both in forthtelling and foretelling.[24]

ii. In this confusion, the only remedy is a proclamation and a living out in discipleship of the Christ who reveals God and our true nature and grants full forgiveness to needy men and women. At times one senses the theological scholarship of Charles Gore and P T Forsyth and maybe Bishop Frank Weston, Anglo-Catholic controversialist but no mean thinker, brooding over Figgis. It was a period of acute Christological controversy. In each era the same questions occur. Theology is like a spiral staircase; mutatis mutandis, the same scenes reappear at the next window. The Hibbert Journal Supplement of 1909 'Jesus or Christ' can be compared with the Myth of God Incarnate of 1977. Figgis' position is an avowal of the historical Jesus with a frank admission of much of Albert Schweitzer's standpoint against that of Harnack. Jesus would be a stranger in the world. The 'boneless Christ' of the liberals has, he says, little appeal. It is Jesus who was crucified, who showed us that to die is life, who was raised, who draws men and women to himself. A subtle and still relevant historical position is adopted on the Resurrection, a refusal either to rule it out a priori as did J M Thompson of Magdalen College, Oxford, or calling the actual occurrence of the Resurrection, which is not recorded in Scripture, an 'historical event'. The parallels with Bultmann, Marxsen and David Jenkins are striking. With echoes perhaps of Alfred Loisy, Figgis ties together history, tradition and present experience as all germane to a full exploration of the 'Christ event'. He follows his mentor, Mandell Creighton, in a still perceptive discussion of the role of tradition in establishing historical data. The 'quest for the historical Richard the Third' provides Figgis with an opportunity to show how the tools of the secular historian can be used in New Testament scholarship. A modern New Testament scholar, Professor Kenneth Grayston, noted its penetration.[25]

Three riders emerge. Most people are like children asking of a story, 'Is it true?' When New Testament scholars dodge that question, they need a reminder of its inevitability. Then there is Creighton's point that the presuppositions of the critic's mind need examination no less than those of the orthodox. Again there is the role of the church Figgis sees as the 'supreme historical document'. It is mere folly to leave it out of account. This is an interesting foreshadowing of 'Form Criticism', though Figgis' conclusions, like those of Vincent Taylor later, would not be that of a Dibelius or a Bultmann. Figgis goes on to state the distinctiveness of Christianity in our apologetic – the similarities with other systems will not win people to the faith. If we cannot make the leap of faith or if the evidence runs against us, then let us have the 'courage of our doubts' and face the music. This is a position taken in our day by Wolfhart Pannenberg. It takes the risk of investigation, which Sir Karl Popper showed to be at the heart of scientific investigation. The Christian runs the risk of refutation.[26]

iii. Christianity must retain its sense of mystery and the miraculous. Figgis arrived at faith, like P T Forsyth, through agony. Like Luther he knew the fearful 'Anfechtungen' (a word stronger than temptations) which rack his kind of temperament. 'To others faith is the bright sanctity of unclouded vision, to me it is the angel of agony, the boon of daily and hourly comfort'. Faith is in the supernatural grace of God revealed in Christ – 'leave out if you must the mysterious birth, the availing death, the empty tomb and the sacramental presence and what have you left? Would it be very much to live by? Would it be anything to die for?' Don Cupitt now tells us there is nothing worth dying for.[27] We must not try to rationalize the mysterious – that is why Figgis rejects transubstantiation. Creeds themselves in a profound way are symbols pointing to the mystery of Christ which is experienced and unfathomable. Figgis does not dodge the issue of miracles. He sees them like Barth as a clue to the openness of the universe. Any 'closed' system is anathema to him whether in science, politics or the church. 'Miracles are but the expression of God's freedom, the truth that he is above and not merely within the order of nature. Disbelief in them really leads on to pantheism'. Figgis sees, like Barth, creation itself as grace. He does not in a debate with J M Thompson conceive of miracles as 'breaking the laws of nature' nor does he use them as an apologetic bolster to Christology. 'Christ did miracles therefore he is the Son of God'. *That* ploy went out finally with J B Mozley, whose views Baden Powell (not the chief scout!) exploded. But he will not allow the Father to be the slave of his universe.[28] That issue is wide open again as a perusal of the works of Maurice Wiles would show.[29] I find, with Jenkins, petty miracles unworthy of God but if he has raised his Son what can he not do? Surely God is not exhausted by his universe?

iv. Lastly Figgis sought always to secure personalism in his setting forth if the faith. Like any Evangelical Figgis asserted that 'faith is personal trust in a Person'. The human burden of sin can be rolled away at the foot of the cross. Like G A Studdert Kennedy (Woodbine Willie), he could talk of making the 'great gamble with Christ'. Yet while he stressed conversion and was what William James called the 'twice born', he never would make conversion the criterion of being a Christian. The faith is personal but never individualistic. It is not the faith of an élite, even a spiritual elite. This is the danger of what Figgis called 'Puritanism' in any age.[30] It was Wesley's danger when he demanded assurance and then wondered to Melville Horne 'that they did not stone us'. They did, of course! All this is underlined by the place of the eucharist in Christian devotion. The sacrament is utterly central to the ministerial life. Figgis' point is relevant again when 'experience' becomes a criterion of true faith.

Figgis, several times in his writings, rapturises the sense of being part of the great wholeness of the church. Like the little boy on his first day at school cheering the first eleven, all the heroes are ours. St Athanasius, St Augustine, St Francis, St Catharine (of Siena, I presume but it could be the mythical lady of Alexandria or the great mystic of Genoa), Wesley, Newman are all *ours*.[31] We are rich to their achievement, their holiness and love. John Scott Lidgett[32] had similar eulogies of all the saints, a sense of Catholicity Now, said Hobsbawm, 'most young men and women at the century's end grow up in a sort of permanent present lacking any organic relation to the public past of the times they live in. This makes historians whose business it is to remember what others forget, more essential at the end of the second millennium than ever before'.[33] The cynic might mutter 'romanticism' but others will see it as a 'cordial for drooping courage'. Figgis called it the 'Fellowship of the Mystery', James Moffatt called it 'the thrill of tradition', which is the real Catholicity. As a contemporary P T Forsyth shared this, so later did Bernard Lord Manning the Cambridge historian, who was very like Figgis in his impact on his contemporaries. For Figgis true 'self discovery' – still very much a catchword – is to be found in the sacramental and prayerful life of the fellowship of the church. We might want to add much more due to the advance of the sciences of humanity but Christian 'Koinonia' can still claim to be the place where many men and women have found themselves because they have found a Lord and a loving community.

The same themes emerge again and again in Figgis – the givenness of revelation, the centrality of Christ and his Cross, the other worldly, not world renouncing nature of Christ, the cost of discipleship, - 'unless we can be the church of the poor, we had better cease to be a church at all', - the glory and scandal of the church set in a world crying out for his message.[34] We could do worse than look again at John Neville Figgis – brilliant Cambridge historian, gourmet and bon viveur, monk, prophet to his day and generation. Let the last word be with Bernard Lord Manning (1892-1941), lifelong nonconformist who died, like Figgis at the height of his powers.[35]

He describes Figgis' last university sermon at Cambridge in June, 1918. It seemed that Paris was about to fall to the Germans. 'Big Bertha's' shells were falling on the capital. 'Figgis was nearing the end of his time on earth. As he moved up the aisle of Great St Mary's in his scarlet Doctor of Letters' Hood and his white preacher's bands, he was more bloated and unhealthy looking than ever, but he was also more tired and feebler. The bloated look they said came from his regular frequent pendulum motion between Mirfield fasts and

Cambridge feasts but the feebleness came from the last enemy that shall be destroyed. He walked with difficulty, leaning on a stick. In his raucous harsh loud voice he croaked through the bidding prayer and we sat for the sermon. The mood was one of gloom ...

Figgis, of course, did not fail. He went straight to the point. Here is the situation. What about it? Figgis announced his text and began his sermon in a way that I can never forget. 'The Lord sitteth above the water-flood and the Lord remaineth a king for ever. *Does He?* Manning previously had said in his sermon 'Figgis was, I take it, easily the most brilliant historian produced in that generation by Cambridge. He was one of the most evangelical preachers of the Cross who, taught by our own Forsyth, led the way from the shallows of the so-called liberal so-called theology. He foresaw and foretold the poignant struggles which were lying ahead for the church and the faith. He foresaw and foretold the challenge of the new morality to the Christian way of life. He foresaw and foretold the challenge of the totalitarian state to the prerogatives of Christ the King in his church. He foresaw and foretold the resurrection of paganism (this was *1936*) naked, unashamed, aggressive. Yet in church and university he missed his way; or rather the Anglican church and Cambridge missed their opportunity with him.[36] He has no living memorial in the multifarious schools and parties of Anglicanism ... he had no office worthy of his talents; and his historical work, pregnant as it is with most of the substance and ideas which have engaged the attention of the last and the present generations of historians, is but a rough sketch of what he should have done'.

Little of the theology of the first twenty years of this century is read now save for Von Hügel, Gore and Forsyth. But a reading of the corpus of John Neville Figgis is still strangely exciting and relevant.

References

1. D L Morgan, *The Great Awakening in Wales*, Epworth, 1988; M A Noll et al, *Evangelicalism*, OUP 1994; D W Bebbington, *Evangelicalism in Modern Britain*, Unwin, Hyman, 1989
2. W H S Jones, *The Story of St Catharine's College Cambridge*, Heffer 1951, pp 166-7; E E Rich (Ed), *St Catharine's College 1473-1973*, 1973, pp 232-4; M G Tucker, *John Neville Figgis*, SPCK 1950; R E Dolman, *Birmingham MA Thesis on Figgis, ExpT March 1996, pp 169ff*
3. W G Fallowes, *Mandell Creighton and the English Church*, OUP 1964; L Creighton, *Life and Letters of Mandell Creighton*, 2 Vols, London 1905 (note vol 1, p 372)
4. G R Elton, *F W Maitland*, Weidenfield and N, 1985
5. H Butterfield, *Lord Acton*, Historical Association 1948; For Figgis on all three: *Churches in the Modern State*, Longmans 1913, pp 227ff
6. G O'Collins, *The Second Journey*, Paulist Press 1978

7. A Wilkinson, *The Community of the Resurrection*, A Centenary History, SCM 1991, pp 118-9, 139-41

8. G Dangerfield, *The Strange Death of Liberal England*, 2nd Ed Paladin 1970. I draw upon and revise my own earlier article, J N Figgis, Anglican Prophet, used with permission, Theology Oct, 1975; E R Norman, *Church and Society in England 1770-1970*, OUP 1976,pp 220-278; K Robbins, *On Prophecy and Politics*, Some pragmatic reflections in *Protestant Evangelicalism*, Blackwell 1990, pp 281-296; R H Tawney, *Religion and the Rise of Capitalism*, Pelican 1948, p 280

9. K W Clements, *Lovers of Discord*, SPCK 1988, pp 19-48; P Hinchliff, *God in History*, OUP 1992, pp 198-222

10. Q Skinner, *The Foundations of Modern Political Thought*, Vol 2, CUP 1978; cf O O'Donovan and J L O'Donovan, *Bonds of Imperfection*, Eerdmans 2004,

11. W D J Cargill Thompson, *Political Thought of Martin Luther*, Harvester Press 1984; ibid, *Studies in the Reformation, Luther to Hooker*, London 1980

12. D G Nichols, *Church and State in Britain since 1820*, RKP 1967; ibid, *The Pluralist State*, Macmillan 1975; D Newsome, *Gore and Figgis*, JEH vol 17.2, 1966, pp 227-41

13. J S McManners, *Church and State in France, 1870-1914*, SPCK 1972

14. Churches, pp 46-7, 88, 250; J M Turner, *Some Problems of Church and State in England*, Epworth Review, Jan 1976, pp 56-64

15. J N Figgis, *Some Defects in English Religion*, London 1917, pp 40-107; ibid, *Anti-Christ and other Sermons*, Longmans 1913, pp 150, 191, 243, 267

16. J N Figgis, *Civilisation at the Cross Roads*, Longmans, 19123, pp 127, 161

17. A N Wilson, *C S Lewis*, Collins, 1990, pp 163ff

18. *Civilisation* p 44; J N Figgis, *The Gospel and Human Needs*, Longmans, 1909, p 47

19. *Anti-Christ*, p 31

20. Cited in A J P Taylor, *The Trouble Makers*, Panther 1969, p 106

21. *Civilisation*, p 91, 34; J N Figgis, *Hopes for English Religion*, Longmans 1919, p 146; J H Moulton, *The Neglected Sacrament*, Epworth, 1919, pp 23-37

22. H Butterfield, Ed C T McIntire, *Writings on Christianity and History*, OUP 1979, pp 248ff

23. e.g. J H Hick, *An Interpretation of Religion*, Yale 1981; W Cantwell Smith, *Towards a World Theology*, Philadelphia 1981

24. E J Hobsbawm, *Age of Extremes. The Short Twentieth Century 1914-1991*, Michael Joseph 1994

25. *Gospel and Human Needs*, pp 56-91, esp. p 63; *Civilisation*, pp 121-178; pp 235ff *King Richard the Third and the Reverend James Thompson*

26. *Gospel and Human Needs*, pp 59, 64, 65, 68; Louise Creighton, *Life and Letter of Mandell Creighton*, London 1905, vol 1, p 216; J N Figgis, *The Fellowship of the Mystery*, Longmans 1912, p 28; K Popper, *The*

Logic of Scientific Discovery, Hutchinson 1968; *Conjectures and Refutations*, R K 1983; W Pannenberg, *The Apostles' Creed in the Light of Today's Questions*, SCM 1972. etc

27. *The Gospel and Human Needs*, pp 15, 55, 21; D Cupitt, *After All. Religion without Alienation*, SCM 1994, p 90
28. Anti-Christ*, p 228*
29. e.g. M Wiles, *God's Action in the World*, SCM 1986
30. *The Gospel*, p 78, 108; *Anti-Christ*, p 81; cf J N Figgis and H J Clayton, *Persecution by the Puritans*, 1908 pp 9-35
31. *Anti-Christ*, pp 287ff
32. John Scott Lidgett, *Apostolic Ministry*, Culley 1909, p 13
33. E J Hobsbawm, op cit, p 3
34. *Fellowship of the Mystery*, p 100
35. B L Manning, *More Sermons of a Layman*, IP 1944, pp 34ff
36. G R Elton said the same in his Preface to the Harper edition of the Divine Right of Kings in 1965
37. Recent Books and Articles
    Mark D Chapman, *Concepts of the Voluntary Church in England and Germany 1890-1920. A Study of J N Figgis and Ernst Troeltsch*, in Zeitschrift Für Neuere Theologiegeschichte. 2, 1995, pp 37-59; Mark D Chapman, *Blair's Britain. A Christian Critique*, DLT 2005, chapter 7; G D H Cole (Ed) *The Pluralist Theory of the State Selected Writings of G D H Cole, J N Figgis and H J Laski*, Routledge 1993; Mark D Chapman, *J N Figgis*, in The New Dictionary of National Biography

Principal Writings of J N Figgis

History

The Divine Right of Kings, CUP 1896, 2nd Ed 1914, Pk Harper 1965
English History Illustrated from Original Sources 1660-1714, Black 1902
Christianity and History, Finch 1905
From Gerson to Grotius 1414-1625, CUP 1907 2nd Ed 1916, Pk Harper 1960
Churches in the Modern State, Longmans 1913
The Political Aspects of St Augustine's City of God, Longmans 1921, 2nd Ed USA 1963

Theology

The Gospel and Human Needs, Longmans 1909
Religion and English Society, Longmans 1910
Civilisation at the Cross Roads, Longmans 1912
Anti-Christ and Other Sermons, Longmans 1913
The Fellowship of the Mystery, Longmans 1914
The Will to Freedom, Longmans 1917
Some Defects in English Religion, Scott 1917
Hopes for English Religion, Longmans 1919

Articles

'*Warburton'* in *Typical English Churchmen*, London 1902

Political Thought in the Sixteenth Century, Cambridge Modern History volume 3, 1904

Peter Canisius and the German Counter Reformation, Cambridge Historical Review XXIV, p 18ff

Articles on *Arminianism, Calvinism, Creighton, Newman, Puritanism, Toleration, S L Ollard and Crosse*, A Dictionary of English Church History, Mowbrays 1912

Erastus and Erastianism, A Journal of Theological Studies Vol 2, 1901

Edited with R Vere Lawrence

The Works of Lord Acton

1. *Lectures on Modern History*, Macmillan 1907
2. *Historical Essays and Studies*, Macmillan 1907
3. *The History of Freedom and other Essays*, Macmillan 1907
4. *Lectures on the French Revolution*, Macmillan 1910
5. *Selections from Correspondence with Newman, Gladstone etc*, Macmillan 1917

Chapter 3

Theologian of Righteousness

Peter Taylor Forsyth (1848 – 1921)

A M Allchin speaks of an 'ecumenism in time,' whereby we can be more attuned to a thinker of the past than with some of our contemporaries. Tradition is thus the 'living faith of the dead,' not the 'dead faith of the living.'[1] P T Forsyth is one of those whom I find strangely contemporary. He still 'rings my bell,' even if some of his judgements are now unfashionable and even perverse.

First, a brief look at his life, then his writing in its context, then some assessment and criticisms. In the year 1840 in Aberdeen, Elspet Macpherson was housekeeper to Peter Taylor, a merchant. On his death he left her his house. She married an ex-bookseller, Isaac Forsyth, a postman earning eleven shillings a week. Their house became a boarding house for university students, including George Macdonald, later so to influence C S Lewis. Peter Taylor Forsyth, named after his family's benefactor, was born in 1848. His school days were spent in the world of ships, the docks, the seaside and students. He became dux of his school, then took a first in classics at the university, becoming, on graduation, assistant to the professor. The Taylors and the Forsyths were Congregationalists, so P T Forsyth never had quite the high Calvinist background of theologians like John and Donald Baillie later.

Forsyth spent a year in Germany as a pupil of Albrecht Ritschl at Göttingen. The historical nature of revelation, as against the stress on experience of Schleiermacher, is vital to Forsyth, who absorbed a great deal of nineteenth century German theology. Frederick Denison Maurice – whose style might, like Forsyth's, be called 'fireworks in a fog' – was a key influence. Christ the head of the human race, the declaratory nature of Baptism, the amazing integration of his thinking, are reminiscent of Maurice. Dora Greenwell, that remarkable woman theologian who constantly pointed to 'a work not our own,' was also influential, as was Baldwin Brown.

Forsyth was a student for a short time at Hackney College, Hampstead. After ordination in 1876 he held a series of Congregational pastorates: Shipley, near Bradford; St Thomas' Square, Hackney; Cheetham Hill, Manchester, and Clarendon Park, Leicester. He was bright, liberal tending to radicalism. Art, music, politics – the 'left' of mainstream Liberalism – absorbed his energy. His first major book was *Religion in Recent Art* (1889), analysing the Pre-Raphaelites, though his *Pulpit Parables for Young Hearers* (1886) shows him to have been a pioneer of 'Family Worship.' He always treated children as worthy of respect. Forsyth was in Bayreuth in 1882 for the first performance of Wagner's *Parfisal*, that strange tale of suffering and redemption, half pagan, half Christian, without which no BBC Good Friday would be complete. In 1893 an article appeared, which made the great R W Dale exclaim, 'Who is this P T Forsyth? He is redeeming an old word – grace!'

1894 was the turning point. He was appointed minister at Emmanuel Church, Cambridge, the university centre of Congregationalism. He was ill; his wife died as soon as they arrived. He was too ill to receive his Aberdeen DD in person. Catholic writers talk much of a 'Second Journey,' sparked off by crisis like bereavement. Forsyth tells us that 'from a lover of love, he became an object of grace.' He had no fear of biblical criticism, he was never anything like a fundamentalist, but recovered a stress on redemption rather than inevitable progress. 'I cannot remember since boyhood passing a day without pain, but I think my life a piece of disheartening self-indulgence when I read missionary biography and track its quavering red line of apolistic succession from the beginning till now' (*Missions in Church and State* p41).

He remarried in 1898 a much younger woman, Bertha Ison – theology began to burst out of him – that amazing creativity which follows 'the Second Journey.' Charles Wesley and John Henry Newman are parallels. Several small books from the 'Cambridge' period are pointers for what was to come. So many of the characteristic phrases and paradoxes poured from a man almost to ill too preach. *God The Holy Father* (1897), *The Divine Self Emptying* (1895), *The Taste of Death and the Life of Grace* (1896), *Christian Perfection* (1899), *The Charter of the Church* (1896), *Intercessory Services for Public Worship* (1896) – Forsyth, like J H Jowett at Carr's Lane, Birmingham, was one of the first Congregationalists to use responsive forms. The themes here are crystal clear – no 'fog' here. 'More,' said J K Mozley, 'like a thunderstorm circling around.'

Fatherhood was in the air in the 1890s. John Scott Lidgett, the Wesleyan who wrote a fine book on the *Fatherhood of God* (1902), recalled W B Pope, Methodism's greatest systematic theologian, shouting to him on a railway platform, 'John Scott, I have won a great victory. I've got 'em to change the Catechism from "What is God? An infinite and eternal Spirit" to "Who is God? Our Father."' Forsyth would say, 'Yes, but a *Holy* Father.' He is never remote, but 'other.' He is the Father who reconciled the world to himself. He skates on thin ice over the atonement, but never separates the Father from the Son. There are seeds here of an approach which we can find in J K Mozley, and more recently in Jürgen Moltmann and Frances Young. Moltmann can talk of a crucified God, reminiscent of Charles Wesley:

'The Immortal God for me hath died,
My Lord, my love is crucified.'

Yes, of course there is the risk of Patripassionism, but Forsyth avoids it. Here is Frances Young, but it echoes Forsyth eighty years before:
'I would still maintain that a properly Christian response to the problem of evil has to begin with the cross, with an understanding of atonement. We do not

begin by explaining evil away, justifying God, excusing him for the mess he has made of his creation. We begin by contemplating the story which tells of God taking responsibility for the evil in his world, entering it himself, taking it upon himself ... in all its horror, cruelty and pain' [2]

The Holy Father the Divine 'Kenosis,' the cross at the heart of history, discipleship as following the true and living way of the cross – all these are in these little books of the practical theology of a pastor. Some of the flashes of lightning still light up the sky.

'Do not say God is love, why atone? The New Testament says God has atoned. What love!' (*Holy Father* p4). Forsyth argues for 'Kenosis' (self-emptying), but could counter the later argument which Temple was to use, 'Where was the Creative Word when Christ was in his cradle?' by saying 'The earthly Christ was not all of Christ. The whole Christ was there, but not all that is in Christ.' "Totus Christus sed non totum quod in eo est," says Calvin (Ibid p18). 'The church may wander far, but as even Goethe says, she must return to adjust her compass at the cross' (Ibid p23).

Forsyth's early comments on perfection need to be seen, not in the context of John Wesley's teaching of perfect love, the two great commandments, but Keswick Convention style stress on entire consecration, or the 'Second Blessing' teaching of some contemporary Methodists like Thomas Cook, who stressed experience rather than aspiration, risking the dangers of smug self-satisfaction. This Forsyth abhorred, and said so. Faith, new birth, sanctification co-exist, they are not successive stages.

'Penitence, faith, sanctification always co-exist. They do not destroy and succeed one another. They are phases of the same process of God in the one soul ... Love is but faith in its supreme and perfect form' (Ibid pp99, 100). 'Our perfection is not to rival the Perfect, but to trust him ... The height of sinlessness means the deepest sense of sin. If we ever come to any such stage as conscious sinlessness, we should be placing ourselves alongside Christ, not at his feet' (Ibid p102).

'Perfection is wholeness ... and yet,' (and this is wholly Wesleyan) 'we enter heaven by a decisive change, and not merely by a progressive purification. And this is the very marrow of Protestant divinity and Evangelical Faith' (Ibid p111). 'It is certain that the perfect man will be the last to know how perfect he is.' Newton Flew finds Forsyth exhilarating, but an echo of Ritschl acquiescing in sin rather than seeking release from it. But he can hardly convict Forsyth, as he does Ritschl, of having a defective view of sin and grace. Forsyth always sees the Kingdom in the light of the cross, not the other way round. The stress here is on the relationship and ethics, rather than mystical experience, and anything approaching 'deification' seems remote from Forsyth's stress. Grace is supreme –'Yea, the hard placid matron, whose family was well brought up and floated out, who was a patron of society, a sponsor for all new-comers, a chaperon with whom you could go anywhere, she was outside the Kingdom, and poor Magdalene, poor

Gretchen, the poor slayer of her unborn child might be in' (Ibid p125). And finally – and this is pure Maurice – 'individual perfection is not possible apart from the perfection of all, especially as that is antedated in Christ.' In its context, this was dynamite.

In 1901, at 53, Forsyth became Principal of Hackney, soon to be New College, the Congregationalist College where he had been an uneasy student. The college was affiliated to the University of London. Forsyth soon was lecturing in theology, becoming Dean of the Faculty of Divinity in 1911. He became Chairman of the Congregational Union in 1905, at the time when his church was in a furore over R J Campbell's 'New Theology,' pure Hegelian immanentalism, which poured from the marble pulpit of the City Temple. Bishop Charles Gore and Forsyth began a friendship which included an onslaught on the 'New Theology.' 'Theological quack,' said Forsyth. When Campbell appeared on the platform, cries of 'Quack, quack, quack,' were heard, while others, at times of theological debate, would cry, 'Forsyth, Forsyth,' till he spoke. Keith Clements has recently outlined again this controversy, which ended with Gore luring Campbell back into the Anglican fold of his Oxford period and re-ordaining him. Campbell died in 1956, an honoured Canon of Chichester, his latter books as dull in their orthodoxy as his earlier ones had been superficial in their radicalism. [3]

The crisis of Forsyth's later years was the First World War, which he first saw as a Godly crusade for righteousness against pitiless militarism. At the turn of the century he had spoken of the 'cursed, cursed, cursed Sultan;' now it was the Kaiser! If you want a statement of the Just War, the *Christian Ethic of war* (1916) is worth a perusal, if only to reject it. Like Karl Barth, he saw the old world falling apart, and his old teachers tarred with the brush of liberalism which had no word for a disintegrating Europe, and whose pacifism was no match for blood and iron! But very quickly he came to see that all were guilty, and in the *Justification of God* (1917) produced the greatest piece of Christian apologetic in World War One. But to this we must return. I want now to analyse the major output of writing, which is a very large corpus, most of it lectures written at white heat. Forsyth's daughter says the desk shook as he wrote day after day, and then he would sink exhausted on his couch, his manic exertions followed by depression and debility. How this frail man produced all he did while running a poverty-stricken college, preaching all over the kingdom, and active in the University, is amazing. I divide the corpus into five areas, all of which were set out in the books of the Cambridge period of Forsyth's life.

1. The Work of Christ

Here are three books: *The Cruciality of the Cross* (1909); *The Work of Christ* (1910) and *The Justification of God* (1917). When Dr Frederic Greeves lectured on Systematic Theology at Bristol, he always began his treatment of Christology with the **work** of Christ – atonement – rather than with his

Person.   Precedents include Martin Luther's spiritual director, von Staupitz –
'Begin with the wounds of Christ,' or Melancthon – 'Christ is known by his
benefits.' Frances Young (again) is a contemporary example, which made the
contribution in *The Myth of God Incarnate* (1977) so different from the rest of
that controversial book.   So Forsyth, like George Tyrrell, and the historian
John Neville Figgis, began with 'that strange man on the cross,' a phrase
which occurs in all three.   But the quest for meaning begins with 'God's
holiness which issues to man in love, acts upon sin as grace, and exercises
grace through judgement' (Cruciality p5).   That holiness is divinely satisfied
once for all on the cross.'   The moral centre of all authority is the cross.
Forsyth anticipates the 'Form Critics' like Dibelius in 1908 by pointing out that
the Gospels are 'Kerygma,' statements of the cross, not biographies of a
spiritual Christopher Columbus.   It is the Word which produces Bible and
Church alike.   As always, Forsyth does not divide Father and Son.   God is
always the initiator. 'The prime doer in Christ's cross was God.   Christ was
God reconciling' (Cruciality p27). 'The feeble Gospel preaches God was ready
to forgive, the mighty Gospel preaches God has redeemed (Ibid p52).
Forsyth rules out crude propitiation or substitutionary theories, though he is
nearer Anselm than Abelard at times.   The atonement did not produce a
grace, it flowed from grace.   Like Maurice, he shows that it is the race that is
redeemed, not just individuals.

Of modern British theologians, Frances Young comes the nearest to Forsyth,
both in the stress on God's initiative, and the moral aspect of atonement.
'Atonement means a conviction that God has somehow dealt with evil, with
sin, with rebellion.   Perhaps the nearest we can get to expressing this is to
say that on the cross God in Christ entered into the suffering, the evil and the
sin of his world, he entered the darkness and transformed it into light, into
blazing glory.   He took responsibility for the existence of evil in his creation;
he bore the pain of it and the guilt of it, he accepted the consequence into
himself and in his love reconciled his holiness to sinful and corrupt humanity,
justifying the ungodly, accepting man just as he is' [4]   Forsyth or James
Denney might have written that! Forsyth sees Christ as bearing the penalty
of sin but not penally. 'A man who loses his life in the fire damp where he is
looking for the victims of an accident, pays the penalty of sacrifice, but does
not receive its punishment.   I think it is useful to think of Christ as taking the
penalty of sin – but I refuse to speak of his taking its punishment' (Work
p162).   Frances Young calls that 'facing the music of his own creation.'
Forsyth moves again into this area in *The Justification of God* (1917).   The
awful evil of war almost overwhelms him.   The Ritschlian idea of the Kingdom
as 'the organization of humanity through action inspired by love' is not
enough. No, the Kingdom breaks in with the cross. 'It is not the cleansing of
the site for the heavenly city, it is the city itself descending to a world which
could tear its heart out in war. 'The cross of Christ, with its judgement,
grace, its tragic love, its grievous glory, its severe salvation and its finished
work, is God's only self-justification in such a world' (p37).   Forsyth has no
false millenarianism either – Christ is crucified, 'in agony to the end of the
world,' as Pascal says (p158).

2. So From The Work We Move To The Person

Here are Forsyth's greatest writings, certainly the most systematic: *The Person and Place of Jesus Christ* (1909), surely his masterpiece, and *The Principle of Authority in Relation to Certainty, Sanctity and Society* (1913), his most massive and complex work. My old teacher, Rupert Davies, in *Religious Authority in an Age of Doubt* (1968), has a notable and sympathetic analysis of the *Principle of Authority*, showing Forsyth's immense debt to Ritschl, his stance on the absolute revelatory nature of Christ, and his Kantian assertion of the Holy as absolute moral authority rather than fascinating mystery. Davies, in a logic chopping exercise, shows us that Forsyth cannot claim certainty for his position, but only certitude. Who can ask more? I am not persuaded that we can emerge beyond what Forsyth asserts. Can one live by more than faith? The *Person and Place* assumes the cruciality of the cross. It is critical of the Patristic models of Christology as 'substance;' Forsyth indeed is as sceptical of the value of the Chalcedonian definition as William Temple was to be. Self-emptying love is the key to Christology. Forsyth draws on much German material and can be directly compared with Gore, H R Mackintosh, and the combative Bishop Weston, who all stressed *Kenosis*, but Forsyth never fell into the trap of deciding which attributes Christ threw off, nor the other trap, which has been called 'Rift Valley Christology' – up, down and up again, with the Incarnation appearing as an interval, and not a symbol of perpetual self-offering, since (the inevitable Charles Wesley!).

> 'He emptied himself of all but love,
> And bled for Adam's helpless race.'

That love and self-offering define how we look at the attributes of God anyhow, for 'there was a cross in the heart of God before there was a cross on the hill of Calvary,' which is to put Forsyth with Abelard and Horace Bushnell at this point. There was no release from self-offering, for it was of the nature of God. Humanity was taken up into Godhead, too. From what Christ does we can reach back to the *Kenosis* and forward to the *Plerosis*, the fullness of the Christ who is the head of the whole human race.

There is some magnificent polemic here, with Harnack's 'religion of Jesus' in the firing line, and a pre-dating of Hoskyns' essays in *Mysterium Christi* and *Essays Catholic and Critical*, with the assertion that 'as far back as we can go, we find only the belief and worship of a risen, redeeming and glorified Christ, whom they could wholly trust, but only very poorly imitate, and in his relation to God could not imitate at all' (Person p44).

Forsyth's Christology does not, I think, answer all our contemporary questions. I think that his handling of the attributes of omnipotence, omniscience, omnipresence, as to be defined by love and self-giving, is luminous (the Methodist theologian, W F Lofthouse taught this also), but his theory of the retraction of the attributes at the Incarnation (for all the world like an aircraft retracting its undercarriage in flight!) won't really do. Nor could we today, I think, follow his view that Christ was indeed sinless but did not know it, therefore his temptations were real. There was almost insuperable weakness in Kenotic theory at that sort of point. When I first read it, as a precocious schoolboy, it seemed to me that Donald Baillie's Christology of the 'paradox of Grace' is more credible than the Gore-Forsyth style of approach. Christ is the union of supreme grace and perfect faith. Need we push it further? In no way does this eliminate the pre-existence of the Logos, nor does it limit the redeeming initiative of the Godhead.

3. Ecclesiology

Forsyth belonged to no ecclesial party, but sought to recover in the Free Churches a positive view of the nature of church, ministry and sacraments, and of the movements for church unity, in contrast with the merging of church activity with philanthropy and politics. It was Campbell who said, 'The atonement needs to be repeated on the altar of human hearts ... Go with J Keir Hardie to the House of Commons and listen to his pleading for justice to his order and you see the atonement.' To Silvester Horne the 'ballot box was the sacrament of humanity.' Forsyth's writings in this area are diverse and intense.

The Charter of the Church – The Spiritual Principle of Nonconformity (1896), a Cambridge period polemic, stressed grace as we might expect. For a high churchman, a Catholic Evangelical like Forsyth, this meant opposition to any establishment of religion. Let the Establishment act like a sister among sisters. Rupert Davies was still having to say precisely that in 1983! Any episcopal monopoly is to be resisted. How Mauricean though is the phrase, 'It was a race which Christ redeemed and souls are members of it. And he redeemed men in a Kingdom' (Charter p41). For Forsyth the apostles had no successors – shades of the 'Shaliach' controversy! – as such. The successor of the apostles was the New Testament, not bishops. Bishops there may well be in a united church, but only if Free Church ministers are accepted as true ministers. 'It is very odd. It is something else than odd. For the rich madame who will not recognise people in business because she is set on being recognised by the aristocracy who snub and ignore her, is not only amusing, but when she parades her religion as the reason, she is, let us say, pathetic' (Ibid p55). Fighting talk, very fin de siècle! Sacerdotalism is rejected, but not replaced by individualism or charismatic enthusiasm as today. *Rome, Reform and Reaction* (1899), contains an analysis of the Reformation. *Faith, Freedom and the Future* (1912) saw Forsyth analysing the Calvinist system into a centralised form, as in Presbyterianism, and a more localized form in Congregationalism, with Anabaptists to the left. Here are the roots of Bernard Manning's pleas for the reunion of the two elements, following fusion with some of the Churches of Christ.

But it is *The Church and the Sacraments* (1917) which shows the mature Forsyth looking to the future. Unlike his contemporaries A S Peake and J S Lidgett in Methodism, but with J H Moulton and Mandell Creighton, he did not envisage organic union in our time in England, but rather what he called the 'United States of the Church,' a form of federation. Lesslie Newbigin harshly renounced this as 'reunion without repentance,' but it is where we still are in Britain! It is amazing how church leaders have shifted their ground back to where Forsyth and Moulton stood in 1917. I am still with Peake and Lidgett, but Forsyth has proved the more realistic.

On sacraments, Forsyth sees 'mere memorialism' as more dangerous than realist doctrines of 'real presence' for, after all, we believe in the Resurrection and the Holy Spirit, and have tryst with a living Lord at the Eucharist. But it is the treatment of Infant Baptism which is still worth exploring. Here is the declaratory sacrament of prevenient grace. The influence of Maurice is strong here. 'If you object that Baptism can mean nothing to the child because he knows nothing of it, must you not object that the cross means nothing to him because, while he was even without life, Christ died for his ungodliness … Yet to remember and take home the cross is salvation' (Church and Sacraments p173). A child is given a christening mug by grandma, who later dies. 'Where is grandma?' 'She is in heaven now.' 'Did she love me before I could speak?' 'Yes.' 'Did God love me before I could speak, too?' 'Yes.' Sacraments are Christ's love tokens to his church. Baptism is not primarily an act of the parents, nor of the child, but of the church, and of Christ in the church. It is our individualism that has done most to ruin the sacrament of Baptism among us (Ibid p177). 'It signifies regeneration, but it does not mean that the rite regenerates the child. It is anticipatory, proleptic. A Baptism <u>unto</u> the confession of Church faith may be as true to the Gospel Grace as a Baptism <u>upon</u> it, and less individualist' (Ibid p181). Forsyth anticipates much of what Donald Baillie, Herbert G Marsh (whose book of 1943 is not as well known as it merits) and W F Flemington said a generation afterwards. [5] He avoided the mischief done later by a comparison of Infant Baptism with circumcision, which is found in Calvin, and Wesley too. So we have a full-blooded reformed sacramentalism here, rare in the Congregationalism of his day, though the renaissance of a more Genevan style, associated with Bernard Manning, Nathaniel Mickelm, J S Whale and Forsyth's pupil, Lovell Cocks, was a logical successor of Forsyth's stand. On the ordained ministry, there is much here for contemporary protestants to explore, with the contemporary dangers of a misunderstanding of the nature of the 'Priesthood of all Believers' in the name of charismatic enthusiasm. Such a priesthood is not about status and office, but about prayer and sacrifice. Forsyth is adamant that the ordained minister is a minister of the Word – the whole great chord of Christ, Bible, preaching, sacraments. *Positive Preaching and Modern Mind* (1907) is perhaps still the most prophetic book ever written on preaching. Its theme is not technique or style, but theology. The preacher represents the 'Great Church' – a notable Forsythian phrase – in the local church. 'Biblical preaching preaches the Gospel and uses the Bible, it does not preach the Bible and use the Gospel' (Positive Preaching p37). 'He is to preach to the church from the Gospel so that with the church he may preach the Gospel to the world. He is to preach to the church that he shall also preach from the church' (Ibid p79). So the preacher is sacramental. 'The real presence of Christ crucified is what makes preaching. It is what makes of a speech a sermon and a sermon a Gospel. This is the work of God' (Ibid p82).

Now Forsyth could offer 'Gospel' to children as well as adults, but what he would make of some 'all age worship' beggars the imagination. Neville Ward's terse comment is relevant. 'The decay of the power of preaching is one of the great pains in the life of the church just now. Affectionate and forbearing church goers who truly love their minister, both for himself and for the Christ who in some mysterious never adequately defined way haunts every ordained person, confess in moments of painful honesty that, while thanking God for the rest of the priest's work, as soon as he announces his text (or in some more radiant way signals the start of the sermon) they just have to switch off their minds if they are to keep sane' [6]. Have we reduced everything now not to 'what Jones can swallow,' but what the Cubs and Brownies can understand? Forsyth would recall us to what preaching actually should be – 'the organized Hallelujah of intelligent faith addressed to men but offered to God' (Positive Preaching p97 cf p95), and he bids ministers remember who they are. 'We are not the fire but we live where it burns. The matter we handle in our theological thought we can only handle with some protection for our face. It is one of the dangerous industries' (The Soul of Prayer p73). What was a cri de coeur in 1907 is now a desperate matter. Preaching must assume almost no detailed biblical knowledge in our hearers, the reasons for which are complex, but one of which is the retreat from theology Forsyth dreaded.

Forsyth is still explosive on ordained ministry – sacramental but not sacerdotal. 'An authoritative Gospel in a humble personality.' Thomas D Meadley, sometime Principal of Cliff College, told me that he tried to get some of Forsyth's insights on to the agenda of the Anglican-Methodist Conversations team in the 1960s, but the discussion was geared in the direction of Anglican norms, which Free Churchmen too tamely followed from 1920 onwards.

To Forsyth the ministry is seen as a gift of God to the church. The minister is not primarily a secretarial functionary (complete with Amstrad, but thin on books!). He is the organ of the common priesthood of the church. 'Not a brilliant personality but a consecrated one.' We might ask where is the great classical Reformed doctrine of the ministry, learned in the Word of God, the servant not of the institution but of Christ?

4. Spirituality

P T Forsyth was a theologian of righteousness, of the holiness which stems from the Holy Father. Towards the end of his years – he was now in his late sixties – came two gems of spiritual life. *The Soul of Prayer* (1916) contained some material from an earlier book, where he was 'twinned' with Dora Greenwell. Old emphases loom large. 'Prayer is the assimilation of a holy God's moral strength' (Soul p12). Prayer is agonizing, wrestling, 'asking with a will,' like the scene in Gethsemane. 'We will come one day to a heaven where we shall gratefully know that God's great refusals were sometimes the true answers to our truest prayer. Our soul is fulfilled if our petition is not' (Ibid p14). Forsyth would have no room for the petty prayers to a God who seems to have a particular regard to the petitions of a sub-culture. 'We pray for the removal of pain, pray passionately and then with exhaustion, sick from hope deferred and prayer's failure. But there is a higher prayer than that. It is a greater thing to pray for pain's conversion than its removal … It is to make it serve the soul and glorify God. It is to consecrate its elements and make it sacramental. It is to convert it into prayer' (Ibid p42). Is there a spirituality for ministers? Yes – intercession. 'The intercessory private prayer of the minister is the best corrective of the critical spirit or the grumbling spirit which so easily besets and withers us today' (Ibid p77). Public prayer should be in the main liturgical, with room for free prayer, as Christ on the cross fell back on the liturgy of his people, the Psalms.

This Life and the Next, the Effects on this Life of Faith in Another (1919) ends Forsyth's literary output. He anticipates by years the stress on eschatology of a Dodd or a Wainwright. Forsyth reveals an almost Eastern belief in the Communion of Saints, which leads to his assertion of the propriety of praying for the dead. 'Prayer for the dead is healthier than tampering with them. Prayer is our supreme link with the unseen. We should resume prayer for the dead were it only to realize the unity of the church and our fellowship with its invisible part' (This Life and the Next p34). And dare we still say at a funeral, 'There are those who can quietly say, as their faith follows their love to the unseen, "I know that land. Some of my people live there. Some have gone abroad there on secret foreign service which does not admit of communication. But I meet from time to time the Commanding Officer, and when I mention them to him, he assures me all is well" ' (Ibid p37)?

Nothing here in Forsyth is more reminiscent of F D Maurice. 'We are all predestined in love to life sooner or later if we will. Death is not final' (Ibid p16). 'Were we in hell, it is still God's hell' (p37). If this is universalism, it is an anticipation of the precise way in which Barth turned the flank of post-Calvin 'double-predestination.' And the end – and this is one of the best things Forsyth wrote – 'The Christian idea is not happiness and it is not power, but it is perfection, which is the growth of God's image and glory as our destiny' (p87). And to that 'great Catholicism' (the phrase is Forsyth's) Wesley and Newman would have cried 'Amen' – three men of the Second Journey.

5. Conclusion

Completeness necessitates a very brief glance at the rest of the corpus. Forsyth was an extraordinary polymath. His first book was on modern art. His *Christ on Parnassus* (1911) links all the arts to theology, a rare thing for a Protestant theologian to dare, but faith 'affects the whole man and the whole society' (Parnassus pvii). 'A gospel which saves society must also save its culture' (pviii). This book contains the oft-quoted defence of Gothic architecture. 'This style is the purest, most adequate and most congenial expression of the Christian spirit in architecture' (p176), but 'If Christianity were an aesthetic religion the Gothic cathedral would be its finished and perpetual type, the fit garment of a worship the most imaginative and beautiful the world knows – but Christianity is not an aesthetic religion, it is an ethical... Its worship centres in an active Saviour who is more than a Godly spectacle... A vivacious critic once said that it was the devil that invented Gothic architecture to prevent the people from hearing the Gospel... The Church must be primarily an auditorium, even when it is not preaching but prayer that we have in view' (pp189-191). *Marriage, its Ethics and Religion* (1913) is notable for Forsyth's comments on the rights of women. The little noted (except by Alec Vidler) and never reprinted *Theology in Church and State* (1915) is paralleled by the writings of J N Figgis at the time.

More important is the material on social ethics, typified by *Socialism, the Church and the Poor* (1908) and the address to the Congregational Union of 1905, entitled *A Holy Church, the Moral Guide of Society* (in The Church, the Gospel and Society pp5-64). Forsyth knew early poverty – forgetting his daughter's birthday in absence of mind, he says, 'Forgive your father who never knew a birthday party.' 'Christ's poor' had a place in his heart, and even if he did not espouse Charles Gore's socialism, he could lambast the materialism of Edwardian society. Contemporary stress on justice finds an echo in Forsyth. 'Christian holy love may take the form of benevolence on the one hand, or the conciliation on the other, but it must also, for public purposes, take the form of righteousness.' There is much more sympathy for the capitalist than Gore, whose social background was very different from Forsyth's. 'Can a Christian be a capitalist? Of course he can, but the social peril of immense wealth in non-moral hands looms large... the pursuit of wealth as the one object of life can be more fatal to the soul than bouts of vice' (Ibid p45, cf p39, 41). What is striking is that Forsyth should have taken that theme for his 'key note' address in 1905, bringing theology and social concern together. This was the year before the great Liberal election 'landslide' of 1906. There is no doubt on which side Forsyth's vote would be cast!

So we end. It is, believe me, a heady experience to read again the corpus of Peter Taylor Forsyth. No theologian of the past asks or answers all <u>our</u> questions. One cannot be a blind disciple of anyone from our age or any other. Here was a foreshadowing of much of Karl Barth and the renewal of

Reformed theology. Barth would surely echo Forsyth when he said, 'When Christ's finality is gone, Christianity is gone' (The Person and Place of Jesus Christ p11). Like Barth, Forsyth is suspicious of 'religion' which is not just 'all the excellent things the Mayor can open' (Ibid p17), but the Ayatollahs also. Like Schillebeeckx in our day, he sees Christ as the 'sacrament on earth of God's real presence' (Ibid p30). The risk is that it is a package deal which you take or reject. There is no middle way with a theology like this.

In the end I concur with Gordon Rupp. 'Forsyth's emphases are lively and modern. It seems likely that he will take his place among preachers and theologians who will be read profitably for many generations to come, not on grounds of theological antiquarianism but as speaking the language of the centuries which makes all Christians contemporary.' [7]

More recent books to be noted:
Trevor Hart (Ed)   Justice, the True and Only Mercy
T & T Clark 1995   Essays on the Life and Theology of Peter Taylor Forsyth
Alan P F Sell (Ed)   P T Forsyth Theologian for a New Millennium URC 1999

References

1. A M Allchin, *The Dynamic of Tradition*, DLT 1981 p1
2. F Young, *Face to Face*, Epworth 1985 p58
3. K Clements, *Lovers of Discord*, SPCK 1988 chapter 2 pp19ff
4. F Young, *Sacrifice and the Death of Christ*, SPCK 1975 p94
5. D M Baillie, *The Theology of the Sacraments*, Faber and Faber 1957
6. H G Marsh, *The Origin and Significance of New Testament Baptism*, Manchester 1941; W F Flemington, *The New Testament Doctrine of Baptism*, SPCK 1948; N Ward, *Enquiring Within*, Epworth 1988 pp66-7
7. A M Hunter, *P T Forsyth*, SCM 1974 p7

Chapter 4

John Wesley's Pragmatic Theology

Introduction

In recent years the transatlantic Evangelical Revival has come into the centre of historical research with its pivotal emphasis of bible, cross, conversion and activism. It was well under way before John Wesley began his work and he was deeply influenced by it. Thus, "simple chronology disposes of the stereotypes of the whole Revival as a chain reaction from the Aldersgate Street experience and of John Wesley as a solitary Moses striking the rock of petrified Anglicanism to release a sudden stream of revival."[1] Bearing in mind the variety of Evangelicalism we need to avoid a stereotyped Wesley as well as nostalgia or using Wesley as a panacea for *our* problems.[2]

Wesley's background needs brief analysis. His first influence was, of course, his parents. Although Samuel and Susanna Wesley were children of ministers who had left the Church of England in 1662, they both became Anglican when teenagers. They were High Church Anglicans with Susanna much more Jacobite than Samuel, hence their famous quarrel, the reconciliation of which led nine months later to John's birth – such are the contingencies of history! Puritanism and Caroline Anglicanism with its emphasis on the sacraments were very much held together by Wesley. While he could appeal to "men of reason," with the Cambridge Platonist John Smith, he saw no real gulf between religious experience and the age of reason, between the use of electricity, folk remedies and the supernatural.

The truest knowledge of God is that which is kindled within us by the heavenly *warmth of our hearts*. That which enables us to know and understand aright the things of God must be a living principle of holiness within us.[3]

None of the influence of his early days – personal or intellectual – were ever forgotten. For example, the theology of Arminianism, characterised by such features as those found in the Remonstrance of 1605:

- Divine election conditional on human faith.
- Human faith foreknown to God.
- Atonement intended for and available to all by the Holy Spirit.
- Divine Grace indispensable but not irresistible.
- It is not certain that all believers will persevere to the end.

This was reflected for Wesley through the Caroline Anglican tradition and made him the odd man out in the Evangelical Revival, save for John Fletcher. From the Carolines also, especially Jeremy Taylor's *Holy Living and Holy Dying* (and we must add Thomas à Kempis), came the stress on utter devotion to

Christ. This was linked with emphasis of Eastern Christianity which he acquired from writings of Macarius the Egyptian.

So also, Wesley was introduced to the Cappadocian fathers especially Gregory of Nyssa, who taught a vision of perfection – of disciplined and aspiring love – and a clear doctrine of the Holy Spirit.[4] An early sermon of Wesley, *The Circumcision of the Heart* (January, 1733), was only slightly altered but never refuted by him and is included in the *Forty Four Sermons.*

"Let your soul be filled with so entire a love of him that you may love nothing but for his sake," says Wesley – his stress being upon "faith which works by love," Wesley's Arminianism was, says Geoffrey Nuttall, an "Arminianism of the heart."[5]

He took the Moravian emphasis on justification by faith, the need for new birth and the assurance of salvation (which could be both gained and lost). This contrasts with the Calvinist stress on 'election' and 'final perseverance,' though Wesley's emphasis on grace was Calvin-like: "Wherein may we come to the very edge of Calvinism? In denying all natural free will and power antecedent to grace. But God will grant that grace to all."[6]

The late Gordon Rupp, following French models, used to say that there were three ways of looking at humanity in the eighteenth century. First, *the optimism of nature* – the Enlightenment view that humanity was fundamentally good and perfectible. In a sense Wesley believed that humanity was perfect and good before the Fall. He even said that there were no volcanoes before the Fall.[7] Second, the *pessimism of grace* – the Calvinist view that humanity was fundamentally evil but could be rescued by God's elective grace, of which preaching was a means. Third, the *optimism of grace* – there is no limit, given the conditions of a fallen world, to what God can do with the human heart. Holiness, happiness and the transformation of the human heart are possible together.

Imagine a triangle, the base of which is the priority of God's universal love and the two sides the need for personal faith and no limit to be set to God's grace. Many Catholic and Protestant elements come together here which made Wesley rather different from most other leaders of the Renewal.

Wesley As A Theologian

I do not put Wesley in the mould of an Augustine or an Aquinas or a Calvin. His style was what Karl Barth called "irregular dogmatics," by which he means a theological style closer than others to the actual preaching of the gospel – the commentary, the sermon and the hymn are examples of what Barth meant. Much of what Wesley said was evangelical commonplace and very much of his age. We must beware the tendency always to want to drag him somehow into our controversies. In the seventies, for example, we had

Wesley the 'liberation theologian,' and now Professor Geoffrey Wainwright is aligning Wesley with his own deep and proper concern with the doctrine of the Trinity.[8] But certain actions and beliefs do stand out.

Action And Reflection

Action and reflection came together. Consider for a moment the experience in Aldersgate Street, 24th May 1738. Wesley felt his heart "strangely warmed," that he did trust in Christ as Saviour, not because of some emotional preaching but through a reading from Luther's *Preface to the Epistle to the Romans.* Here is the probable passage:

'Faith is a living, daring confidence in God's grace, so sure and certain that a man would stake his life on it a thousand times. This confidence in God's grace and knowledge of it, makes a man glad and bold and happy in dealing with God and all his creatures; and this is the work of the Holy Ghost in faith. Hence a man is ready and glad without compulsion, to do good to everyone, to serve everyone, to suffer everything in love and praise of God who has shown him this grace. And thus it is impossible to separate works from faith as to separate heat and light from fire.[9]'

Wesley's heart was warmed and his mind enlightened by this passage, which connected justification by faith and God's gracious initiative with our active response and growth in grace. Franz Hildebrandt, who was Martin Niemöller's curate in Hitler's day, was right to point to the strong link between Luther and Wesley.

Appeal To Tradition

Not many bothered with Luther in the eighteenth century. Wesley saw his own Anglican tradition light up in a way that made Cranmer's liturgy and the Thirty-nine Articles say the kind of thing Luther was saying. When Wesley talked about tradition, he meant not only the Fathers of the early centuries but the Anglican Fathers also.[10]

After May 1738, Wesley went off across Germany to Herrnhut to "see how the Christians lived," i.e. those Moravians who played such a profound role in his journey to Aldersgate Street. It seems that the Herrnhutters were not sure of his soundness! Wesley and Zinzendorf clashed on Christian perfection. Zinzendorf said that it was only imputed righteousness and not change in status:

Jesus, thy blood and righteousness
My beauty are, my glorious dress;
Midst flaming worlds, in these arrayed,
With joy shall I lift up my head.[11]

Wesley, drawing on the Early Fathers avowed a change in nature. Righteousness was imparted as well as imputed. Charles Wesley's hymns pushed that further, almost to deification at times, though normally God and human beings are one in glory:

Finish then thy new creation,
Pure and spotless let us be;
Let us see thy great salvation,
Perfectly restored in thee.
Changed from glory into glory,
Till in heaven we take our place,
Till we cast our crowns before thee,
Lost in wonder, love, and praise![12]

Commitment To Mission

Wesley did not begin his open air evangelism at this point, but was pushed into it by George Whitefield in Bristol. He found it worked – and it gave others assurance of their salvation, if not himself! The Mission with centres in London, Bristol and Newcastle began in earnest in 1739 and Wesley's part in it did not end until 1791 though its style had changed. Of course, the Mission did not depend wholly on Wesley, as Heitzenrater has recently insisted – Wesley did not ceaselessly ride a horse! A careful study of his journal reveals that after the early days, Wesley usually never went far away from London between November and March. His journeys were also carefully planned and monitored. Later he usually changed the horse for a coach fitted out as a prayer room, library and a place where he could do a great deal of writing.

But how could revival continue and converts grow in grace? Remember that it wasn't wildfire – about one thousand five hundred converts a year on average up to seventy-two thousand members of society in 1791 in Great Britain.[13] The great increase in numbers were a nineteenth century phenomenon matching greater population increases. The early converts often had some religious background. About sixty per cent were women, some quite wealthy spinsters and widows as well as an army of women servants. Then there were artisans – shoemakers, cordwainers, carpenters, saddlers, harness makers, coopers, weavers, spinners, shopkeepers, school teachers, miners, tinners – what came later to be the 'aristocracy of labour.' Nobodies could become somebodies – perhaps a notable work of Methodism.[14] The early societies were often to be found where the parish system was weakest, and Wesley 'cannibalised' such groups, integrating them into *his* Connexion.

Organisation Into Small Groups

When issuing the first volume of Methodist hymns in 1739 Wesley affirmed that "the gospel of Christ knows no religion but social, no holiness but social holiness. Faith working by love is the length and breadth and height of Christian perfection." By that he did not mean social righteousness or politics but the fact that converts need to belong to a group, a truth he learned in part from the many Anglican religious societies of the day but also from the Moravians and from French Catholics like Count Gaston Jean-Baptiste de Renty (1611-49).[15] These Methodist societies became basic organisational units. Then there were the 'bands,' whose members met in a kind of corporate confessional with the aim of pressing on to perfection. "Do you desire to be told your faults to your face plain and home?" Methodists still sometimes use the old phrase 'in band,' that is, hold your tongue! The bands were too intense and too sectarian, however, and died by and large in a generation.

Methodism could not be just a holiness group. Its constituency was widening. Two elements in Wesley's thinking – salvation as an instant gift and experience, and as a steady progress through devotional means – tended to split apart into two different versions of holiness.[16] As Gordon Wakefield has put it:

"Wesley went on to claim that entry into perfection might be instantaneous like first conversion. The doctrine not only aroused opposition; it led to some scandals within the Methodist Societies, extreme claims and fanatical scenes."

But Wesley never claimed perfection for himself, "and always stood at some distance from his own movement. What must never be forgotten is that for him, perfection was perfect love, the keeping of the great commandments and the test was whether one loved one's enemies with a heart cleansed of hatred."

The 'class meeting,' as small groups of people belonging to a society, became normative. If a Bristol sea captain called Foy saw in such groups a good way of getting a penny a week to pay for the New Room, Wesley seized upon the structure to do more than collect money. Here was the key means of nurture and evangelism. In 1783 in Bristol, for example, there were fifty seven classes with nine to eighteen members. In Sunderland the classes were larger. The classes needed lay leaders – men and women who were the real pioneers of growth. The societies then needed leaders for worship, and the lay preaching system developed, based on the apprentice system, which is still in operation to this day.[17] Some preachers were part-time, others full-time – ministers in embryo almost inevitably. The societies were arranged into geographical units called 'circuits' – a term taken from the law and from religious orders. Furthermore, realising that many of these early preachers were of limited ability – though a very youthful army of great physical energy – Wesley ensured that they did not stay in any one circuit for long. The three volumes of the *Letters of John Pawson* give evidence of what the itinerancy was really like. The itinerants were not dissenting pastors, though not a few became such.

The class was Wesley's reply to the frequent phenomenon of a rapid revival petering out – like "a rope of sand," as he said to Whitefield – such as the great Cambuslang Revival of 1742. Wesley's generalisation of revival is a trifle unfair, for I think even Wesley had vested interests in portraying it thus. But on the whole it was fair enough.[18]

Importance of Worship

For worship, Wesley was in no doubt that his people should have the *instituted means of Grace* at the parish church (especially Holy Communion), but he also advocated the use of *prudential means of Grace* which became characteristic of the societies. This included activities like the 'preaching service' which may have been derived from the University sermon, or the medieval 'prone' (sermon), or from dissenting models which were around.[19] Hymns could provide a drip-feed of theology 'lined-out' by the preacher – an oral process which was an aid to people's memory. Methodist theology came alive in hymnody – its loss could be fatal! The straightforward expository sermon was delivered in a service at five in the morning, or after Evensong – becoming later when the lighting of chapels by gas encouraged evening worship in the early nineteenth century.

Then there was the 'lovefeast,' copied from the Moravians, which was a service of testimony and prayer with cake and water – a "democratised folk eucharist," as John Walsh called it. It was not an open meeting but required a ticket to attend as the young Jabez Bunting found as a teenager.[20] The 'watchnight service' was held, not necessarily at the New Year but often when there was a full moon, to avoid getting mugged on the way home! The 'Covenant Service'[21] was borrowed from the Puritans – Joseph and Richard Alleine – probably first used in 1755. It was a tremendous act of personal and corporate rededication, recently adopted in modern forms by the Church of South India and the Church of Scotland in the New Book of Common Order. The modern forms are benign compared with:

Lord Jesus wilt thou undertake for me?... I come Lord; I believe Lord; I throw myself upon thy grace and mercy; do not refuse me! I have not whither else to go. Here I will stay, I will not stir from thy door; on thee will I trust and rest and venture myself. God hath laid my help on thee and on thee I lay my hope for pardon, for life, for salvation. If I perish, I perish on Thy shoulder; if I sink, I sink in Thy vessel; if I die, I die at thy door. Bid me not go away for I will not go.

Christ indeed "has many services to be done" – which might result in "sailing against the wind, swimming against the tide, steering contrary to the times;

parting with our ease, our liberties and our accommodations for the Name of our Lord Jesus." *That* is scriptural holiness.

Pragmatic Theology

The whole pattern emerged without a highly planned system. It was inspired pragmatism. The preachers became more and more like ministers. What of the sacraments in the societies? The situation in America drove Wesley to even more pragmatic action. The War of Independence had driven most Anglican priests back to Britain, and there was no bishop in America. Wesley, believing that he had found precedents for ordination by presbyters in emergency, set apart Thomas Coke (already an Anglican priest) as superintendent, and then others as presbyters for America. Coke went over the Atlantic to set apart Francis Asbury as superintendent on Christmas Day 1784. He called himself bishop and acted most effectively as one. Charles Wesley was furious and wrote scurrilous verse:

Wesley his hands on Coke hath laid
But who laid hands on him?...
A Roman emperor, 'tis said,
His favourite horse a consul made
But Coke brings other things to pass
- He makes a bishop of – an ass!

There followed ordinations for Scotland which Ronald Knox called "Gretna Green ordinations,"[22] because Wesley had said it was proper for Scotland but the presbyters must not celebrate the sacraments south of the border! After Wesley died, English preachers such as John Pawson either continued to exercise a full ministry or wished to. The itinerant preachers soon became the Wesleyan ministry, and the Methodist Societies became the Methodist Connexion. Wesley early on had defended his style: "Methinks I would go deeper. I would enquire what is the end (i.e. purpose) of all ecclesiastical order? Is it not to bring souls from the power of Satan to God and to build them up on his faith and love. Order then is so far valuable as it answers these ends; if it answers them not, it is worth nothing"[23] We can call that pragmatic evangelicalism.

It is worth noting, at this point, what that astute Roman Catholic journalist, Clifford Longley, said in 1988. "Wesley did not leave behind a systematic theology... His memorial was the Methodist movement, itself a living thing rather than a set of ideas. It took its deepest inspiration not from him, however, but from his brother... Wesleyanism at its simplest definition is a choir founded by John to sing the hymns of Charles – and to live accordingly. This is its heart, its spirituality."[24]

But there is more than hymns, vital carriers of theology though they are – or should we say were? *Did* Wesley leave a systematic theology? The American scholar, the late Albert Outler, was right to call Wesley a "folk theologian" who minted theology for plain people. It was the balance and stance which matter, not the detail on which, frankly, Wesley could be confused and change his mind, as he did. Dr John Walsh in a brilliant recent article, "John Wesley – a Bicentennial Tribute," calls Wesley a 'both-and' man, which can be substantiated in many ways. He believed in a network of private religious societies or revivatising cells both to regenerate the church, and to exercise a missionary concern for the unchurched. Wesley said, "I look upon all the world as my parish"; though we might note that Whitefield used similar phrases! Again, he believed both in ministry in little places and also having everybody combined in a Connexion which he ran autocratically. Vivian Green called him "granite in aspic,"[25] for Wesley held both a low view of human nature and original sin and also the optimism of grace. As Walsh expresses it, the Christian life for Wesley was one of "ceaseless, cheerful activism." He saw the essence of perfection as perfect love for God and neighbour. He was both a fervent evangelical and also a sacramentalist, as was his brother. Wesley believed passionately in justification by faith but equally in Christian perfection. Although he was Protestant to the core, he also had catholic and orthodox elements in his theology. His faith was individual, and even individualistic at times, though he once advocated the community of goods (influenced no doubt by William Law whose views haunted him).[26] He had both love and concern for the poor and a hatred of accumulated wealth. He was involved at the end in the Antislavery Movement and believed that church and society should be transformed, though we cannot claim that Methodism ever achieved that.[27]

His personal life was a paradox. He was an Oxford don, obsessively neat and tidy, who held to the maxim 'cleanliness is next to godliness.' But he could also rub shoulders with the poor. He would tramp through the London streets in the snow collecting pennies for the poor – a sort of one man Christian Aid campaign. He encouraged experimental religion and didn't mind if people got excited, though Charles was more realistic and, on one occasion, had a bucket of water ready if the ladies became noisy again! But he also insisted on discipline and would rid the societies of crackpots, of which there were not a few.[28]

The use of scripture, tradition, reason and experience are not an inaccurate summary of his theological method, so long as we recall that the first three are standard Anglicanism going back to Richard Hooker, and note clearly that scripture was the "centre of gravity of his thinking" as George Croft Cell put it. Scripture is central, illuminated by the whole tradition, confirmed by the disciplined use of reason, verified by personal experience. Modern Methodism has seen this as some sort of quadrilateral but it is not a quadrilateral of equal sides, at least not if we are true to Wesley, which I fear we are often not.[29]

So, in summary, we can say that Wesley was both evangelical and catholic; he believed in faith and good works, in scripture and tradition, in revelation and reason though not when they contradicted one another. God's sovereignty and human freedom are held in tension as are universal redemption and conditional election, assurance of pardon and also the quest for Christian perfection – with its possible loss and recovery. Is all this just a 'pick-n-mix' pot-pourri derivative from the forces which played upon him? In some ways, the answer must be "Yes!" Gordon Wakefield is right to say, "Wesley was not original in anything he said or did except in so far as originality may consist in the ability to borrow, steal or adapt and unite in one whole items from various schools and systems." He could be influenced by the latest book he read – and he was reading for three quarters of a century. But I think the French scholar, Jean Orcibal, is right when he says, "Wesley was most original when he was most derivative, a theologian whose originality lay in his ability to select, assimilate and reconcile while yet remaining within the boundaries of a definite system."[30]

Contemporary Considerations

What then for today? Methodism split after Wesley's death or rather different parts of his system acquired autonomy. Methodism, too, became a world communion with considerable diversity, now brought under the umbrella of the World Methodist Council. An extraordinary amount of the old 'skeleton' remained, but Methodism now has to accommodate styles of society quite different from the early industrialism of the time when the system gelled. It did not – and could not – save England from revolution but it did produce a lifestyle which enabled ordinary people to become educated and often politically articulate. The consequence was men and women of thrift, frugality, reliability and initiative who would move marginally – and occasionally much higher-up the social scale. If poor they might become 'respectable poor.' The paradox is the later Wesley's attitude to the inevitability of the secularisation of Evangelical Arminianism into religious respectability combined with responsibility. Did temperance become a substitute for perfect love – "all pride, poverty, pianos and the stuff of self-reliance"?[31] Dare one call it scriptural holiness for the sparrows rather that the eagles? The role of Sunday schools, Friendly Societies, Trade Unions, Civic Government at every level, the Labour Party and, earlier elements of the Liberal Party, would reveal Methodist influence at most levels of English society. What of scriptural holiness? Thinking and practice split along the lines of revivalism. On the one hand, there were figures of the holiness movement such as Lorenzo Dow, James Caughey, Phoebe Palmer, Thomas Champness, Thomas Cook, Samuel Chadwick and their followers. The other line of thinking and practice, which stressed nurture and spiritual growth, can be found in Richard Watson, William Burt Pope, John Scott Lidgett and Robert Newton Flew.[32] Here R W Dale's astute criticism of Wesley's holiness doctrine is pertinent. Dale said that "the class meeting is perhaps the most striking and original of all the fruits of the Revival but in ethics it has a great weakness. Voluntary service – yes. Moral endeavour – yes. But the doctrine of Christian Perfection remains where Wesley left it – it has not entered the world of politics."[33] Wesley indeed had no systematic doctrine of applied perfection. He had no better prescription for the social problems of industrial capitalism than the injunction to give wealth away for fear of corruption.

Hugh Price Hughes brought together experiential holiness with a radical Liberalism which was prepared to use legislation for moral purposes. Scott Lidgett was to enter the political world in a rather different way with a transformist theology, linking with F D Maurice and fostering the later stages of the Forward Movement, including Central Halls, the Bermondsey Settlement, National Children's Home, the Wesley Deaconess Order and other progressive movements. Let us not forget, too, that the Wesleyan tradition produced an extraordinary generation or two of missionaries who were utterly disposable, at the behest of the Missionary Society.[34] Men and women, self-disciplined, self-respecting, often self-educated and sometimes self-absorbed, could have been crucial in producing a "viable class society" to use H J Perkin's phrase.[35] Why was England so peaceable in the 1930s at a time of gross economic deprivation? We might pause to remember that, in the 1980s, Methodism produced both prime minister Margaret Thatcher and the leader of the opposition Michael Foot, though neither remained Methodist. The role of the 'lapsed Methodist' is fascinating! It produced, too, a man like Sir Herbert Butterfield, Professor of Modern History at Cambridge who taught some of us to "hold to Christ and for the rest to be totally uncommitted."[36]

I end with a recent summary of Wesleyan theology by Geoffrey Wainwright with which I am in total agreement.

Allowing for the lapse of two hundred years, there is a close correspondence between the classic ecumenical movement and the profile of John Wesley that informed Methodists and others would recognise. Wesley's vision, program and praxis were marked by the following six principal features. First, he looked to the scriptures as the primary and abiding testimony to the redemptive work of God in Christ. Second, he was utterly committed to the *ministry of evangelism* where the gospel was to be preached to every creature and needed only to be accepted in faith. Third, he valued with respect to the Christian tradition and the doctrine of the church a *generous orthodoxy* wherein theological opinions might vary so long as they were consistent with the apostolic teaching. Fourth, he expected *sanctification* to show itself in the moral earnestness of and loving deeds of believers. Fifth, he manifested and encouraged *a social concern* that was directed towards the neediest of neighbours. Six, he found in the *Lord's Supper,* a sacramental sign of the fellowship graciously bestowed by the Triune God and the responsive sacrifice of praise and thanksgiving on the part of those who will glorify God and enjoy him for ever. These are the features which must be strengthened in contemporary Methodism, if we are to maintain our historic identity, speak with significant voice on the ecumenical scene and keep track on a recognisable Christian track as the paths diverge.[37]

References

1. G V Bennett & J D Walsh *Essays in Modern English Church History* (Black, 1966) p 134. See also David Bebbington, *Evangelicalism in Modern Britain* (Unwin Hyman, 1989) pp2ff
2. Richard P Heitzenrater *Mirror and Memory* (Nashville: Abingdon Press, 1989)
3. John Smith *Select Discourses* (1673) pp 2-4; cited in P E More & F L Cross *Anglicanism* (London, 1934) p 229
4. A Outler *John Wesley* (Oxford: Oxford University Press, 1964) pp 9-10. See also J A Newton, "Perfection and Spirituality in the Methodist Tradition," *Church Quarterly Review* (October 1970) pp 95-103
5. G F Nuttall *The Puritan Spirit* (London: Epworth, 1967) p 78
6. In 1745, he asked "Wherein may we come to the very edge of Calvinism? In denying all natural free will and power antecedent to grace. *But God will grant that grace to all.*" In 1765, he said "I think on justification just as I have done any time these last seven and twenty years and just as Mr Calvin does. In this respect I do not differ from him an hair's breadth." *Letters 4*: 298
7. E G Rupp *Principalities and Powers* (London: Epworth, 1952) ch5. See also B Bryant, *John Wesley and the Origins of Evil* (Moorleys, 1993)
8. D G Miller *P T Forsyth* (Pittsburg, 1981) p 63;
   G Wainwright *Methodists in Dialog* (Nashville: Abingdon, 1995)
   R Williams *Resurrection* (London D L T, 1982) p 4
9. P S Watson *The Message of the Wesleys* (London: Epworth, 1964) p 8
10. F Hildebrandt *From Luther to Wesley* (London: Epworth, 1951)
    S J Jones *John Wesley's Conception of Scripture* (Nashville: Abingdon, 1995)
11. HP 225
12. HP 267
13. R P Heitzenrater *Wesley and the People Called Methodists* (Nashville: Abingdon, 1995) pp 140, 149, 181, 183, 199, 237, 265, 288
14. C D Field, "The Social Structure of English Methodism" *British Journal of Sociology,* 18 (1977) pp 199-225
    J Lawson *A Man's Life* (London, 1913) p 113
15. H Bett, "A French Marquis and The Class Meeting" *PWHS,* 18 (1931-32) pp 43-5
    D Dunn Wilson *PWHS,* 35(1966) pp 181-4
    G S Wakefield *John Wesley* (Foundry Press, 1990) p 27
16. J M Turner *Conflict and Reconciliation* (London: Epworth, 1985) pp 51-2

H Cunliffe Jones & B Drewery (Eds) *History of Christian Doctrine* (London: T & T Clark, 1978) pp 473 ff

Wakefield   *John Wesley* p 27

17. M Batty   *Stages in the Development and Control of Wesleyan Lay Leadership 1791-1878* (Peterborough: Methodist Publishing House, 1993) pp27ff

G Milburn & M Batty (Eds) *Workaday Preachers: The Story of Methodist Local Preaching* (Peterborough: Methodist Publishing House, 1993)

18. A Fawcett   *The Combuslang Revival* (Banner of Truth Trust, 1971)

Letters 6:151

H D Rack   *Reasonable Enthusiast* (London: Epworth, 1986) pp 227 f

19. C N Wallwork "Wesley's Legacy in Worship" in: John Stacey (Ed) *John Wesley: Contemporary Perspectives* (London: Epworth, 1988) pp 83 ff

20. John Walsh   *John Wesley: A Bicentennial Tribute* (Dr Williams' Trust, 1993)

T P Bunting & G S Rowe   *The Life of Jabez Bunting* (Woolmer, 1887) p33

21. D Tripp   *The Renewal of the Covenant in the Methodist Tradition* (London: Epworth, 1969)

Wesleyan Service Book (1883)

22. R Knox   *Enthusiasm* (Oxford: Oxford University Press, 1950) p 511

See also J Vickers   *Thomas Coke* (London: Epworth, 1969) pp 101-2

23. Letters 2: 77   *To John Smith, 25 June 1746*

24. C Longley "Pursuing Christian Perfection" *The Times* (29 February, 1988)

25. V H H Green   *John Wesley* (Nelson, 1964) pp 127, 141

26. John Walsh "John Wesley and the Community of Goods" in: K Robbins (Ed) *Protestant Evangelicalism 1750-1850* (Oxford: Blackwell, 1990) pp 25-50

27. H D Rack   *Reasonable Enthusiast* pp 551-4

28. E G Rupp   *Religion in England 1688-1791* (Oxford: Oxford University Press, 1986) p 369

29. Wainwright   *Methodists in Dialog* p 304

R Clutterbuck   *Classical Christianity* (Sheffield: Cliff College, 1996)

S J Jones   *John Wesley's Conception of Scripture* (Abingdon, 1995)

J B Cobb   *Grace and Responsibility; A Wesleyan Theology Today* (Nashville: Abingdon 1995)

Ted Campbell "The Wesleyan Quadrilateral: The Story of a Modern Methodist Myth" in *Methodist History* 29 (1990-1) pp 87-95

30. Wakefield   *John Wesley* p 22

See also Jean Orcibal "The Theological Originality of John Wesley and Continental Spirituality" in R E Davies and E G Rupp (Eds) *History of the Methodist Church in Britain* vol 1 (London: Epworth, 1965) pp 81-111

31. C Binfield   *So Down to Prayers* (Dent, 1977) p 91

    See also David Bebbington "Holiness in Nineteenth Century British Methodism" in: W M Jacob & N Yates (Eds) *Crown and Mitre* (Boydell Press, 1993) pp 161-174

32. For a fuller analysis see J M Turner, "Victorian Values − or Whatever Happened to John Wesley's Scriptural Holiness," *PWHS,* 46:6 (1988) pp 165-184

    J M Turner   *After Thompson: Methodism and the English Working Class* (Halifax Antiquarian Society, 1989)

33. R W Dale   *The Evangelical Revival* (London, 1880) pp 31 ff

34. E Norman   *The Victorian Christian Socialists* (Oxford: Oxford University Press, 1987) chapter 8, Hugh Price Hughes

    R E Davies (Ed)   *John Scott Lidgett* (London: Epworth, 1957)

    A Birtwhistle   *In His Armour* (London, 1954)

    M Dickson   *The Inseparable Grief: Margaret Cargill of Fiji* (London, 1976)

35. R Colls   *The Pitmen of the Northern Coalfield: Work, Culture and Protest 1790-1850* (Manchester university Press, 1987)

    H J Perkin   *The Origins of Modern English Society 1780-1980* (Routledge and Kegan Paul, 1969) chapter 9

    E Royle   *Modern Britain: A Social History 1750-1985* (Arnold, 1987) pp 97 ff

36. H Butterfield   *Christianity and History* (Bell, 1949) p 146

37. Wainwright   *Methodists in Dialog* pp283-4

Chapter 5

The Last of the Wesleyans

Henry Bett (1876 – 1953)

In the period between the First and Second World Wars Handsworth College, Birmingham[1], had an extraordinary pre-eminence in Methodist scholarship – indeed, probably only Mansfield College, Oxford and Westminster College, Cambridge could surpass it in the academic 'firepower' of its staff. W F Lofthouse taught firstly Old Testament, then Theology and Philosophy (and anything else including Sociology and social ethics) and was Principal from 1925. W F Howard taught New Testament, becoming an internationally known Johannine scholar. C R North (whose first book was on Islam) taught Old Testament, laying the foundations for his notable contributions to post-exilic prophetic studies when Professor at Bangor. The fourth of the famous quartet was Henry Bett who taught Church History and History of Doctrine and was resident Tutor, which involved pastoral duties and the care of the College property.

Bett was a product of the late Victorian Wesleyanism in Lincolnshire and in many ways a Wesleyan to his finger tips. He was clearly one of those referred to by G G Findlay [2] in articles on ministerial training in 1901-02 stating that in his College (Headingley) he had men of university calibre and other men who were barely literate, with the implication that the former were not being given the stimulation which they needed from overworked tutors. Bett had little of the advantages of the later university trained men, but while exercising a notable pastoral and evangelistic ministry, he maintained academic interests which brought him his Manchester MA and were amazingly wide ranging.

His first book was *The Hymns of Methodism* (Kelly 1913, with revisions and enlargements, Epworth 1920 and 1945, with the help of a 'friend and former colleague' A R George). Bett displays here a thorough knowledge of eighteenth century literature, in which context the Wesleyan corpus of hymnody is set. The fascinating problem concerning which hymns were penned by John Wesley is partially solved. He anticipated much of the more recent interest in Charles Wesley shown by Bernard Lord Manning in the thirties and more recently by Donald Davie [3] who quotes Bett frequently – 'the indispensable Dr Bett' he calls him. From 1913 onwards Bett was a tireless enthusiast for Wesley's hymns and earned his richest reward in being nominated as one of the editors of the 1933 Methodist Hymn Book in which much of the Wesleyan corpus was retained: some 'Bettian' insertions are notable such as the two hymns of his 'liebling' Dora Greenwell (MHB 259, 381). Bett would have had more Wesley and Watts if the 'sons of Zeruiah' had not got the better of him. More 'flabby and sentimental verses of the modern poetasters' got into the book than were to his taste. A second book in this genre followed a year later with the *Spiritual Maxims of Angelus Silesius* (Kelly 1914), the German mystic, one of the many byroads down which Bett would wander with complete mastery of his material.

The transfer form Circuit life to Handsworth College in 1923 saw the flowering of Bett's scholarship.

Three medieval studies revealed a grasp of European languages – ancient and modern – and a penetrating ability to expound the complexity of medieval theology and philosophy which was notable in a man who was largely an autodidact, though linked with the University of Manchester. It is interesting that the two leading Methodist historians of the day – the other was Herbert Workman of Westminster College, London – were attracted to medieval history. Bett's three books in this field are remarkable for the strange way in which he chose three figures who were hardly on the academic sky line at all in 1925 but in the last twenty years have come into greater prominence than for centuries – and Bett's books (and those of Workman) are cited not infrequently by Catholic scholars.

The first book was *Johannes Scotus Erigena, a Study in Medieval Philosophy* (CUP 1925). This claimed to be the first full scale English treatment of "this supreme monument of art in the midst of the sandy wastes of the desert". Erigena's 'aphophatic' approach to God has recently been interpreted by John Macquarrie in his *In Search of Deity* (1984). The ground of his choice can be found in Bett's clear, concise analysis of this Eastern-style scholar, largely out of place in ninth century Europe. *Joachim of Flora* (Methuen 1931) followed – a book in much the same style. The recent renaissance of interest in Joachim, the later 'spiritual Franciscans' and the whole medieval theological underworld – the whole notion of an Age of the Spirit following the Ages of the Father and the Son – reveals that Bett has travelled the road before. [4] The same is the case with *Nicholas of Cusa* (Methuen 1932). Again Bett was a pioneer, for no English book had hitherto appeared on Nicholas. The enormous spate of scholarship on what the Dutch polymath Heiko Oberman calls the 'Masters of the Reformation'[5] and their 'forerunners' has swept past Bett's contribution, but he can stand as an English precursor here along with Workman's contemporary work on Wyclif and Hus. Bett, too, was eminently readable, a matter underlined by the rash of little books and articles on English style which he produced at the time – *How to Write Good English* (Allen and Unwin 1929), *Some Secrets of Style* (Allen and Unwin 1932), and *Wanderings about Words* (Allen and Unwin 1938).

This was still the age of the essay, a genre in which Bett excelled. Three books of notable essays backed up the three medieval books – *Studies in Religion* (Epworth 1929), *Studies in Literature* (Epworth 1929) and *On Second Thoughts* (Epworth 1931). The first includes brief pieces on miracle and prayer (which were soupçons to a later study), Eckhart, Mysticism, Joachim and the doctrine of the Eucharist, where Bett, the doughty evangelical protestant, breaks a lance or two with realist theories of the real presence, oddly ignoring Bucer and Calvin. The more literary book ranges from Walter Von der Vogelweide through Wesley's Journal to 'What is Poetry?', Theophile Gaultier and Dora Greenwell, of whom more later.

This spate of books (by the standard of modern tutors so busy relating to students at every hour of the day that they have little time for thinking let alone writing!) did not dry up, but Bett moved into other fields, notably back to his own beloved Methodism. Three books – two slender, one major – followed. *The Early Methodist Preachers* (Epworth 1935) is a model of the lecture-book and reveals a sharp historian's eye looking at Wesley's preachers. "With the exception of half a dozen of the earliest preachers who were soldiers, they were nearly all from that social group which lies between the working class and the middle class – skilled artisans, small tradesmen, small farmers, clerks, schoolmasters and the like - a class from which a great deal of what is best in English life has always come…" That sociological observation has been underlined by recent work like that of Dr Clive Field [6] – who has shown the enormous numerical proportion of artisans – neither 'lumpen proletariat' nor bourgeoisie – who found in early Methodism a way to meaning, purpose, thrift, prosperity, respectability and heaven!

Bett's Fernley-Hartley lecture comes next – *The Spirit of Methodism* (Epworth 1937). This is, perhaps, Bett's outstanding book – beautifully written, yet scholarly evocation of early Methodism. Bett trails his coat at times and reveals an alliance in thought on several issues with Bernard Lord Manning. A glance at *Essays in Orthodox Dissent* (1939) which Manning published two years after Bett's book will show the convergence. Bett, like Manning, had an instinctive historian's suspicion of ecclesiastical power and a more than merely prejudiced fear of episcopacy. This comes out in Bett's third chapter, 'Wesley, Methodism and the Church', which harks back at times to J H Rigg. Bett's book did not appear in the bibliography of Volume 1 of the History of Methodism – an odd slip, but then such naughty thoughts as those of Bett and Manning were best 'hushed up' in 1965! – the chickens have since come home to roost. Bett was not converted, as was his colleague W F Lofthouse, to support the Church of South India scheme, including bishops, which obtained Conference support in 1934. Nor (high Wesleyan though he appeared) was he much impressed by the *Methodist Sacramental Fellowship* (established in 1935) and engaged in dialogue with Dr J E Rattenbury over what he thought an isolation of the Eucharist from other means of grace.

Two theses pulsate through the book: Wesley marks the end of the dominance of Calvinism (Manning would not have liked that!) by which he implies any doctrine of double predestination rather than Calvin's churchmanship to which he was not averse, and he marks the consummation of the Reformation in stressing the importance of religious experience in determining the patterns of Christian doctrine. At the time when Karl Barth was questioning not only the liberal tradition but any theology of experience, Bett asserted that Wesley was the precursor of Schleiermacher and made penetrating comments on the links here between Moravian, Wesley and the great father of liberal Protestantism. This interpretation was eclipsed very quickly, but now we all seem to be existentialists! Bett clearly follows in the wake of Herbert Workman and George Eayrs [7] here, and it is worth opening up again the question of what really does characterise Methodism – the doctrine of Christian holiness or the priority of religious experience. Were, after all, the theological critics of Methodism from Dean Tucker to E B Pusey right in seeing the dangers of the stress on what they were inclined to call 'salvation by feeling'?

Bett's answer was to state that the "religious contribution of Methodism was … the recovery of the evangelical witness and the evangelical experience – the spiritual fact that real penitence, real faith, a real surrender of the heart and life to Christ, brings an assurance of the pardon and the peace of God, from which a sense of wonder and joy naturally spring and which leads directly to an intimacy of religious fellowship and a zeal of passionate evangelism". A pamphlet written in 1938 *What Methodists Believe and Preach* (Epworth) (200 years after Wesley's Aldersgate Street experience) underlines Bett's summary of the Methodist stance – "Repentance, faith, conversion, the assurance of sins forgiven, witnessed to the believing soul by the Spirit of God, when we cast ourselves on the mercy of God in Christ; and then all that results from this: a sense of wonder and thankfulness and joy, the practice of spiritual fellowship and the steadfast pursuit of holiness in our own lives and an impassioned evangelism that seeks to proclaim the glad news of salvation – the message which we ourselves have heard and believed – and the redemption that we have experienced in our own souls – to all the world." Perhaps Bett ends up with the best of both worlds. Theologically he clearly saw Methodism as grounding belief in experience rather than in tradition or scripture, vital though they may be. In an earlier essay he stated that "it must not be forgotten that what Schleiermacher in Germany did deliberately and scientifically as a theologian was done instinctively and practically by the Wesleys and the early Methodists in England" [8] Is this the way to circumvent Kant? The debate, I suspect, is not closed.

If anyone thought Bett a mere pietist they must look at another vein of his scholarship which, again, was curiously a decade or two before its time. In 1929, the year Bett had six books published, there appeared *Nursery Rhymes and Tales* and the *Games of Children* (both Methuen) anticipating the remarkable work of Iona and Peter Opie [9] in this field. In 1939 when a great Russian scholar, Professor Nicholai Arseniev, failed to appear to lecture on an occasion organised by the student body at Handsworth, Bett held a prestigious audience spellbound with an impromptu address on nursery rhymes, no doubt including 'Eena, Mena, Mina, Mo' with its equivalents in several European languages in which in each case the racial enemy is identified. [10] Research of this kind must have occupied many hours of Bett's time, as must the material packed into *English Legends* (Batsford 1950, 2nd ed. 1952), a most recondite and amusing compilation of legends, romances and tragedies, saints and relics, demons and goblins, monsters and giants.

The book is full of odd, sharp remarks (a mine of children's stories for the preacher) and beautifully illustrated by Eric Fraser including 'What Peeping Tom saw in Coventry' and the 'Tempting of St Dunstan' by an equally voluptuous medieval lady!

Henry Bett was a notable preacher – W F Lofthouse once remarked that his sermons were apparently very simple (this was said also of R N Flew) and beloved of ordinary congregations, but also provided matter for a theologians' retreat. The volume *The Exalted Name* (Stockwell 1929) typifies his preaching style, which was carried to the lengths and breadth of England when he was President of the Conference in 1940-41, those dark days of the Battle of Britain and the Blitz when a convinced pacifist sat in Wesley's chair. Bett as a preacher was an evangelical, always stressing the lure of Christ and our response. The 'wonder why such love to me', that 'work not our own' (Dora Greenwell's phrase), which was at the heart of his own devotion and prayers, was remembered long afterwards by those who heard him pray in College Chapel.

Bett retired in 1943, but his pen was not stilled. In 1949 there appeared *The Reality of the Religious Life* (1949), a comprehensive study of Providence, prayer and miracle. Bett was an evangelical but not what today would be called 'conservative evangelical'. Here, in fact, is a choice blend of liberal evangelicalism and the philosophical insights of F R Tennant and A E Taylor. The approach is rather different from the lexicographical analyses of biblical theology then becoming normative (Bett wrote almost nothing on the Bible!) or the secular forms of logical analysis in vogue in philosophical circles. Bett's approach is still out of fashion, but no less interesting for that. Book reviews like that on W R Matthews' *Problem of Christ on the Twentieth Century* [11] (1950) revealed a theological and critical acumen which was still needle sharp. But the finest contribution of these years was the culmination of his long interest in the Victorian poet and evangelical mystic Dora Greenwell.

A brief and beautifully written biography appears in 1950 *Dora Greenwell* (Epworth) and a year before his death an edition of Miss Greenwell's most remarkable book *Two Friends* (Epworth 1952, with introduction by H Bett) with its startling modernity such as an acceptance of evolution and openness in theology (a contrast to the hounders of the authors of *Essays and Reviews* and its warm tribute to Methodism. "Methodism is eminently social – its idea is that of journeying Zionwards in companies, gathering as they go … You see what with class meetings and prayer meetings and preachings, Wesleyans have so much more means than church people.") I am glad that *Hymns and Psalms*, which has also used so little material from fragile, ailing Victorian lady poets, have retained two of Dora Greenwell's poems:

"Thy reign eternal will not cease;
Thy years are sure, and glad, and slow;
Within thy mighty world of peace
The humblest flower has leave to blow."

"Yea, living, dying, let me bring
My strength, my solace from this spring,
That he who lives to be my King
Once died to be my saviour."   (HP 415 221)

A glance at the *London Quarterly and Holborn Review* [12] between 1920 and 1953 will reveal a succession of reviews and essays which, when we add the rich material provided for that journal by Howard and Lofthouse, shows the astonishing output of Handsworth College. Bett's life was not an untrammelled one. His first wife died in 1930. They had two daughters and a son. He married again. In 1935 he was awarded the rare degree of D Litt. by the University of Manchester for the medieval trilogy.

Of his role as a tutor, many tales are told of his preaching and his prayers and of his coughing and sneezing if a student should succeed in 'ringing Henry's bell' which presumably meant saying or praying something with which he violently disagreed. 'Uncle Henry' he was, in a way impossible for Lofthouse or Howard – one did not, I think, call *them* 'uncle' and every college needs an avuncular heart. Oddly enough, folklore tells us that his lectures could be dull – why goodness knows! – unless some student could distract him by asking "Dr Bett, do you believe in a personal Devil?" or something of the sort to relieve the tedium of the Arian controversy, that church historian's graveyard.

When it is remembered that for many Methodist ministers the theological college was their only sniff of a broader religious life than that of the chapels, the role of the college tutors was all the more important. The ministers, who most influenced me as a student, were two 'Handsworth men' and their love of Charles Wesley's hymns which they imparted to me (and Watts and Dora Greenwell) came direct from Henry Bett – that portly frock-coated Wesleyan historian who loved children's games and nursery rhymes as well as Methodism and was, I think, the only college tutor to have written not only poetry but a novel *The Watchnight* (Paul, nd). We salute Henry Bett – Methodist historian – who could range so widely where now only experts dare go. Perhaps we ought not fail to refuse to be intimidated by experts who too easily put fences up. And maybe telling a story is as important as exploring a concept. Bett could clearly do both!

References

1. J M Turner (Ed), *Queens' Essays*, Queen's College 1980 Foreword and Ch. 1
2. G G Findlay, *London Quarterly* XCV Jan. 1901, pp 108-32
   XCVIII July 1902, pp 97-118
3. B L Manning, *The Hymns of Wesley and Watts*, Epworth 1943
   D Davie, *A Gathered Church: The Literature of the English Dissenting Interest, 1700-1830,* Routledge and Kegan Paul 1978

Ibid, *Dissentient Voice: Enlightenment and Christian Dissent,* Notre Dame, USA 1981

4. N Cohn, *The Pursuit of the Millennium,* Mercury Books 1959
    M Reeves, *Joachim of Fiore and the Prophetic Future 1976*
    H Leff, *Heresy in the Later Middle Ages* 2 vols. Manchester 1966
    M Reeves, *The Influence of Prophecy in the Later Middle Ages,* OUP 1969
    M Lambert, *Medieval Heresy,* Arnold 1977

5. H A Oberman, *The Harvest of Medieval Theology,* Harvard 1963
    Ibid, *Forerunners of the Reformation,* Philadelphia 1981
    Ibid, *The Masters of the Reformation,* CUP 1981

6. C D Field, *British Journal of Sociology XXVIII,* No. 2, June 1977, pp 199-225

7. W J Townsend, H B Workman & G Eayrs, *A New History of Methodism* Vol. 1. Ch. 1. (H B Workman), Hodder and Stoughton 1909; G Eayrs, *John Wesley: Christian Philosopher and Church Founder,* Epworth 1926; cf. H M Hughes, *The Theology of Experience* Kelly 1915; E S Waterhouse *The Philosophy of Religious Experience* Epworth 1923

8. *Spirit of Methodism* pp127-8, *What Methodists Believe and Preach* pp 4-5, *Studies in Religion* p 19

9. I & P Opie, *The Lore and Language of Schoolchildren* 1960

10. cf. W Bett (Ed), *The Words and Wisdom of Henry Bett* Epworth 1955

11. *Methodist Recorder* 18 Jan, 1951

12. E.g. Oct 1924, Jan 1926, July 1927, Apr 1931, Jan 1932, July 1935, July 1936, Oct 1937, July 1938, July 1940, Oct 1940, July 1941, Apr 1945, Apr 1947, July 1950
    Also *Proceedings of the Wesley Historical Society* VIII, IX, XIII, XIV, XV, XVIII

Chapter 6

The Christian and the Study of History

Sir Herbert Butterfield (1900 – 1979)

Do we live in an age with no sense of history? Ireland, the Middle East and Poland believe this. Maybe the historian is needed to slay the legends, to be the herald of what J H Plumb [1] called "the death of the past". There are also New Testament scholars like Professor Dennis Nineham [2] who appear to imply that the distance between ourselves and the people of the New Testament world is such that we can hardly communicate with them. If Nineham is right, then the whole enterprise of ancient history, not to speak of archæology, and anthropology, seems somewhat futile, and it is doubtful if the new fashionable use of sociological categories will help either. Relativity takes over – unless it is the case that Nineham is stuck with rather outmoded views of how an historian works. Let us look at the contribution of one historian to the use of history by the Christian – the late Sir Herbert Butterfield, who was a Methodist and, though he would have disclaimed the title, a "lay theologian".

Herbert Butterfield was born in 1900 at Oxenhope, between Keighley and Halifax. His father, who left school at the age of ten, was a woolsorter and later a petty clerk, the very epitome of the "labour aristocracy", that crucial group who bridge the gap between the working and the lower middle class. These are the folk to whom Methodism traditionally made its appeal – men of integrity and responsibility. Albert Butterfield led his "class" of working men in the local chapel. Young Herbert was sent to Sunday school, hated it, and went to chapel worship instead. Men like Albert Butterfield (and, higher up the scale Margaret Thatcher's father) encouraged their children in the virtues of self-education, thrift and hard work, individual choice and achievement, the pursuit of excellence, which produced a very high proportion of Methodists at universities after World War 1. "It was a Methodist ethic which found the English liberal political and social tradition congenial." [3] At a time when the "work ethic" is subject to scrutiny and criticism in the West, we do well to realize that Christianity has nearly always produced the thrifty person of integrity. There is evidence that the "black-led" churches are doing this now, and will not easily be patronized by guilty products of upper-crust education who may accuse them of social elitism.

Herbert had early aspirations to authorship; he preached as a teenager, an exercise in communication which stood him in good stead later; went up to Peterhouse, the "historian's college", at Cambridge. A double first was followed by a Fellowship at a very early age. In his twenties he was a visiting Fellow at Princeton during the era of Prohibition. A lifelong teetotaller,

Herbert drank while in the USA – a liberal protest at totalitarian temperance morals. There is something very nonconformist in that!

Herbert Butterfield's first book was *The Historical Novel* (1924). Points made there remained with him – that often a novel catches the spirit of an age as well as a piece of "scientific" history-writing. Stories and legends accrue round any great character, and often tell us what such a one was like. In his last book Butterfield applies this to Winston Churchill. There are hundreds of unverified "Churchill" stories. Are not the Gospels full of the same sort of material – not *ipsissima verba*, but full of verisimilitude?

'*It is wrong to assume – as people so often do – when they are dealing with the Scriptures – that if an event has not been demonstrated with mathematical certainty, it has been proved not to have happened at all.*' [4]

The "redaction critic" concerned with the author's intention is concerned with what has been commonplace to historians. It has not unduly worried them – it is the person who pretends to have no pre-suppositions who is likely to be misleading.

The next book was of quite a different genre. Butterfield, in 1929, produced a large-scale work on the *Peace Tactics of Napoleon, 1806-8*. Three aspects of the revolutionary epoch are germane now. First, the historian of diplomacy has no illusions about power or about revolution. The romanticization of revolution, common in the age of Mazzini and common again in some Christian circles a few years ago, had a touch of naïveté about it. It may have been right for young Wordsworth to toast the Revolution of 1789 –

Bliss was it in that dawn to be alive,
But to be young was very heaven!

- Yet the movement from idealism through the terror of Napoleon is haunting and repetitive. The lesser Napoleons of today are a warning to idealists and ideologues. Nevertheless, Butterfield is not an ally of reaction – he reminds us how like hatred of Communism was earlier suspicion of democracy, and how much the Marxists mimic earlier Christians. Second, Butterfield was a true son of Action in seeing the destructive element in power, and his Augustinian sense of human wilfulness and cupidity are only paralleled, I think, in Reinhold Niebuhr. The big book on Napoleon was followed by a short but brilliant biography in 1939, and in the next year *The Statecraft of Machiavelli* (1940), a glance at the kind of statesman who saw the power of his own state as being paramount, no ideology, no desire to impose a religion or political system – simply *realpolitic*. Diplomacy, incidentally, throws up patterns of human behaviour which change little across the centuries. One of Butterfield's outstanding essays, buried in a *Festchrift* to D B Horn, was on styles of diplomacy beginning with an analysis of the visit of the Assyrian Rabshakeh to the king of Judah, indulging in propaganda to the people behind the king's back – not much different from some use of "the media" today and a great deal more effective. Maybe the gulf between one age and another is not impassable!

Third, the big book on Napoleon showed a method of doing history which is of lasting value, much needed now. He would imaginatively let himself be attracted to each side in order to understand them almost from inside. He called this the process of "self emptying" in conscious quotation from Philippians or the hymn "And can it be". Next he would sort out his criticisms of each side's errors and exaggerations and discern the residue of the truth in each position, what he frequently called "picking up the other end of the stick" – not always the "right" end! He would then reconcile the truths at a higher level of insight, what he often called the "last analysis". In his own religion he has reconciled "evangelical" and "liberal", and came out as what we would call "critical orthodox" – neither reductionist nor fundamentalist. These days we are more prone to shout slogans and to fail to see the other person's viewpoint. Siren-voices are telling us that unless we always "take sides", we are automatically on the side of the *status quo*, which always assumes to be replaceable by something better. The "cross-bencher" is thus at a discount. The "Butterfieldian" version of Hegel's dialectic is of great value. "The owl of Minerva" may be a bird that extremists would love to shoot, but she is of great value, and liable to become extinct.

In 1931 Butterfield, then a young don beginning to develop lecture techniques, which made him a "star" among undergraduates later, produced a small book, *The Whig Interpretation of History*, only 132 pages in length, but packed with ideas, as readable now as then. For very few of the ideas expressed did he need to repent. Basically, it is an attack on the idea of progress – what is discussed is the tendency in many historians to write on the side of Protestants and Whigs, to praise revolutions provided they are successful, to emphasise certain principles of progress in the past, and to produce a story which is the ratification, if not the glorification of the present. The Whig view still rears its head, not least when we assume that somehow living standards must get better and better, that communities may not decay or even wither away, forgetting that we may be "one with Nineveh and Tyre". The historian is more reconciler than avenger. He cannot easily arrange the men of the past as friends and enemies of progress. We simply have to enter into minds *unlike* our own, which means that there are enough similarities. We must not always study the past with reference to the present, but in its own right. "The true historical fervour is the love of the past for the sake of the past", so that, for instance, we see Magna Carta as a feudal document and not as an anticipation of the great Reform Bill or Mr Gladstone's first government. Sometimes analogies have to be destroyed, for the chief aim of the historian is the elucidation of the unlikeness between past and present, and his chief function is to act in this way as the mediator between other generations and our own, for in the end "it is nothing less than the whole of the past with its complexity of movement, its entanglement of issues and its intricate interactions which produced the whole of the complex present". [5] This scintillating little book was seen by Professor G M Trevelyan as an attack on much of what he stood for, so much so that he handed to Butterfield his vast collection of papers on Charles James Fox, implying that he was the one to write a definitive life of Fox, - a fantastic backhanded compliment! Alas, the book on Fox was never finished.

For us, the *Whig Interpretation* puts a question mark against a lot of assumptions about progress which are still around. Butterfield produced a sequel to the *Whig Interpretation,* a little book called *The Englishman and his History* (1944) – which E H Carr described as a eulogy of things English produced under the pressure of war, only to be countered by Butterfield, who revealed that the book was a rewrite of lectures actually given in Berlin of all places in 1938. But the book is a vindication of some of the Whigs and their contribution – not least Nonconformist Whigs!

It seemed that Herbert Butterfield was destined for a quiet and fruitful life as Professor of Modern History in Cambridge. Another very large book was gestating on *George III, Lord North and the People, 1779-1780* – 400 pages on one year of British politics! The book came out in 1949, but was overshadowed by a remarkable story. In 1948, Butterfield was pushed into giving two courses of public lectures in Cambridge – one on *The Origins of Modern Science, 1300-1800* is an attempt to interpret the rise of the scientific method as an episode in European history of supreme importance eclipsed only by the rise of Christianity. The audience was large, the book popular. But the lectures on *Christianity and History* surpassed all bounds – eight hundred undergraduates listened to him at 12 noon on Saturdays for a whole term. The two books, together with *George III,* were published at the same time. Butterfield was a "best-seller" in two spheres. As a student at Cambridge at the time, I remember my room mate, an agnostic, pushing his copy of the *Origins* at me, saying, "This will rock your faith", only for me immediately to push *Christianity and History* at *him*, saying, "And this will rock your agnosticism". "Good God!", he said, "the same fellow!" It was a quite remarkable feat. The *Origins* showed how the rise of the modern scientific world-view reduced even the Reformation and the Renaissance to the rank of mere internal displacements within mediæval Christendom. The role of secularization on modern history was expounded by Butterfield long before theologians had heard of it. He showed, too, how the idea of progress, and indeed evolution, came from historical thinking long before Darwin was born.

Christianity and History I would rate one of the ten most important books in Christian theology written in Britain since the second World War. We can only pull out a theme or two still relevant to us now. He wrote, he said, prophetically – for a time not of progress but of cataclysm. Themes like human sin and cupidity and the nature of judgement loom large, also the need to repent of that self-righteousness against which Jesus fought so hard. History is too flexible ever to be hardened into the concept of "righteous" nations who have the right to imagine that they can wage wars "for righteousness" – a theme picked up in more detail in *Christianity, Diplomacy and War* (1953). Butterfield saw the individual as of infinite value but flawed:

It is essential not to have faith in human nature. Such faith is a recent heresy and a very disastrous one ... What history does is rather to uncover man's universal sin. [6]

If you remove the safeguards of civilized life, chaos and anarchy reign, illustrated when Butterfield recalls the Liverpool Police Strike of 1919, which led to riots like those of Toxteth in 1981. [7] On the combination of judgement and promise, of which the Old Testament is full, there is great penetration - judgement often enough comes from "the penalty of God's formidable non-intervention". Conflict in history is usually "tragic" rather than simply good versus evil, *that* war is at a higher level, or in the individual himself. In any case the goal of history is the manufacture of human souls. The process is more like a composer making it up as he goes along or like a father teaching a boy to ride a bike on an indefinite stretch of sand. What matter the odd course, so long as the boy rides the bike? The lectures reach their climax with a profound discussion of the Incarnation and the typical Butterfieldian comment that what really matters in Church history is the slow leaven of Christian love, the work done by humble men over the face of the earth – "the most moving spectacle history presents". [8]

The conclusion is the famous closing passage:

'... if one wants a permanent rock in life and goes deep enough for it, it is difficult for historical events to shake it. There are times when we can never meet the future with sufficient elasticity of mind, especially if we are locked in the contemporary systems of thought. We can do worse than remember a principle which both gives us a firm rock and leaves us the maximum elasticity for our minds, the principle, hold to Christ and for the rest be totally uncommitted.'

Lest anyone is so foolish as to think that this means other-worldliness or an apolitical stance, this passage is glossed in a later essay:

'... holding on to this one piece of rope, this one affirmation of ours – taking our stand so to speak on this one rock, the living Christ – we are better able to be free and flexible about everything else. We can prevent ourselves from making gods out of mundane things or out of mere abstract nouns. It is important that we should recognize our liberty and exercise it thoroughly.' [9]

So he means that nothing – no state or nation or class or church or society, has total sovereignty. This is what Paul Tillich used to call "Protestant principle", and we do well not to forget it in an age of totalitarianism.

From 1949 to 1960 Butterfield's output of sheer range and penetration was amazing, though later on the pace slackened somewhat, and becoming Master of his college, Regius Professor and Vice-Chancellor, sucked him into university politics, in which he proved a sagacious chairman. I fear history was a little the loser. One of my academic memories of Cambridge is

Butterfield's course on "Renaissance and Reformation" (never published) and that remarkable *tour de force* on the Diplomatic Revolution of 1756, when he showed how in one crucial year the whole of European and indeed world history was changed.

But we must ask now what he has to say in his later books to the Christian. *Christianity in European History* (1951) shows the role of the faith and the Church in changing cultures – urban Rome, the significance of Constantine's conversion, not wholly an evil incidentally, the Christianization of barbarian peoples, a phase not to be repeated unless civilization breaks down, the familiar Butterfieldian stress on the leaven in the meal.

There can be no doubt that those who merely preached the Gospel without *arrière-pensée*, those who preached purely for the salvation of souls and assumed that man was born for eternity, always worked better in the cause of civilization than they ever knew or purposed. [10]

Ecclesiastical power was abhorrent to Butterfield. He has no solace for those who imagine that Christians in positions of power are better than others – they are often enough too self-righteous and too inflexible. The meat of this little book, however, is a brief penetrating statement of the impact of secularization, much of it a representation of ideas originally Christian, especially Christianity in its "insurgent" forms. England had nonconformity, Germany got rid of it. This is a sobering thought when nonconformity in religion is somewhat under a cloud! The danger of secularization is that abstractions like "society" come to be more important than individuals. Butterfield predicted long before some Christians became besotted with it – how often were the blessed words "the secular" used in the '60s as a slogan! – that secularism could lead to dark pagan mythologies, superstition, irrationalism, with the Christians having the greatest opportunity for a millennium in offering purpose and meaning to its Gospel.

'Those who preach the Gospel, nurse the pieties, spread New Testament love and affirm the spiritual nature of man, are guarding the very foundation, dealing with the problems of civilization at its very source and keeping open the spring from which new things will still arise.' [11]

Much of the argument of this short book is elaborated in a survey *Christianity in History* in the *Dictionary of the History Ideas II* (1973), pp. 373-412.

History and Human Relations (1951) picks up many of the same themes – the tragic element in modern international conflict, Marxist history, a typical piece of Butterfieldian dialectic still worth reading in the age of President Reagan and liberation theology. The element of fear in international affairs is the recurrent theme, the chief element indeed in big-power conflict, a theme picked up again in *International Conflict in the Twentieth Century,* published in 1960, containing much that is now, very belatedly, being said by Christians who seemed to have other things on their minds when Butterfield was warning of things to come (the military dictatorships of Right and Left were predicted in 1951).

'The greatest war in history could be produced without the intervention of any great criminals who might be out to do deliberate harm in the world. It could be produced between two powers both of which are desperately anxious to avoid conflict of any sort.' [12]

On the other hand, Butterfield, whilst admitting that every nation in Europe has taken to aggression when it suited them to do so, says that to refuse to arm against a potential aggressor is to help create the very evil of which we complain. We must do this without "barbarizing" ourselves, and maybe any policy involving the nuclear bomb would do precisely that. Butterfield was no pacifist, and I am not sure where his argument really leads us – possibly to a piling-up of conventional arms which aren't exactly children's toys! Certainly his point stands that it hardly will do for undergraduates who couldn't wheedle sixpence out of a college porter to lecture Bismarck on diplomacy – the same would apply to the armchair Christian diplomat too! History is always complex; the range of choices for the statesman is often limited. Sometimes silence is golden.

Along with that great defender of the Church of England, Lord Clarendon, we must sadly accept the fact that the affairs of the world would be worse if we were governed by ecclesiastical statesmen. The Christian who feels that his religion has anything to contribute to the politics of today must realize that the outsider is going to be very cautious of him. He had better disguise his message as common sense! [13]

So we can be slightly cynical about Ian Paisley, Mikarios, Bishop Muzorewa and Canaan Banana, and sceptical of Wolsey and Richelieu, though the latter was a consummate statesman! This does not mean that Butterfield was against the "radical"; far from it. He supported what he called an "insurgent" form of Christianity so long as it didn't achieve power! Then it would be too assertive and self-righteous, the danger of the "Nonconformist Conscience" in any age. On the other hand, sometimes

Until some act of violence occurs, we do not realize there is a problem to be solved … in the imperfect state of our own internal order, it is clear that it requires an act of violence to secure that a topic is in any effective sense put on the agenda at all. [14]

A neat counterbalance to the point about anarchy! This is the typical Butterfieldian dialectic.

In 1955, and then in 1981, posthumously, Sir Herbert produced two books which are not so relevant to this article. *Man on His Past* (1955) showed skilfully how the modern conception of historical scholarship developed – the Göttingen school; the gigantic contribution of Van Ranke, to whom Butterfield clearly owes much; Acton, who again was a formative influence on so many. Butterfield began here with what he was familiar with. In his last book he starts at the beginning and shows how Hittites, Egyptians, Chinese and Greeks thought of history and what they wrote. *The Origins of History* (1981) is "caviare to the general", but in the middle of it are outstanding chapters on the Bible as history. It is not necessary to espouse outmoded views on *heilsgeschichte* – there is only one history, after all – to see the amazing contribution of the biblical historians. They alone of ancient peoples asked for penitence from their own people as well as support from God. Promise always went hand in hand with providence and judgement. Yahweh was the God of history rather than of nature, with the Exodus the centre of the story. No doubt the biblical expert might find Sir Herbert lacking in some of his detail – he hadn't read all the latest monographs – nevertheless, like the *Origins of Modern Science*, it shows amazing range and a mind willing ceaselessly to pick other brains around him. It is the integration that is the mark of the true scholar. One other book of the 1950s, *George III and the Historians* (1957) was very much an historian's book – a full-scale dialogue with the school of Sir Lewis Namier (only a fellow giant would take *him* on!). With that we are not concerned now, although one chapter of that book, "The Historian and His Tools", is a first class introduction to historical method.

Right at the end of Butterfield's life an American scholar, C T McIntire, edited *Writings on Christianity and History*. Published in July, 1979, Sir Herbert was able to read it just before his death. The book is the best introduction to Sir Herbert's thinking in the area most likely to appeal to the general reader. The short biography and assessment by McIntire can be supplemented by the chapter in Maurice Cowling's *Religion and Public Doctrine in Modern Britain* (1980) – one of those important books which ecclesiastical reviewers seem to have ignored. We can only pick up some key points from these essays by way of summary. The essay on *God is History* (1950) I would rate the most brilliant single piece Sir Herbert ever wrote. How can we believe in Providence and freedom in a scientific universe? Only Nicolas Berdyaev [15] of modern writers on Providence surpasses it, I think.

Nothing is more important [he says] than that we should recover the sense and consciousness of the Providence of God – a Providence that acts not merely by a species of remote control but as a living thing operating in all the details of life – working at every moment, visible in every event. Without this you cannot have any serious religion, any real walking with God, any genuine prayer, any authentic fervour and faith.

Perhaps people are too overawed by laws of nature, thinking of them like Acts of Parliament rather than hypotheses. To look at Providence, we need three levels of analysis, each of which can be true at the same time.

If you go on a journey, and at the end of it ask: "Why are you here now?" you may answer, "Because I wanted to come" or you may say, "Because a railway train carried me here" or you may say, "Because it is the will of God";

and all these things may be true at the same time on different levels. So with history: - we may say at the first level of analysis that men's actions make history and men have free will – they are responsible for the kind of history that they make. But then at a different level we find that history, like nature itself, represents a realm of law; its events are in a certain sense reducible to laws. However unpredictable history may be before it has happened, it is capable of rational explanation once it has happened, so much so that it becomes sometimes difficult to imagine that it ever had been possible for anything else to have happened or for history to have taken any other course.

Now to take an example we can see the long term causes of the first World War, but the men of 1914 cannot be let off blame for blunders of colossal proportions. And what of the Providence "in whom we live and move and have our being?" – "It is Providence who puts us in a world where we run the risks that follow from free will and responsibility" – a world which has its regularities and laws we do well to know about. God does not interfere with planetary movements or history; we are all perhaps like the people we see in dreams – when we stop dreaming they no longer exist, and when God stops His work of creating and maintaining the universe we ourselves and all this fine pageantry of stars and planets simply cease to exist any longer. It is not meaningless to praise God for a new day or the Spring. It is because God is in everything, in every detail of life, that people so easily think they can live as if He didn't exist.

Another essay written in 1977 called *Does Belief in God Validly Affect the Modern Historian?* returns to the question more sharply. How do we see the hand of God in History? We must not bring God in as a "God of the gaps", when we have no other explanation. Christians too easily drag in the Holy Spirit as an explanation of, say, the Evangelical Revival. If God is not everywhere, He is nowhere. This is very reminiscent of Bonhoeffer and Charles Coulson. [16] Does the historian run the risk of "methodological atheism"? That risk *was* run by Christian historians as diverse as J N Figgis, B L Manning, [17] the late Dom David Knowles, that monk of terrifying historical thoroughness, his lay friend Herbert Butterfield, and the formidable Norman Sykes. The issue is complex, and it is always a risk too easily to name the name of God. Perhaps we don't see God in history, if we don't see Him in our inmost beings. There is no Exodus without a burning bush – and no doubt the rest sat round and picked blackberries! The Exodus was a small "hiccup" in Egyptian history which never recorded defeats! Maybe mass unemployment in Liverpool is a judgement on the slave trade, which made it prosperous. Yet where there is a judgement, there is always a promise and hope is renewed. So we have the constant theme for Butterfield of determinism, contingency and providence – in the end *people* make history from "shoeblack to sovereign Lord", to use Carlyle's phrase; but we have to learn, where we are unfree also. You won't get a flourishing "Junior Church" if there are only pensioners on the estate nearby!

Butterfield then turns to his old theme of the conflict of right and wrong in history. The "war for righteousness" is rejected. How easily the churches fell for it in 1914! – even P T Forsyth, [18] the greatest theological mind of the day, in 1916 published his worst book, preaching a war for righteousness against Germany, though his mood changed rapidly, and the *Justification of God,* the sequel, marked a change of stance. It would be a salutary thing if men would recognize that in the case of "many of the world's conflicts the struggle is not between right and wrong but between one half right that is too wilful and another half right that is too proud". [19] Can we today still espouse the concept of the Just War or its twin brother Just Revolution? Is it too slick for radicals, rightly opposed to racism, to condemn as "implicit racists" those Christians who are uneasy about the Programme to Combat Racism's support for groups pledged to use violence for the purpose of liberation? Do we indulge in political utopianism? Do we sometimes want our opponents to appear more wicked so that we can be justified in our aggression? - C S Lewis[20] had some pungent thoughts on *that* phenomenon which appears on both sides. The "left" will paint a right-wing dictatorship as black as possible, any change is merely "cosmetic", the "right" always finds the international Communist conspiracy under every bed. Does Butterfieldian dialectic push us on to the side of the *status quo?* "Double-think" is too easy an area and the kind of indignation which is directed to one side only. World Council of Churches' statements appearing to condone the military take-over of Poland as a lesser evil than anarchy (Luther's old argument!) contrast strangely with support of guerrilla anarchy elsewhere. The next block of essays is about the Bible – spin-offs from the more, massive treatment in *The Origins of History.* The God of history, providence and judgement appears again as does the "suffering servant" – the only example of a nation with a national mission which didn't involve aggrandisement. *The Modern Historian and New Testament History* (1974) should be compulsory reading for biblical scholars, bringing them comfort and discomfort – comfort in that the secular historian is right always to distrust the ecclesiastical mind. *Why* do New Testament scholars appear to assume that Paul's letters are always accurate as against Luke, that obviously biased historical theologian? Memoirs and diaries are notorious for lapses of memory, as a look at recent editions of Gladstone's *Diaries* reveals. Discomforting in that Butterfield (quite different from Michael Goulder or Willi Marxsen [21]) shows the utter centrality of belief in the Resurrection.

At any rate it seems totally impossible to discover any personal ambition or vested interests which could have induced the disciples and the preachers to carry out a sort of hoax. They must have known they were going to almost certain death. [22]

Short shrift to the "Gnostics!" If the Gospels are aimed at communicating a particular view, is that surprising? A lot of sources the historian has to handle are similar. If we read Marxist historians like Christopher Hill or Eric Hobsbawm or E P Thompson, we allow for their bias, but we needn't thereby assume that they are liars or make it up! The scepticism and odd sleight-of-hand by which some "redaction critics" shut off all knowledge of the "mortal Jesus" (John Coventry's phrase), yet seem to know so much about the communities to which the Evangelists address themselves need some probing. We then have *The Establishment of a Christian Interpretation of World History* (1963) – Eusebius, Augustine, the division of history into five monarchies which was the norm before the eighteenth-century Germans "invented" the "Middle Ages" and "modern times". A question stabs out: was Constantine, so eulogized by Eusebius as God's instrument, the Christian Cyrus, really the "curse of Christendom", as R M Benson dubbed him? Can Christianity survive its establishment? We might beware the traps before we say a resounding nonconformist "No!", especially if we had an LEA grant for youth work for that bright lad at theological college! The radicals who now say we should have nothing to do with those who hold power can easily be impaled on the horns of an awkward dilemma here. It is not easy to initiate change without power, as Wilberforce and Shaftesbury knew well.

An interesting point here is Butterfield's rejection of any cyclical view of history. Augustine saw that the idea of Christ returning to be crucified again in another repetition of the cycle would turn the whole salvation story into a kind of cosmic puppet-show. What then of the boy on the bike on an indefinite stretch of sand going round and round? I think there is a point worth teasing out here: the biblical Christian has Ecclesiastes as well as Revelation in the canon.

I end with two typical Butterfieldian attitudes. The historian above all needs humanity and imagination – while Hitler was alive it was necessary to fight him and stop his cruelties, destroying his power; but it would be good if an historian could explain how a boy of ten playing in an Austrian street could be like that. [23] Under the skin we are sinners all! The whole process of emptying oneself in order to catch the outlook and feeling of men not like-minded with oneself is an activity which ought to commend itself to the Christian.

Then there is the historian as prophet. [24] The world, he says, may be secular, but it will not stay secular. The hungers, anxieties and nostalgias which favoured the success of Christianity in the Roman Empire are going to operate in the same way again over a still wider world. And in the world-conflict of religions which is bound to come (that is a contrast to John Hick and Cantwell Smith) and which can hardly be said to have begun as yet, our church will have no special privileges. It will demand only freedom of conscience. In the ancient Roman Empire it did not need even that, for it won the victories partly through the readiness of Christians to accept martyrdom. He sees new styles of Christianity not tied to Græco-Roman culture emerging in Asia and Africa.

The twentieth century seems to me to require what is called the "insurgent" type of Christianity – not the kind which binds up the fortunes with the defence of the *status quo*. By "insurgent" Christianity I do not mean cheap or noisy agitation of the pursuit of novelty for its own sake. I mean the kind of Christianity which, instead of merely cherishing tradition and idealizing it, is constantly ready to return to first principles, to make fresh dips into the Gospels and the New Testament revelation.

Liberals and reductionists get a warning – liberals in 1900 would have tied Christianity to the things which happened to be fashionable in the year 1900. Maybe the Wiles, Cupitts, Kents and Ninehams of our day are in the same jam – faith is judged by what the latest Arts Faculty atheist can swallow! Butterfield disclaimed the title of "lay theologian", but could engage in doctrinal niceties at crucial points. The Christian must hold together belief in the Jesus of history and the living Christ – "continuous with the historical Jesus, yet one with whatever God exists, showing us in this earthly life all that the human mind could grasp of the nature of God". His essential Methodism emerges when he asserts:

I wish I could convince them that this is the greatest moment in a thousand years for the preaching of Christianity and they can safely leave the results to Providence! [25]

One last shot from Butterfield as an old man, a sentence which may reflect his long friendship with David Knowles:

I would say that sometimes I wonder at dead of night whether during the next fifty years Protestantism may not be at a disadvantage because a few centuries ago it decided to get rid of monks. Since it followed that policy, a greater responsibility falls on us to give something of ourselves to contemplation and silence and listening to the still, small voice. [26]

Despite his disclaimer, Butterfield *was* one of the great lay theologians – C S Lewis, T S Eliot, Basil Willey, T E Jessop, B L Manning, D M Mackinnon can parallel him. He was one of that very small company who could engage with total integrity across the disciplines, a great teacher, a self-effacing man who "held to Christ", believing the infinite value of human beings, and making history an exciting and compelling exploration.

For recent assessments of Butterfield, see John W Derry: "Herbert Butterfield", in J Cannon (Ed): *The Historian at Work* (1980), pp 171 ff., M Cowling: *Religion and Public Doctrine in Modern Britain,* vol. 1 (1980), and A R Coll: *The Wisdom of Statecraft: Sir Herbert Butterfield and the Philosophy of International Politics,* Duke University Press, Durham, USA (1986), John Clive: *The Prying Yorkshireman, Herbert Butterfield and the Historians Task,* Collins Harvill (1989), C T McIntire: *Herbert Butterfield. Historian as Dissenter,* Yale University Press (2004)

Major Works By Herbert Butterfield

The Historical Novel	CUP 1924
The Peace Tactics of Napoleon	CUP 1929

The Whig Interpretation of History	Bell 1931
Napoleon	Duckworth 1939
The Statecraft of Machiavelli	Bell 1940
The Englishman and his History	CUP 1944
George III, Lord North and the People	Bell 1949
The Origins of Modern Science, 1300-1800	Bell 1949
Christianity and History	Bell 1949
History and Human Relations	Collins 1951
Christianity in European History	Collins 1952
Christianity, Diplomacy and War	Epworth 1953
Man in his Past	CUP 1955
George III and the Historians	Collins 1957
International Conflict in the Twentieth Century	Routledge 1960
"Christianity in History" in Dictionary of the History of Ideas, II	
	Scribners 1973, pp 373-412
Writings on Christianity and History,	Ed C T McIntyre OUP 1979
The Origins of History	Eyre Methuen 1981

References

1. J H Plumb;   *The Death of the Past,* Macmillan (1969)
2. D E Nineham;   *The Use and Abuse of the Bible,* Macmillan (1978)
3. C T McIntyre (Ed);   *Writings on Christianity and History* (1979), p xxi
4. *Writings,* pp 97 pp 110
5. *Whig Interpretation of History,* Bell (1950), pp v, 2, 9, 10, 19.
6. *Christianity and History,* Bell (1949), p 47
7. *Writings op cit,* p 59
8. *Christianity and History,* p 136
9. Ibid., p 146; *Writings* p 256
10. *Christianity in European History,* Collins (1952), p 32
11. Ibid., p 55
12. *History and Human Relations,* Collins (1951), pp 19-20
13. *Writings op cit,* p 38
14. *International Conflict in the Twentieth Century,* Routledge and Kegan Paul (1960) p 32
15. N Berdyaev;   *The Meaning of History,* Geoffrey Bles (1936)
16. D Bonhoeffer;   *Letters and Papers from Prison,* Fontana (1959), p 103; C A Coulson;   *Science and Christian Belief* (1958) p 41
17. J M Turner;   *"J N Figgis: Anglican Prophet",* Theology, vol 73, Oct 1975, pp 538-44; *Bernard Lord Manning as Church Historian; Journal of the United Reformed Church History Society,* vol 1, No. 5, May 1975, pp 126-38
18. P T Forsyth;   *The Christian Ethic of War,* Longmans Green (1916);   *The Justification of God,* Duckworth (1916)
19. *Writings op cit,* p 48

20. C S Lewis;   *The Screwtape Letters*, Bles (1942) pp 40-3;
                 Reflections on the Psalms, Fontana (1961);
                 History and Human Relations op cit p 122
21. John Hick (Ed);   *The Myth of God Incarnate*, SCM (1977) pp 48 ff
22. *Writings op cit*, p 102
23. N Stone;   *Hitler*, Hodder and Stoughton (1980). *A brilliant short account.*
24. *International Conflict in the Twentieth Century of cit*, pp 105 ff;
                 Writings, pp 253-256 ,259
25. Ibid., pp 256, 260
26. Ibid., p268

Chapter 7

Gordon Rupp (1910-86) as Historian

In many ways Gordon Rupp was the *guru* of the more theologically minded Methodists of the period after the Second World War, the era of 'biblical theology', now rather unfashionable. His influence coincided with a brief renewal in Methodism of a rich Protestantism which had an appeal to not a few students in the confusions of the post-war world. In the 1970s newer theologies and political liturgy not to Rupp's taste began to predominate. As a preacher (or speaker) he was able, remarkably, to be *en rapport* with any congregation, with a range of illustrations and metaphors from art and church history to the latest TV programme and detective stories old and new. He said that his own consistent vocation was that of a Methodist preacher.[1] Rupp believed – here he was solidly Methodist – that a theology that could not be preached was not of great importance, which revealed, perhaps, a lack of interest in the more philosophical side of theology. It certainly gave an hortatory side to his historiography.

Gordon Rupp's roots were in London – he was always a Cockney *gamin*, said Gordon Wakefield.[2] Born within a stone's throw of Thomas More's old house, he worked as a bank clerk before becoming a student of history at King's College, London, where Norman Sykes, that great encourager of students, was beginning his career as a teacher and writer. 'Professor Norman Sykes as teacher, tutor and friend is the one from whom largely derives whatever ideals I have of the *Verax historicus*.'[3] The late Dr Dorothy Farrar told me that Rupp wept openly when the news of Sykes' untimely death was conveyed to the joint Anglican-Methodist Conversations Committee in 1961. Sykes never created or encouraged a 'school' but gently pushed his pupils in clear directions – Rupp, Best, Kent, Walsh, Collinson, the late G V Bennett are good examples. For Rupp the agenda set by Sykes and Charles Smyth was the theology of the English Reformation. The Methodist ministry then claimed him. At Wesley House, Cambridge, his teachers were Dr Maldwyn Hughes, beloved and honoured by all his students, and Dr Newton Flew who guided his historian's mind from 'duty to vocation'.[4] Like Sykes, Flew had the skill of suggesting research topics that could last a lifetime. With R E Davies and P S Watson,[5] Rupp was to popularize modern Luther studies in Great Britain with the rise and fall of Hitler, the German church struggle, Karl Barth, the second was and consequent German division and reconstruction as the back cloth. History, theology and current affairs are not divisible.

But the first agenda – and the last – was England. From the manse at Chislehurst, where Rupp was minister during the war, came two books. The first was *Is this a Christian Country?* (1941), one of Dr Alec Vidler's Christian newsletter series which included Barth's famous *Letter to Great Britain from Switzerland.* Rupp pleads for a 'sane, reasoned and Christian patriotism' finding roots for it in Reformation scholars like Tyndale whose *Obedience of the Christian Man* so neatly balanced Luther's *Freedom of the Christian Man.*

The 'great layman' (Henry VIII) was, however, a much more sinister figure, as Tyndale came to realize! History, Rupp avows, is not just a matter of the 'shape of Cleopatra's nose', sheer contingency, but also of the tent peg of Jael, wife of Heber the Kenite, Oliver Cromwell and the 'Smiths, Browns and Robinsons' of the 'Puritan left', who gave us so many of our liberties. The first freedom of the Christian is freedom to obey God and to proclaim his word. Rupp stresses that priesthood of all believers or apostolate of the laity which is not bland equality of lay and cleric but an equality in suffering, prayer and sacrifice. 'Priesthood makes us worthy to stand before God and to pray for others. For to stand and pray before God's face is the prerogative of none except priests' (Luther).[6] Rupp makes a point here which occurs again in his last book. 'Despite Lecky it was Puritanism rather than Methodism which saved us from a French Revolution for the decisive influences were exerted before 1688.' In fact there are phrases and paragraphs here which are developed many times in Rupp's writings, not least his estimate of Wesley's preachers. 'Not pale young curates, profound, distinguished and unintelligible; his helpers, a few parsons, tradesmen and ex-soldiers were more like a gang of highway-men, conspiring together to go round England, calling the miners of Wales and Cornwall, the workers of the North, the soldiers of the French camps to stand and deliver the Word.' Here was theology preached and sung with Watts and Charles Wesley 'a sane protection against religiosity or sentimentality.' In the dark days of war there was no complacency. The shadows of false prophets fall across the path. 'We had not realized that there was no guarantee for any generation that the barbaric floods may not come in if the dykes go unwatched.'[7]

From the apprenticeship of the pre-war and wartime period stem six agendas which occupied Rupp for the rest of his life – spent at Wesley House as Flew's assistant (1946-7), Richmond College (1947-52), Cambridge (1952-6), Manchester as Professor of Church History (1956-67) and finally Cambridge again as Principal of Wesley House (as Hughes predicted) and as Dixie Professor of Ecclesiastical History in the History Faculty – Sykes' old chair. The agendas were:

1. The English Reformation and its consequences.
2. Luther, his friends and antagonists.
3. Methodism.
4. The spirituality of ecumenism.
5. God working in history.
6. The communication of the Gospel to all who would hear.

Rupp's first major book, stemming from his Archbishop Cranmer Prize Essay, was *Studies in the Making of the English Protestant Tradition mainly in the Reign of Henry VIII* (1947). The English Reformation was not wholly a political conspiracy or a political event. It had after all 'something to do with the beliefs of Christian men.' Rupp seeks to show the combination of ideas and theologies which can be easily forgotten. Here we have the legacy of the Lollards, 'the secret multitude of true professors', as Foxe called them; the Cambridge Reformers meeting in the 1520s at the White Horse Tavern ('Little Germany') between King's and St Catharine's bringing to England new insights from Luther; Barlow and Tyndale with his Bible and his concept of obedience; the tricky negotiations of Henry VII and the protestants in Europe. Justification by faith was as much the belief of Cranmer as of Luther – the role of Calvin was not yet on the agenda in England. Rupp's book is racy and readable, appearing just before the massive work of G R Elton and A G Dickens. Dickens fills out Rupp's insights and shows the growth of protestant theology and tradition in the English Church. This became almost an established orthodoxy (along with Elton's stress on the political and intellectual role of Thomas Cromwell) in interpretation from 1955 to 1980. The picture is now seen to be more complex. What was the Reformation *like,* asks Christopher Haigh, suggesting (especially in Lancashire) the continuing grip of Catholicism, the unpopularity and lateness of Protestantism. Haigh dovetails into J J Scarisbrick's picture of an English people taking ill to Protestantism imposed on them by political fiat and new style protestant clergy, 'old priests' writ Calvinist. Patrick Collinson's studies, more sympathetic to Protestantism, show that it was the late Elizabethan period which saw the triumph of Protestantism with its iconoclasm and opposition to old feasts and fasts. So ideas and idealism are downplayed along with Whig interpretations – Rupp was, no doubt, a right royal Methodist Whig!

The Reformation no longer appears as the historic matter of Tyndale's Bible, Cranmer's Book of Common Prayer (now almost a museum piece of cathedral and Oxbridge college chapels!), Foxe and his Martyrs and a God who paid particular attention to his Miltonian Englishman. Even Watts and Wesley, so beloved of Rupp, are now 'golden oldies' rather than the staple of dissenting and Methodist hymnody. It is significant that Rupp added *Thomas More* (1978) in a later 'coffee table' style book following up *Six Makers of the English Religion* (1957) of whom Bunyan is now the most written about.[8]

But Luther was to be Rupp's main concern. Here he was the supreme interpreter and populariser to British readers hiding formidable scholarship behind a lively style. He began with a demolition job on Peter Wiener's *Martin Luther – Hitler's Spiritual Ancestor.*[9] Wiener appears as a propagandist who repeated the caricatures of Grisar, Denifle and Brentano. His misquotations and selective quoting was brilliantly savaged by Rupp. Trevor-Roper's onslaught on Lawrence Stone was a similar exhibition of *odium historicum* but Stone was a foeman worthy of Trevor-Roper's steel and gave as good as he got.[10] Behind Wiener was a more significant scenario, for even William Temple had seen Luther with that curious Anglican myopia as Hitler's long-term spiritual ancestor.[11] Misunderstandings about the Reformation prevailed still in the Anglo-Catholic pamphlet *Catholicity* (1947) which so aroused Free Church scholars. Rupp wrote at the time when anti-German feeling, fuelled by men like Vansittart, blazed up. His polemic reflected his passionate concern for European reconstructions. The fireworks can be forgotten, no one repeats the canards now, save on Luther's anti-semitism on which Rupp wrote later with no attempt to whitewash Luther.[12]

Rupp was now on the scene overnight as a major Reformation scholar. The Birkbeck lectures at Cambridge followed in 1947, to be published in 1953 as *The Righteousness of God*. A popular version came first – *Luther's Progress to the Diet of Worms* (1951, 2nd ed. 1964). Here is Rupp the populariser. The style is exciting, the story carries the reader along but the footnotes reveal the scholarship underlying the mounting of the story, historians need to be able to be vulgar! Rupp could do it brilliantly even if not all would follow his enthusiasm for Luther the man. 'Who in 1510 could have imagined that within a generation there would exist new forms of Christian language and worship clothed in new forms of Christian institutions and discipline, new pieties capable of growth, of transmutation and development, of nourishing innumerable holy souls?'

The Birkbecks were of a different order. Summarizing Luther's Wittenberg lectures for English readers, showing Luther the theologian wrestling with the relationship of grace and faith, the two Kingdoms, church, ministry, sacraments. This must be Rupp's most significant work, since it introduced so many British readers to the width and depth of modern Luther research and the significance of Luther for Christianity, even if Protestantism was developed in quite different directions by a Calvin here and a Wesley there, but which dominated protestant approaches to the heart of the matter and to the interpretation of St Paul almost until the last decade. E P Sanders and others have shown that the Judaism of St Paul's day was not the caricature of the Protestants and the weighting of interpretation has moved away from the exegesis of classical Protestantism shown in Luther, Calvin, Wesley and Barth. I would, though, hazard the guess that any modern analysis of Paul if it is to be, in F F Bruce's phrase, a 'plenary' interpretation cannot ignore the Augustinian succession, even if the psychology of Martin Luther is no longer on the agenda. The ARCIC document on Justification is one pointer, another is the Czech J M Lochman's *Living Roots of the Reformation* (1979). Lochman sees justification by faith as enabling us to see people in right standing with God, not as workers or performers. Cut off from justice, faith becomes sentimental. In a performing society, capitalist or communist, we must look to faith again to enable us to value people. It might save us, too, from guilt ridden 'frantic philanthropy' (Rupp's phrase) which can be a substitute for Gospel – a secular spin off of misunderstood Protestantism.[13]

Rupp claimed that 'Luther's doctrine of justification by faith and his conception of history recover that eschatological context which modern biblical theology is interpreting anew' but he also prophetically admits that 'the characteristic language, forms, institutions, disciplines which began four hundred years ago have come to the end of their journey as evangelical and pastoral vehicles however imperishable their value to the trained and instructed within the household of faith.' That prophecy has long been fulfilled.[14]

Sir Herbert Butterfield,[15] reviewing the 'Birkbecks', was concerned that Rupp would overplay his propensity to humour but saw that 'he takes us through darker tunnels and thornier paths, into worlds well beyond the frontiers of wise cracking', on indeed to the frontiers between history and the 'bright empire of theologians'. The procession of essays on Luther carries on from 1942 to the end when *Old Man Luther* appeared posthumously, a soupcon to what could have been a major work to balance the stress on the period before the protestant 'map makers' of the plan of salvation.[16]

Continental scholarship has recently explored what Rupp called 'the dark side of the moon' – later scholasticism and mysticism, the sociological setting of Lutheranism on which Rupp was not expert. To compare Rupp with John Bossy [17] who stresses continuities showing that religion did not turn protestant over-night (if ever!) or with the influential R W Scribner whose sociological approach gives students a quite different 'feel' of the Reformation compared to Bainton or Rupp, reveals a great change in historical mood and historians' priorities allied to new insights from anthropology and sociology. History as 'story' or biography is displaced by history as underlying social process. Somehow both are part of the wholeness of historiography. Much of the new history seems 'caviar to the general.' The pioneering works are more readable though they need now to be supplemented by the sobriety of Heinrich Bornkamm and Cargill Thompson (more in Rupp's tradition), the massive erudition of Heiko Oberman whose 'Luther' is much more 'medieval', more apocalyptic, more obsessed with the Devil than Rupp's somewhat warmer, human figure. Oberman may well be right but more than changes in historiography are at stake here!

No one can know Luther who only Luther knows. The 'Birkbecks' were followed by the Fernley-Hartley Lecture of 1953 on *Patterns of Reformation*, not published in its final form until 1969. The role of the city in the Reformation had been made clear in Bernd Moeller's pioneering studies.[18] Rupp illustrates this insight with a brilliant character sketch of Oecolampadius, the Reformer of Basel, showing the place of humanism in Reformation patterns, largely independent of Luther, and the lay Reformer Vadianus, who was the epitome of moderate reform in the little town of St Gall. His biographer, Kessler, is Boswell to Vadianus' Johnson. Very different were Karlstadt and Müntzer. Karlstadt emerges as the prototype Puritan – with that hatred of visual imagery and iconoclasm which need psychological analysis, for its pervasiveness in Protestantism cannot entirely be attributed to the printing press; a legalistic view of the Sabbath; a high view of lay participation with an attendant ambivalence towards intellectual élitism. Karlstadt liked to be called 'Neighbour Andrew', suppressing his doctorate, but was 'Dr' again when it suited him to lobby at Wittenberg. Luther was not amused! His type is recurrent, the awkward radical who cannot exist without the institutions they profess to despise. Perhaps Müntzer with his more aggressive militancy – 'away with all that crap about mercy' – and support of the peasants' cause was even less to Rupp's taste but he gives a sympathetic portrait of a man whose liturgical skills were the equal of a Cranmer. In the 1960s Müntzer was the hero of the Marxist G D R, before they moved over to find a stranger hero in Luther himself for the 1983 celebrations! Rupp sees him as representing the underbelly of medieval suppression and oppression, the poor asserting their right to a place in the sun. Here was a characteristic contribution to the 1960s revival of interest in that radical Reformation which ran alongside the magisterial Reformation of the 'big three' – Luther, Zwingli and Calvin.

Historical studies have gone through revolutions since Rupp began his career. Fernand Braudel and the *Annales* school with their 'total history', the recent stress on social structures, populations studies and the stress by Marxists – pioneered in Britain by Roy Pascal of Birmingham[19] – on the role of the bourgeoisie in the rise of the Reformation faith, the effort to articulate the faith of the common people, often very different from the leadership and the élite, were quite distinct from Rupp's personalism and at times Whiggish style. Fashions change, however; the so-called 'New History' is now becoming less normative. There are signs of a return to a more chronological style with narrative and story at the heart of it.[20]

Did Gordon Rupp make any particular contribution to historical thinking? He repeatedly makes a point often overlooked by his peers. Dr John Kent, for instance, complains that those whom he calls 'committed church historians' try hard to disconnect Christianity from the violence and intolerance of the post-Reformation era.[21] Rupp was not one who dodged this issue. He takes seriously the analysis made by Paul Hazard,[22] Herbert Butterfield and much earlier Norman Sykes of the vital significance in European history of the period between Bossuet believing and Voltaire disbelieving, the crisis of the European conscience which could be interpreted as secularization or dechristianization. The church, says Rupp, lost its hold tragically both on great traditions of letters, science and human thought and on the search for justice and liberty. There was ecclesiastical introversion, failure of nerve, failure in compassion. This was the terrible legacy of the Wars of Religion which followed the Protestant and Catholic Reformations – the most important factor in the making of European unbelief. Here are the roots of the estrangement of masses of modern men and women from religion.[23] This is the 'unacceptable face' of Church history. Rupp was to elaborate the point about the fragmentation in European thinking in several ways.

While defending a proper Christian conservatism – Hooker, Wesley, Burke, Newman, Shaftesbury are carriers of it – he notes 'Great are the temptations which occur when Satan appears as an angel of light but the most sinister of all temptations to the Church is that which comes, as it came to the Wesleyans and the Roman Catholics in the nineteenth century, when the angel of light is disguised as Satan and when the call of the divine truth, divine compassion and divine justice is unheard and unheeded because it is embedded in an ideology atheistic, unchristian, anti-clerical and profane.'[24] *That* tradition, which was to produce a whole philosophy of political and social action in Marxism, was one consequence of the great schism in European life. Rupp's only full analysis of this crisis came in his last book *Religion in England 1689-1791* (1986) where he sees it as a fragmentation of the Christian catholicity into mystics, moralists and rationalists typified by William Law, Joseph Butler and William Whiston who pushed orthodoxy to its Socinian limits. Rupp, too, coined the phrase the 'priesthood of *un*believers' for his search for a universalism of Christian compassion and Christian listening to what apparently alien traditions had to say. Churchmanship and worldmanship are to be one, an insight from Frederick Denison Maurice and one of his mentors, John Scott Lidgett.

Another characteristic of Rupp's approach was his placing of the Methodist tradition within a basically Augustinian profile of humanity but distinguished from Calvinist theologies especially Anglo-Calvinism, as Rupp calls the Whitefieldian wing of evangelicalism. He repeatedly adopts a phrase from the French Catholic, M Rondet, the 'optimism of grace'. He distinguishes this from the 'pessimism of grace' of Calvinist and Jansenist and the 'optimism of nature' of the Enlightenment. This is a fundamentally eighteenth-century optimism about the possibilities of change in human nature which the late Professor Roger Anstey saw as a link between Enlightenment and Evangelical Revival.[25] Rupp's philosophy of history, while akin to that of his fellow Methodist Sir Herbert Butterfield, always had at its heart a Wesley-like optimism despite the tragedy he never dodged.

Rupp wrote much occasional material about his own Methodist tradition, as well as being co-editor of the four volume *History of the Methodist Church in Great Britain* (1965, 1978, 1983, 1988). World Methodist theological colloquies were not complete in the 1950s or 1960s without a historical *tour de force* from Gordon Rupp.[26] With all their brilliance they seem almost 'triumphalist' now, especially as elements in the tradition so dear to Rupp are tending to drain away into either a generalised left-wing politicisation or a reviving conservative evangelicalism owing much to a neo-Pentecostalism which has always been in tension with classical 'Wesleyanism' in one form or another since Wesley's early days when he confronted what Luther would have called 'Schwärmerei'.

Rupp's espousal of Methodist and Free Church traditions keyed in with the revival of Reformed theology typified by B L Manning and J S Whale in Congregationalism. But his high Wesleyanism, with its Arminian theology and sacramentalism, was not incompatible with the liberal Anglo-Catholicism typified by A M Ramsey. Both Ramsey and Rupp were doomed to be bitterly disappointed by the breakdown of the Anglican-Methodist reunion scheme, though Rupp was to respond characteristically with full support for the Cambridge Federation of Theological Colleges. Federation might be a *pis aller* ('union without repentance', said Lesslie Newbiggin) but it is realistic.

Gordon Rupp was a formidable exponent of the ill-fated scheme which was on the agenda from 1955 to 1982. With his old mentor, Norman Sykes, he outlined the historical problems in 1958.[27] In 1962 he was able to defend the 'clerical integrity' of those who were prepared to go into the ecclesiastical and political wilderness in 1662[28] but he was 'Protestant Cavalier' not 'Protestant Roundhead' and could not stomach what was claimed to be the same integrity which caused the Methodist dissentients to submit their Minority Report of 1963 negating the basis for the scheme. Barrett, Snaith, Jessop and Meadley were not quite able to convey what was not only a theological reaction but a 'gut' reaction of many Methodists, especially in the North and South West, to any alignment with Anglicanism or any form of the historic episcopate. If (as Max Warren shows) Bernard Manning could not understand what made a Conservative Evangelical Anglican 'tick', Rupp could not quite 'hear' what Methodists from the avowedly dissenting traditions were saying. Rupp reverted to the style of polemic which he had turned against the hapless Wiener. *Consideration Reconsidered* (1964), *A Dissentient View of the Dissentient View* (LQHR July 1963), *Meadley's Medley* (LQHR April 1964) and *Chaos and Old Night* (Frontier 1970) reveal Rupp's desperate concern for an apostolate to England but have, when read now, a waspish and personal tone. For once Herbert Butterfield's warnings were not heeded. Thomas Meadley was right to complain that the Methodists too easily allowed Anglicans to hold the middle ground, calling all the shots while Free Church people had in the theology of P T Forsyth (let alone Luther!) a doctrine of grace which might have been more openly pressed. It is easy to be wise after the event of Anglicans rejecting a Methodism prepared to accept the Chicago-Lambeth Quadrilateral. Rupp's contribution can now, alas, be seen as below the par of his major writing. The polemics of this period are now dated beyond recall.[29]

Much more significant and in line with his Reformation studies was his ecumenical work for the World Council of Churches. From the Stuttgart meeting with Evangelical leaders in October, 1945, when he supported Bishop George Bell, there was ceaseless interpretative work of German rehabilitation and reconstruction. With German reunification now a fact, Rupp would have pointed to those who suffered under Marxist regimes so often 'white-washed' by some of the more naïve leaders of the Protestant churches who were deceived about the real nature of Leninism-Stalinism. Rupp pointed often to the picture Luther drew of Tyranny like a giant balloon with a monstrous face painted on it which in the end bursts so that the house that Joe built crashes down like Adolf's folly.[30]

Finally we come to Rupp's last work. From the Reformation he moves forward to the eighteenth century. The book *Religion in England 1688-1791* (1986) reveals all Rupp's strengths and weaknesses as a historian. In style and range this is his finest work but those who look for sociological analysis and accurate statistics will find it old fashioned. Certainly Rupp at times appears to be walking still in the shadow of Sykes. The work divided neatly into six parts. 'Names and Sects' depicts the church after the Restoration of

1660 and the Revolution of 1688 when Puritanism appeared 'repudiated and discredited' though, like Alph the sacred river, the lost cause ran underground surfacing in 'the persistence of Calvinism, a covenantal view of the terms of salvation, the English Sunday and a national addiction to sermons'. We might add Susanna Wesley's kitchen! Rupp has a notable chapter on the Non-Jurors who went into the political wilderness like the nonconformists, an issue of Christian conscience, as well as being luminous on those who trod more moderate paths. It is never foolish to see reason or the spirit of man as the candle of the Lord.

Part two analyses the dissidents – Protestant and Catholic. Rupp draws on recent studies here, not least those of Eamon Duffy and John Bossy, who show Catholics as by no means in the ghetto in which Newman thought he found them. There are sensitive portraits of characters like Fox, Watts, Doddridge, Challoner and the worship of small groups like confessing churches of Hitler's day and since.

Part three shows the wholeness of faith and the immense pressure of a century of theological, religious and political conflict, ending in Civil War and the familiar Rupp assertion of the splitting of Christian thought into mysticism, moralism and rationalism. This is the English version of the 'crisis of the European conscience' when problems emerged which haunt us still – the place of reason, the nature of authority, the character of the universe and the nature of historical evidence. Rupp picks his way through all this with consummate skill.

Part four, 'Increase of Charity', reveals that those like the late G V Bennett and John Walsh who speak of renewal of religion before Wesley are correct – the SPG, Religious Societies, the SPCK, charity schools, the hospitals were signs of the 'small awakening'. No more than Sykes does Rupp repeat the convenient but inaccurate tale of a church so dead that nothing could rouse it 'until Wesley like a solitary Moses struck the rock of a petrified Anglicanism'.[31] The great revival had many antecedents and fore-shadowings.

Part five has Rupp on his native heath with a scintillating account not only of Wesley's Methodism but of the Anglo-Calvinism of Whitefield, the Countess of Huntingdon and her circle and that Welsh Revival which produced poetry and hymnody too easily forgotten. No one has shown more clearly the real issues in the split between Wesley and the Huntingdon circle in 1770. Rupp is scrupulously fair here, though earlier he shows Wesley sensing the Moravians as rather like the Triffids in the science fiction story, 'a shapeless mass ever advancing, infiltrating, engulfing, swallowing his converts!' Wesley's whole approach is seen as a balance, a proportion, a 'package deal', in which what he calls 'our doctrines' explain and supplement one another, including 'our hymns' and 'our discipline' – only the skeleton of which now remains. If supplemented by Henry Rack's more astringent *Reasonable Enthusiast* (1989), Rupp provides a superb introduction to Wesley and all his works.

The last section of the book deals with the Establishment – bishops and their clerical subalterns and the 'laics' too – Wilberforce, Sarah Trimmer (the Enid Blyton of the time!), Hannah More and the great Samuel Johnson – here Rupp makes a pertinent comparison with Luther and shows 'the pain of being a man'. I doubt if Rupp wrote anything better than his portraits of Johnson and William Law. Towards the end he chances his arm with a last great swipe at Elie Halévy's thesis about Methodism and Revolution and also the recent sexual interpretation of Methodism which stems from Rattrey Taylor and E P Thompson.[32] This echoes, as we have seen, a paragraph from his first book. Here he is surely right, but no doubt the social historians will say that he lacks the precise social analysis now expected from the historian. But this book is history as biography!

We are given marvellous portraits of people including those faithful 'little people' whose lives (an insight Rupp shares with Sir Herbert Butterfield and Sir Owen Chadwick at the risk of being thought romantic) maintain the church's very fabric. People, warts and all, like John Fletcher, bachelor like, living off scraps, talking to himself, bowled over by his Mary but thinking up theological reasons for not proposing; old Thomas Coram, turned off the council of his own Founding hospital, haunting the grounds handing out gingerbread. But make no mistake, the analysis of great spiritual tomes shows deep learning which makes this Rupp's finest book, despite the flaws, though not the most significant.

As one would expect, cheerfulness creeps in but is always relevant. Epigrams abound which encapsulate immense controversies. Radicals may shudder at 'that most insidious of all radicalisms, innovation based on appeal to tradition, a past that never was'. (p 56) Neo-Victorians are brought up sharp with 'as so often in church history, godliness was profitable, integrity paid dividends and there was movement up the social escalator' (p 149) – *that* about the Quakers! 'Wilberforce making due and lawful use of the machinery of politics and law proved that Christian politics are the art of the *im*possible' (p 526). Social activists might long ponder on that. 'In 1791 two ultimate attitudes to human society were in confrontation between Edmund Burke and Thomas Paine; they still confront one another' (p 554). Rupp's series of essays *Just Men* (1977) abounds in epigrammatic summaries, like that on St Benedict. 'To build an ark not made with hands into which two by two, human and eternal values might enter, to be kept until the waters assuaged and then to be brought safely out into a new world, this was the achievement of Saint Benedict and that ark was his rule' (p 3).

There are also those comparisons across the centuries at which Rupp was so skilled, switching from Luther emerging in friar's habit from the Wartburg to berate his 'militant tendency' to John Wesley freeing Methodism from 'stillness' in 1740 with sermons in full canonicals at six am. In each case a whole Christian style was at stake. In the last analysis, Rupp shows that it was right to look at the eighteenth century from behind rather than from the hindsight of the Victorians and from this stance we have much wisdom even if it needs balancing with the statistics of Virgin's recent book and the de-bunking of J D C Clark.[33]

Gordon Rupp as communicator of the Gospel is not our prime theme but not to mention it would give an unbalanced picture. Theology has to be preached. Rupp's writing up of the Methodist Local Preachers Department report on *Doctrinal Preaching* (1951) is typical of his approach. His preaching often broke all the rules of homiletics – it was more like a great shower of fireworks but one of the rockets would suddenly 'home' in on its target. To be personal, it was a sermon of Rupp in 1952 which 'clinched' my own call to the Christian presbyterate. It was sixteen years before I told the preacher! But that is *precisely* what preaching is about. It is a great pity that so few of Rupp's sermons have survived, unlike the sermons of Austin Farrer found in the attic after his death! Rupp's notes on the back of old envelopes were meant for *that* congregation on *that* day. Perhaps the preacher sometimes eclipsed the historian.

As preacher and historian one can excuse his faults[34] – occasional sentimentality, the muddled statistics. As communicator he was without peer in his generation and made Church history interesting and exciting when so often it is simply deadly dull!

Gordon Rupp was a Methodist in the succession of John Scott Lidgett and Robert Newton Flew who owed so much to other streams of Christian thought especially that following from F D Maurice and liberal Catholicism. None of it was incompatible with the evangelical Arminianism in which he saw Christ as the head of the whole of humanity, the Christ who was the Servant. Rupp saw Church history as an attempt to see in Cinderella in her rags and tears the bride adorned for her husband. In the shame of a sometimes faithless church he could see the glory and he made history, in J B Lightfoot's phrase, 'a cordial for drooping courage'.

Then let us rejoice
In heart and in voice,
Our Leader pursue
And shout as we travel the wilderness through.

References

1. The Sixty Plus and Other Sermons, Collins 1978, p7
2. Obituary, Methodist Recorder, January 1987
3. Studies in the Making of the English Protestant Tradition, CUP 1947, p viii; The Righteousness of God, Hodder 1953, p xii
4. Studies, p viii; Righteousness, pp x-xii
5. e.g. R E Davies, The Problem of Authority in the Continental Reformers, Epworth 1946; P S Watson, The State as a Servant of God, SPCK 1946, Let God be God: An Interpretation of the Theology of

Martin Luther, Epworth 1947; R N Flew and R E Davies (Ed), the Catholicity of Protestantism, Lutterworth 1950

6. Is this a Christian Country?, Sheldon Press 1941

7. ibid., pp 28-9, 45, 46, 53, 65; see also Religion in England 1688-1791, OUP 1986, pp 391 ff, 449

8. For newer interpretations of the English Reformation cf R O'Day, The Debate on the English Reformation, Methuen 1986; C Haigh (Ed), The English Reformation: Revised, CUP 1987; J J Scarisbrick, Henry VIII, E&S 1968, The Reformation and the English People, Blackwell 1984; P Collinson, The Religion of Protestants, OUP 1982, The Birth Pangs of Protestant England, Macmillan 1988; D MacCulloch, Suffolk and the Tudors, OUP 1986; N H Keeble (ed), John Bunyan: Conventicle and Parnassus, OUP 1988; C Hill, A Turbulent, Seditious and Factious People: John Bunyan and his Church, OUP 1988; M Johnson (Ed), Thomas Cranmer: Essays, Turnstone 1990; D MacCulloch, Thomas Cranmer, Yale 1996; Tudor Church Militant, Penguin 2001

9. P F Wiener, martin Luther – Hitler's Spiritual Ancestor, Hutchinson 1944

10. H R Trevor-Roper, 'The Elizabethan Aristocracy: An Anatomy Anatomized', HER 2nd set, 3, 1951

11. 'Malvern 1941': The Life of the Church and the Order of Society, Longmans 1941, esp. p 13: 'It is easy to see how Luther prepared the way for Hitler'; Catholicity: A Report, Dacre Press 1947, pp 20-3

12. Martin Luther and the Jews, Council of Christians and Jews 1972, I Seek my Brethren: Bishop George Bell and the German Churches, Epworth 1975

13. E P Sanders, Paul and Palestinian Judaism, SCM 1977, Paul, the Law and the Jewish People, SCM 1985; J Dunn, Jesus, Paul and the Law, SPCK 1989; J M Lochman, Living Roots of the Reformation, Augsburg 1979

14. Luther's Progress (1964 Ed) p 107, cf J Kent, The Unacceptable Face, SCM 1987, pp 31 ff

15. Cambridge Review cited in J Brooks (Ed), Christian Spirituality, SCM 1975, p 4

16. 'The Old Man Luther' in Faith, Heritage and Witness: Essays for Morris West, Baptist Hist. Soc. 1987; R W Scribner, Cambridge Modern History, v2, 2nd Ed, 1990, pp 69 ff (replacing Rupp's chapter in 1st Ed)

17. R W Scribner, The German Reformation, Macmillan 1986; J Bossy, Christianity in the West 1400-1700, OUP 1985, cf J Delumeau, Le Catholicisme entre Luther et Voltaire, Paris 1971, ET 1977; W D J Cargill Thompson, Studies in the Reformation, Athlone Press 1980, The Political Thought of Martin Luther, Harvester 1984; H Bornkamm, Luther in Mid Career, DLT ET 1983; H Oberman, Luther – Man between God and Devil, Yale 1990; A G Dickens and J M Tonkin, The Reformation in Historical Thought, Blackwell 1985

18. B Moeller, Imperial Cities and the Reformation, Philadelphia 1972

19. R Pascal, The Social Basis of the German Reformation, London 1933

20. L Stone, The Past and the Present, RKP 1981; D Cannardine, The Pleasures of the Past, Fontana 1990, pp 133 ff; J H Hexter, On Historians, Collins 1979; G Himmelfarb, The New History and the Old, Harvard 1987

21. J Kent, The Unacceptable Face, SCM 1987, esp. pp 43, 66

22. P Hazard, The European Mind 1680-1715, 1935 ET Penguin 1964, European Thought in the Eighteenth Century, 1946 ET Penguin 1965; H Butterfield, The Origins of Modern Science 1300-1800, Bell 1949, Christianity in European History, Collins 1951, pp 24 ff; N Sykes, Church and State in England in the Eighteenth Century, CUP 1934, pp 332 ff., From Sheldon to Secker, CUP 1959, ch. v

23. Worldmanship and Churchmanship, Epworth 1958, pp 14 ff, Methodism in Relation to Protestant Tradition, Epworth 1954, pp 29-31, The Old Reformation and the New, Epworth 1967, pp 1 ff., 'Protestantism and Catholicism after 400 years' in D Pailin (Ed) Seventy Five Years of Theology in Manchester, 1980, pp 102 ff., Religion in England 1688-1791, OUP 1986, pp 207 ff

24. Thomas Jackson, Epworth 1954, p 39

25. R Anstey, The Atlantic Slave Trade and British Abolition, Macmillan 1975, pp 157 ff

26. e.g. Methodism in Relation to Protestant Tradition, Epworth 1954; LQHR July 1953, July 1959; R E Davies and E G Rupp (Ed), A History of the Methodist Church in Great Britain, Epworth 4 Vols

27. Conversations between the Church of England and the Methodist Church: Interim Statement, SPCK/Epworth 1958, pp 9-16

28. 'Clerical Integrity – 1662', The Expository Times 1962, cf C K Barrett, ibid July 1962

29. J M Turner, Conflict and Reconciliation: Studies in Methodism and Ecumenism 1740-1982, Epworth 1985, chapters 9,10

30. Sermon 'The Magnificat: 1520', Principalities and Powers, Epworth 1952, pp 47 ff

31. J D Walsh and G V Bennett (Ed), Essays in Modern Church History, Black 1966, p 134

32. J M Turner, 'After Thompson – A Study in Histioriography', Halifax Antiquarian Soc. 1989

33. J D C Clark, English Society 1688-1832, CUP 1968

34. The Sixty Plus, p 104; LQHR Jan 1957, p 12; A History of the Methodist Church in Great Britain, vol 1, p xxxvii. The quote from G C Cell occurs in various forms.

Principal Works of E G Rupp

1941   Is This a Christian Country? Sheldon Press
1945   Martin Luther – Hitler's Cause or Cure? Lutterworth
1947   Studies in the Making of the English Protestant Tradition, CUP
1951   Luther's Progress to the Diet of Worms, Harper
1952   Principalities and Powers, Epworth

1953 The Righteousness of God, Hodder and Stoughton
1954 Thomas Jackson – Methodist Patriarch, Epworth
1954 Methodism in Relation to the Protestant Tradition, Epworth
1957 Six Makers of English Religion 1500-1700, Hodder and Stoughton
1958 (Ed) G R Elton, New Cambridge Modern History, Vol 2, 1st ed. pp 70-118, CUP
1958 Worldmanship and Churchmanship, Epworth
1960 Protestant Catholicity, Epworth
1964 Last Things First, SCM
1964 Consideration Reconsidered, Epworth
1965 (Ed) Davies and Rupp, a History of the Methodist Church in Great Britain, vol 1 Introductory chapter, Epworth
1967 The Old Reformation and the New, Epworth
1969 Patterns of Reformation, Epworth
1970 (Ed) B Drewery and E G Rupp, Martin Luther, Arnold
1975 I Seek my Brethren: Bishop George Bell and the German Churches, Epworth
1977 Just Men, Epworth
1978 The Sixty Plus and Other Sermons, Collins
1978 Thomas More, the King's Servant, Collins
1986 Religion in England 1688-1791, OUP

Chapter 8

British Methodist Historical Scholarship 1893-1993

Wesley Historical Society Centenary

In 1893 a small group of enthusiasts founded the Wesley Historical Society on a shoestring. Its aim was to promote the history and literature of Methodism, to accumulate exact knowledge and to provide a medium of intercourse on related subjects.[1] Richard Green, John Telford, Nehemiah Curnock, John S Simon, H J Foster, F F Bretherton, E S Lamplough and W H Doughty were among the pioneers. From small beginnings came the fostering of both national and local history, regional branches growing after the Second World War with the drive of Wesley F Swift, Maldwyn Edwards, John C Bowmer and local enthusiasts.

In this article I look at three main phases of Methodist historiography – the era of denominational triumphalism, the period of definitive monographs and recent interplay between history and the social sciences.

In 1893 the major resources for those interested in the early period were the biographies of Samuel Wesley and John Wesley (3 vols), George Whitefield (2 vols) and the Oxford Methodists by Luke Tyerman, a keen-eyed and rather anti-Catholic Irishman. Tyerman was a notable historian and user of primary sources whose accuracy is only occasionally assailable. He makes no attempt to disguise his biases – Methodism is the greatest advance in Church History – yet he was no Wesley sycophant either. This is Methodism seen through the eyes of an Irish Protestant. Along with Tyerman, there were the Thomas Jackson editions of the *Works of John Wesley*[2] (still available under the imprint of Zondervan, USA), Jackson's *Life of Charles Wesley* (2 vols, 1841) and his edition of *Charles Wesley's Journal* (2 vols, 1849). To these we add *The Poetical Works of John and Charles Wesley*, edited by George Osborn (13 vols, 1868-72) and the *Lives of the Early Methodist Preachers* (6 vols, Ed T Jackson, 1865), the journals and histories of that remarkable 'Dad's Army' of early preachers without which Methodism would not have flourished. The bibliographies devised by Richard Green and George Osborn are still invaluable though now updated by the bibliographical material assembled by Clive Field in the fourth volume of *The History of the Methodist Church in Great Britain* (1989) and updated annually.

This was the age of denominational triumphalism and British Imperialism typified by the Twentieth Century Fund leading to the building of the Central Hall, Westminster – 'It must be large, it must be central, it must be monumental,' said Sir Robert Perks. 'One can imagine an awestricken whisper running round the grim gargoyles of the Abbey – "the Methodists have come",' was the sentiment of the Methodist Times.[3] In 1907 the union of the 'liberal' Methodist Churches occasioned the first of the new tools – monumental indeed – for scholarship, *The New History of Methodism* edited by W J Townsend, H B Workman and George Eayrs (London 2 vols, 1909). Workman set the tone with an introduction in which he exploited his considerable range as an historian. Methodism, whose primary 'Idea' lies in its emphasis on experience,[4] was not only a part of the Church Catholic but the largest Protestant church in the world and the ultimate logical consequence of the Reformation. This ties in with the thinking of Hugh Price Hughes (d 1902) that Methodism would be *the* church of the twentieth century. The *New History* was a fine achievement, still worth perusal, though the late Victorian period was scantily treated and the title of one section, 'Methodism beyond the seas', betrays an inevitable feeling of Britain being the centre of the Methodist and every other world. H B Kendall's equally monumental *The Origin of the Primitive Methodist Church* (London, 2 vols, 1905) is a mine of connexional and local information; slightly shambolic, disorganized, profusely illustrated, it is at times brilliantly perceptive, not least in the connection Kendall makes between revival and social upheaval. The 'mini' version of 1919 is more analytical and concise.

The reign of Jackson came to an end partly with Nehemiah Curnock's edition of *John Wesley's Journal* (London 8 vols, 1909-16). Here is the epitome of what the WHS stood for – accurate scholarship but with a clear bias towards Wesley himself. The Wesley 'legend' was firmly fixed in the Methodist mind – few would dare risk a Tyerman-like quip at Wesley when he called him a dupe over the John Bennet-Grace Murray affair! Curnock was the very type of inspired amateur who dominated the WHS. John Telford (1851-1936), Connexional Editor from 1905-1934 followed, with the *Letters of John Wesley* (London 8 vols, 1931). The trilogy was completed by the Australian scholar, E H Sugden's, edition of the *Standard Sermons* (London 2 vols, 1921). The redoubtable John S Simon only partially eclipsed Tyerman with his five volumes on John Wesley (London 1921-1934), the last volume completed by his son-in-law, A W Harrison. It would be unfair to demean Simon's achievement by calling it hagiography. He was a meticulously accurate historian, and on the Religious Societies innovatory and still important, but Wesley was his hero and he followed his journeys with tireless devotion.

This brings our story to about 1930. The earlier works were avowedly denominational, including the works on the post-Wesley connexions like the *Centenary of the Methodist New Connexion* (Ed G Packer, 1897), W J Townsend's *The Story of the Methodist Union* (Halifax, 1906) and *The United Methodist Church* edited by Smith, Swallow and Treffry (London, 1932). A flurry of books celebrated Methodist Union, typified by B A Barber's evocative *A Methodist Pageant* (PM Publishing House, 1932) and the more sober *The Methodist Church – its Origins, Divisions and Reunion* by A W Harrison et al (London, 1932).

The first signs of a new approach came from Europe and the USA. No statement on Methodism appears to have had more influence than that of Elie

Halévy in *The History of the English People in 1815* (ET Penguin 1938) – following up on his own pioneering essays in 1906[5] – that the extraordinary stability of nineteenth century England could be attributed to Methodism and its pervasive influence through Evangelicalism in the Church of England and Protestant Dissent. Whenever I give a talk on Methodist history I am asked if Methodism saved England from revolution. While it is difficult to discuss an event which never happened, the 'Halévy thesis' switched the focus of attention from the 'Wesley legend' to the effect of the whole movement. W J Warner's *The Wesleyan Movement in the Industrial Revolution* (London, 1930) showed the social influence of Methodism on an emerging urban industrial 'labour aristocracy' anticipating much later research. Warner consciously sought to follow up the work of Max Weber and R H Tawney, who are so frequently cited but often misinterpreted to infer that capitalism was a side effect of Protestantism. Nevertheless Methodism was seen as a factor in the life style of some of the aspiring artisans who played key roles in industrialisation. Sir Robert Peel, the elder, of Bury is reported to have said in 1787, 'I have left most of my works in Lancashire under the management of Methodists and they serve me excellently well.' Wesley breakfasted with him and feared for his soul![6]

Functional interpretations of Methodism were now on the agenda. Ernest R Taylor broke new ground with his *Methodism and Politics 1791-1851* (CUP, 1935), showing the parallels between the changes in national politics and the political attitudes of the Methodists, spilling over from their ecclesiology as with Alexander Kilham and later on the opposite wing Jabez Bunting. Taylor tends to parallel Halévy in the exaggeration of Bunting's role which was still pervasive until John Kent outlined a more subtle approach, revealing a denomination seeking and not always finding maturity.[7] Taylor's book was superseded in 1984 by David Hempton's *Methodism and Politics in British Society 1750-1850* (Hutchinson, 1984). Taylor was followed the same year by Maldwyn L Edwards whose *After Wesley* (Epworth) broke new ground in what was then called the 'middle period' when the Wesley inheritance was fragmented as it met the challenge of its own great expansion and a society half of which was urbanized by 1850. Edwards claimed that an 'underlying liberalism' battled with a 'dominant Toryism' in Wesleyanism, which is now rather modified to show from poll books and other sources that liberalism was more pervasive at an earlier period.

Edwards had already written on the Wesley period (*John Wesley and the Eighteenth Century* – London, 1933) and later probed the period after the Bunting era in *Methodism and England 1850-1932* (Epworth 1943) which was notable for its interpretation of the Forward Movement. This was a trilogy easily underrated now when the sociological and statistical methods the historian must use are more sophisticated. Robert F Wearmouth's most important book *Methodism and the Working Class Movements of England 1800-1850* (Epworth 1937) followed, opening up the parallels and relationships of Methodism and modes of working class solidarity in the early nineteenth century, especially Chartism.[8] Wearmouth shows the ways in which Methodist styles and techniques – the class systems, class meetings, quarterly meetings, camp meetings, the 'plan' and Conference itself – were picked up by early working class movements. J L and Barbara Hammond, despite their strictures on Methodist quietism, rewrote part of their *Town Labourer* in the light of Wearmouth's researches. 'As a mere exercise in self government and social life, the chapel occupied a central place in the affections and thoughts of people who had little to do with the government of anything else'.[9] A later book, *Some Working Class Movements of the Nineteenth Century* (Epworth, 1948) contains much information about the Radical Societies of 1816-23, the political notions of 1831-5, Luddites and Chartists. This work is now replaced by the fine studies of Edward Royle summarized in *Modern Britain, a Social History 1750-1985* (Arnold, 1987).[10] Wearmouth's *Methodism and the Common People of the Eighteenth Century* (Epworth, 1943) contains a clear account of working class activities and the role of the mob during the Wesley period, anticipating later work by Rudé, E P Thompson and John Walsh.[11] Wearmouth, however, is not entirely dated especially when he shows how Methodism used people's talents, giving them scope in that strange combination of autocracy and democracy which became the Wesleyan system. We shall return to this later.

These books typify the second era of Methodist scholarship, the detailed monograph which, while still denominational, is no longer hagiographical or triumphalist.

Henry Bett's *The Spirit of Methodism* (Epworth 1937) captured admirably the essence of Evangelical Arminianism, underlining again Workman's stress on experience. Here was Wesley anticipating Schleiermacher.[12] This is a disputable interpretation which could become fashionable again. Ernest Rattenbury celebrated the 200th anniversary of the events of Whitsuntide 1738 with the *Conversion of the Wesleys* (Epworth) which has dated rather more than his major studies of hymnody – *The Evangelical Doctrines of Charles Wesley's Hymns* (Epworth 1941) and the more polemical *Eucharistic Hymns of John and Charles Wesley* (Epworth, 1948). Rattenbury's theory of 'personation', the notion that Wesley put himself in the place of those for whom he wrote, is still worthy of critical analysis. These books recalled along with Henry Bett's *Hymns of Methodism* (Epworth, 1913, revised 1945) and the Congregationalist lay historian, Bernard Manning (*Hymns of Wesley and Watts*, Epworth 1943), and R N Flew,[13] a heritage partly recovered in the short period before and after the Second World War when there was a brief revival of the use of classic Wesleyan hymnody, before the flood of modern and later 'charismatic' hymns and religious songs reduced them to the status of 'golden oldies'.

Worship, too, concerned John C Bowmer who explored the theology and practice of Methodism on the Lord's Supper (Dacre, 1951, Epworth, 1961) followed by Frank Baker on the *Love Feast* (1957) and David Tripp on the *Covenant Service* (1969). A fine article[14] by Raymond George on the role of private devotion, and Gordon Wakefield's *Methodist Devotion 1791-1945*

(Epworth 1966) shows the relevance of Methodism in the ecumenical conversation. In a quite different style Leslie F Church explored the role of the ordinary Methodist – a very significant shift away from obsession with the Wesleys – in *The Early Methodist People* and *More about the Early Methodist People* (Epworth 1948, 1949). Drawing upon material in the archives, these were important and too quickly forgotten studies which took up not only the legacy of *The Early Methodist Preachers* (as did Henry Bett in a notable WHS lecture)[15] but the artisans, shopkeepers, soldiers, independent women, servant girls and the odd squire like Robert Carr Brackenbury, who made up the early societies. Here was a pointer to a style of Church History concerned with ordinary people.

We need at this point to add the attention given to doctrine – the USA and Europe take the lead here. No book on Christian perfection has equalled Harald Lindström's *Wesley and Sanctification* (1946) though R N Flew's chapter on Wesley in his *Idea of Perfection in Christian Theology* (OUP 1934) and W E Sangster's *Path to Perfection* (Hodder, 1943), written in the harsh conditions of the London 'Blitz', were notable along with A S Yates on the *Doctrine of Assurance* (Epworth 1952), while Bernard Holland later showed the complexities of the Wesleyan doctrine of *Baptism* (Epworth, 1970).

The WHS was called by Gordon Rupp[16] in 1954, 'our only learned society, the only one with truly monkish possibilities'. There did seem to some of us at that time an obsession with early Wesleyan class tickets and such minutiae – an article on 'Wesley's use of the asterisk' might serve as an example. History can become antiquarianism. H J Hanham[17] speculates whether Methodist concentration on Wesley was not due to an inability to come to terms with the fragmentation of his inheritance not only in England but in America. Changes came in the style of the WHS Proceedings when John Bowmer took over as editor. Bowmer was not only concerned to supervise the whole matter of the categorization and preservation of the Methodist archives but was aware of a whole new tribe of academic historians who brought to Methodist studies a new critical style – the names of E G Rupp, R E Davies, J H S Kent, W R Ward, J D Walsh, J A Newton, A S Wood, H D Rack, J Vickers and others mark the new era. Their articles and books began to shift the style of the WHS Proceedings not least by opening up the nineteenth century. A transition to the newer style marks the *History of the Methodist Church in Great Britain*, appearing in four volumes between 1965 and 1989. The delays in publication made some chapters appear somewhat dated and there was, at times, an inability to break away entirely from older stereotypes of denominational history. Maldwyn Edwards' chapter on John Wesley contrasted sharply with V H H Green's *John Wesley* (Nelson 1964). Green, whose *The Young Mr Wesley* (Arnold, 1961) was outstanding, had a cool academic approach. 'Ultimately John Wesley, like so many of the Christian saints, was self regarding ... the diaries form one of the most consistently complacent documents ever written and the more religious he became the more free from human frailty he appeared to be ... nothing could justify the wild attacks of the neo-Calvinists and the writers in the Gospel

Magazine but their fury, like his wife's rages, may have been provoked by his untouchability, the hard core of his personality.'[18] Green may be harsh but his biography was the most notable of the short biographies since Elsie Harrison's *Son to Susanna* (1937). Wesley could be outrageously insensitive. Even one of his henchmen, John Pawson, was critical after his death.[19] In the History there was some tension in the enterprise between the academic historians and chapters like that of W F Lofthouse on Charles Wesley, simultaneously denigrated by John Kent as 'unfortunate ... little more than hagiography' and hailed by Geoffrey Nuttall as beyond praise.[20] The old fashioned (to some) missiological approach of Allen Birtwhistle 'comes off' because it is superbly written and concerned the *people* which after all is the stuff of history. The three volumes end up by being essays towards the fully comprehensive history needed, with the chapters by Walsh (vol 1), Ward's summary of social change in the early nineteenth century, Kent's approach to Wesleyanism (Vol 2), the monographs of A R George on worship (Vol 1) and ordination (Vol 2) and Rack, Turner and Davies in Vol 3, being markers towards new interpretations.

The new style, the third era of Methodist studies, brings on to the scene also the economic and social historian and sociologists who found Methodism a fertile ground because of well kept records and statistics. Towering above them all was E P Thompson's *The Making of the English Working Class* (Gollancz 1963, Pelican 1968). Thompson takes up Halévy's thesis, turning it into the implication that Methodism stifled working class conscientiousness and radical thought, pushing it into religious activity and to an accommodation with the world of the mill owners like the Akroyds of Halifax.[21] It was a 'psychic ordeal in which the character-structure of the rebellious pre-industrial labourer or artisan was violently recast into that of the submissive industrial worker'. It was the 'chiliasm of the despairing'. This view, which is by no means ridiculous, can be compared with the 'parallelism' theories of Wearmouth who sometimes romanticises the influence of the Methodists on political action – though Nigel Scotland's *Methodism and the Revolt of the Field* (Sutton 1981) and other local studies showed that Primitive Methodism was a source of rural labouring political consciousness. Thompson clearly exaggerates Methodism's influence and needs balancing by the astute Marxist, E J Hobsbawm, in two important and penetrating articles.[22]

John Kent's equally trenchant writings restored the balance. Halévy was deconstructed. Bunting was rehabilitated. On the Wesley period (following Robert Currie[23]) he showed how Wesleyanism operated in the gaps of the parish system, a view underlined by a series of superb articles by John Walsh[24] who in the period after 1965 was the historian most respected by secular historians.

The period from 1965-1990 was a fertile period in Methodist studies both from within Methodism and outside it. W R Ward was outstanding at this time. His *Religion and Society in England 1790-1850* (Batsford 1972), though assuming greater knowledge than was wise, shows the real significance of the fractures in Methodism after 1791. Jabez Bunting is stripped of his mask of either ogre or benevolent dictator in the three volumes of his letters including one on Scotland by Hayes and Gowland,[25] where comparisons of Methodism and the Free Kirk could be illuminating. A D Gilbert gives the reverse of E P Thompson by showing the extraordinary hold that Methodism had on the artisan groups in the late eighteenth century and early nineteenth century, underlined by Clive Field's sociological surveys.[26] Here was not the 'chiliasm of the defeated' but the vitamins of the aspiring, the slightly independent weavers and spinners, croppers, cordwainers and shopkeepers, saddlers and harness makers who dominated the early societies and sometimes moved marginally up the social scale. From their ranks often came the great entrepreneurs who floated Methodism in all its forms – Rank, Firth and Hartley, Ferens, Baldwin and Morel[27] and the extraordinary Wesleyan cousinhood who produced a kind of intellectual aristocracy which spawned the crop of scholars in the mould of the Moultons, Gedens and Findlays, Osborn, Gregorys and Derrys. There is always a danger in overplaying the functional approach to church history. It so stresses the effects of a religious sub-culture that its political and social influences loom larger than the actual life of what is, after all, a religious community. Could H J Perkin's view, that religion is 'an analgesic against the pain of labour' influencing the working class into non-violence be tantamount to saying that Methodism saved England from the Russian revolution through a Labour Party more Methodist than Marxist?

These issues will be found in the WHS Proceedings along with a renaissance of local history which ranges from the glorious amateurism of a study like Eve Chapman's *John Wesley and Co.* (Halifax 1952) and the late Joanna Dawson's work on the great Howarth Round and Nidderdale to studies of Leeds by Colin Dews, York by Edward Royle and Sunderland by Geoffrey Milburn as well as local church studies like Philip Bagwell's *Outcast London* on the West London Mission (Epworth 1987). Local studies form the very life blood of the local branches of the WHS, helped by the policy of depositing vast quantities of archive material in local libraries and in that austere monument of late Victorian piety, the John Rylands Library in Manchester. The outcrop of these sources was outstanding scholarly work typified by Robert Moore's *Pitmen, Preachers and Politics* (CUP 1974) highlighting the miners of the Deerness Valley. Men and women (for here was a community religion which gave women an alternative to the pub) tended to be highly disciplined, self-controlled persons 'willing to train their minds in critical thinking and their voices in harmony singing'. This spilled over into Liberal and early Labour politics. The recent work of Robert Colls[28] has supported Moore's analysis, showing the impact of Methodism, especially Primitive Methodism, in producing self confident, self possessed articulate working class people.

Primitive Methodism has drawn a battery of historians to itself recently. J T Wilkinson lovingly brought to life potter William Clowes and carpenter Hugh Bourne. Julia Werner, Deborah Valenze and Dorothy Graham[29] (secretary of

WHS) have shown the way this paradigm of the evolution of a revivalist group from sect to denomination used women (often amazingly young women) in its evangelism. One itinerant, Miss Elizabeth Bultitude, survived until 1890. The changes from the 'Ranters' of Belper to Peake's Commentary is a Christian saga of immense fascination not least to the sociologist. Oliver Beckerlegge has told the story, from their angle, of *The United Methodist Free Churches* (Epworth 1957). It can be balanced by John Bowmer's *pastor and People* (Epworth 1975) followed by the sophistication of David Gowland's account of *Methodist Secessions, Free Methodism in Manchester, Rochdale and Liverpool* (Manch 1979). Thomas Shaw is always reliable on the *Bible Christians* (Epworth 1965) while E A Rose completes the picture with his studies of the Methodist New Connexion.[30]

The relationship of Methodism to the other Communions is another branch of Methodist Studies. Rupert Davies' *Methodism* (Pelican 1963) has clear ecumenical undertones. Frank Baker's *John Wesley and the Church of England* (Epworth 1970) is authoritative from the Methodist angle. It needs balancing by a study beginning from the Anglican side which can, indeed, begin with Baker's own *Grimshaw of Haworth* (Epworth 1963), Walsh on the early Evangelicals and recent surveys of European Evangelicalism by W R Ward, showing that the revival was a European-American movement of immense complexity.[31] J M Turner's *Conflict and Reconciliation* (Epworth 1985) explored the relationship with other churches following up insights in John Bossy's *English Catholic Community 1570-1850* (DLT 1979), showing it to be part of English Dissent. The subtle links between Methodism and the Age of Reason are revealed by David Bebbington in his penetrating survey of *Evangelicalism in Modern Britain* (Unwin 1989), following up the equally perceptive *Nonconformist Conscience* (Allen and Unwin 1982). The difficulty here is that a surgeon's knife is needed to cut between the Arminian styles of Evangelicalism and those forms with a Calvinist theological basis.

In Wesley studies the 1970s saw the beginning of a new era. The 'Oxford' or *Bicentennial* edition of *John Wesley's Works*, dreamed of by Professor Frank Baker, began to appear and is now well under way with outstanding editorial and interpretive work by W R Ward on the Journal, Baker himself on the Letters, Davies on the early societies, Franz Hildebrandt and Beckerlegge on the hymn Book of 1780. Here is scholarship of a very high order, a tribute to the indefatigable persistence and attention to detail of Frank Baker and now Richard Heitzenrater as General Editor. There are signs, too, that Frank Baker's earlier work on the *Representative Verse of Charles Wesley* (Epworth 1962) is being followed up by scholarly editions of Charles's work also.[32]

My brief is to confine myself to British scholarship, though to make no reference to the earlier work by the Franciscan Maximin Piette or G C Cell, to Martin Schmidt's 'theological biography' or Albert Outler's magnificent rehabilitations of Wesley as 'folk theologian'[33] and Richard Heitzenrater on Wesley's Diaries would be ludicrous.

Henry Rack marked the 250th anniversary of the Wesley's 'Second Journey' with his *Reasonable Enthusiast* (Epworth 1989), clearly the outstanding one volume biography of Wesley this century. Rack was not afraid to break stereotypes, to show the development and context of Wesley's work, and is fully abreast of eighteenth century scholarship. Finally, like a great boulder across the path, is Gordon Rupp's final work *English Religion 1688-1791* (OUP 1986) with its fine treatment of the Wesleyan style of spirituality. Rack will stand authoritatively for some years, though a good deal of work is being done on the early eighteenth century which will make the context of Methodism more clear. Rupp followed in the wake of Norman Sykes, on some measure completing his mentor's work. Newer work will not be able to ignore the social historians like John G Rule and political historians like Lynda Colley.[34]

The history of Methodism after 1932 is found in several summaries by Rupert Davies[35] and the analysis of Conference reports by Thompson Brake in his exhaustive and somewhat exhausting *Policy and Politics in British Methodism 1932-1982* (London 1983). There are notable biographies like Gordon Wakefield on *Newton Flew* (Epworth 1971) and Paul Sangster on his father, *W E Sangster*, while Alan Wilkinson's evocation of the earlier half of the century in *Dissent and Conform*[36] is only excelled by the Free Church sections in Adrian Hastings' *A History of English Christianity*. There is scope here to ask if E R Norman's thesis[37] about clerical and lay elites following secular fashion a decade or so later can be applied to Methodism, which can too easily fall for gaily painted secular bandwagons! What are the sociological reasons for decline? Why did Methodism, for a time, have an appeal to many university students? What ultimate effect did all the ecumenical discussions have? The deluge of reports and pamphlets in the 1960s now seem almost archaeological. Has the Methodist structural St Vitus' dance really achieved anything apart from the abolition of the Wesleyan diarchy of 'leaders' and 'trustees'?

Where are the gaps now? What are the features of the future for Methodist studies? Several areas stand out. We need a full treatment of Methodist worship, following up the basic studies of hymnody and the liturgical studies of A R George, G S Wakefield, G Wainwright and D Tripp. Has Methodist preaching a distinctive note compared with other churches' styles – a whiff, perhaps, of the open air about it? We need, too, a full analysis of the style and impact of Methodist scholarship from Adam Clarke and Richard Watson, following up William Strawson's valuable chapter in the History, volume 3. This would take us back to an era reliant on classic Anglicanism and Joseph Butler through W B Pope to Scott Lidgett. Boyd Hilton's *The Age of Atonement* (OUP 1988) showed the impact on society of a shift from atonement to incarnation in theology. Methodism is not mentioned, a fact eloquent of isolation and neglect. Yet there is a whole slant on Hilton's thesis which could be filled here. In our century it is too easily assumed that there is little beside the giants of biblical scholarship – Moultons and Findlays, Howard, Taylor, Barrett, Hooker, Dunn, Marshall. But where were the 'lay theologians' who operated in other disciplines like Sir Herbert Butterfield, Charles Coulson and Basil Willey.[38] Is there a definable Evangelical Arminianism to be found here, a thread of optimism of grace leading back to Wesley himself? A much larger scale sequel to Langford's essays in this field is needed.

Space has forbidden a look at British Methodism overseas, in itself a fascinating exploration. It is a matter of deep regret that there is no adequate successor to G G Findlay and H W Holdsworth's *History of the Wesleyan Methodist Missionary Society* (Epworth 1921-4, 5 vols). The late Professor E E Rich told me that such a work would take a full time professional historian at least five years including considerable field work.[39] The style of the writing of African and Asian history has changed out of all recognition since Allen Birtwhistle's biographical approach. A fleet of secular historians has now pushed well beyond the stale controversies of Marxists and non-Marxists which marked the post war era.

Denominational history can be nostalgic (the WHS has not always escaped that!) or proof texts and panaceas for the present or future (if only we could get back to John Wesley or even lining up John Wesley behind present concerns as if he were a brooding presence) or it can be a genuine part of our memory without which we are barely alive, like the Florentines after the great flood when all their treasures were lost, who cried, 'Give us our history back'. The WHS has its continuing task precisely here.

References

1. cf R Green, *The Founding of the WHS,* PWHS vol 6, part 4, 1907; F F Bretherton, *The WHS – Its Origin and Progress,* PWHS vol 24, parts 2 & £, 1943; also articles by A W Harrison and F Baker; J C Bowmer, *Twenty Five Years. The Work of the WHS 1943-1968.* PWHS vol 27, part 2, 3, 1969; H D Rack, *Recent Books on Methodism*, Epworth Review, vol 7 No. 1, Jan 1980; C D Field, *British Methodist Studies 1980-1988*, Epworth Review, vol 15 No. 2, May 1988
2. W F Swift, *The Works of John Wesley*, PWHS vol 31, Part 8, Dec 1958
3. Methodist Times, 5 Feb 1903, p 91
4. NHM vol 1, p 7, 27
5. E Halévy, *The Birth of Methodism in England.* Translation with introduction, B Semmel, Chicago 1971; cf J D Walsh, *Elie Halévy and the Birth of Methodism*; Transactions of the Royal Historical Society, vol 25, 1975; D Christie, *Stress and Stability in Late Eighteenth Century Britain*, OUP 1984
6. L Tyerman, *Life and Times of John Wesley*, vol 3 Hodder 1871, p 499
7. John Kent, *The Age of Disunity*, Epworth 1966, ch 2, 3, 4
8. cf J M Turner, *R F Wearmouth 1882-1963. Methodist Historian*, PWHS vol 43, part 5, 1982
9. J L and B Hammond, *The Town Labourer 1760-1832*, Guild Books 1949, p 65, 108

10. cf E Royle, *Radical Politics 1790-1900*, Longmans 1971; ibid *The Infidel Tradition*, Macmillan 1976

11. J D Walsh, *Methodism and the Mob* in C J Cuming and D Baker *Studies in Church History*, vol 8, CUP 1972, pp 213-27

12. cf J M Turner, *Henry Bett – Last of the Wesleyans*, West Midlands WHS Silver Jubilee 1990, pp 14-19

13. R N Flew, *The Hymns of Charles Wesley*, Epworth, 1953; cf H A Hodges & A M Allchin, *A Rapture of Praise*, London 1966; L Adey, *Hymns and the Christian Myth*, Vancouver 1986; ibid *Class and Idol in the English Hymn*, Vancouver 1988

14. A R George in Studia Liturgica, vol 2, No 3, Sept 1963

15. H Bett, *The Early Methodist Preachers*, Epworth 1935

16. E G Rupp, *Thomas Jackson,* Epworth 1954, p 7

17. In S Mews (Ed), *Modern Religious Rebels*, Epworth 1993, p 5

18. V H H Green, *John Wesley*, p 141

19. H D Rack, *Wesley Observed*, PWHS vol 49 part 1, Feb 1993

20. Kent in PWHS vol 35 part 5, March 1966; G F Nuttall, 'John Wesley Presides', London Quarterly and Holborn Review 1966, pp 200-4

21. J M Turner, *After Thompson – Methodism and the English Working Class*, Halifax Antiquarian Society 1989, pp 57-72; cf G Malmgreen, *Women and the Family in East Cheshire Methodism*, in J Obelkevich, *Disciples of Faith*, RKP 1987, pp 55ff

22. E J Hobsbawm, *Methodism and the Threat of Revolution, in Labouring Men*, ch 3, London 1964; *Primitive Rebels*, ch 8, Manchester 1959

23. R Currie, *A Micro-Theory of Methodist Growth*, PWHS vol 36, part 3, Oct 1967; ibid, *Methodism Divided*, A Study of the Sociology of Ecumenicalism, Faber 1968; J Kent, *The Age of Disunity*; ibid, *The Unacceptable Face*, SCM 1987, p 99ff; in H Cunliffe-Jones & B Drewery, *History of Christian Doctrine*, T & T Clark 1978, pp 461ff; HMBG vol 2 ch by Kent on Wesleyanism etc

24. esp. as in 5, 11; cf *The Origins of the Evangelical Revival*, in G V Bennett & J D Walsh (Ed) Essays in Modern English Church History, Longmans 1966; HMBG vol 1 ch by Walsh; *Methodism and the Common People*, in R Samuel (Ed), People's History and Social Theory, London 1981; *Religious Societies. Methodist and Evangelical 1738-1800*, W J Sheil & D Wood, Studies in Church History vol 23, Blackwell 1986, pp 239-302; *John Wesley and the Community of Goods*; In K Robins, Studies in Church History, Subsidia 7, Blackwell 1990, pp 25-50

25. W R Ward (Ed), *The Early Correspondence of Jabez Bunting 1820-9*, London 1972; Ibid, *Early Victorian Methodism*, The Correspondence of Jabez Bunting 1830-1858, OUP 1976; A J Hayes & D H Gowland, *Scottish Methodism in the Early Victorian Period*; The Scottish Correspondence of Jabez Bunting 1800-1857, Edinburgh 1981

26. C D Field, *Sociology of Methodism*, British Journal of Sociology, July 1977, Oral History, Spring 1976; A D Gilbert, *Religion and Society in Industrial England*, Longmans 1976; R Currie, A D Gilbert & L Horsley, *Churches and Churchgoers*, OUP 1977

27. D J Jeremy, *Capitalists and Christian* , Business Leaders and the Churches in Britain 1900-1960, OUP 1990; ibid (Ed), *Business and Religion in Britain*, London 1988; G E Milburn, *Piety, Profit and Paternalism in Methodists in Business in the North East*, PWHS vol 44 No 3, Dec 1983; ibid, *Big Business and Denominational Development in Methodism during the Nineteenth and Early Twentieth Centuries*, Epworth Review Vol 10 No 3, Sept 1983; J M Gibbs, *Morels of Cardiff*, Cardiff 1982; H J Perkin, *The Origins of Modern English Society*, RKP 1969, ch 6, 8, 9

28. R Colls, *The Pitmen of the Northern Coalfield*, Work, Culture and Protest 1890-1850, Manchester University Press, 1987, pp 118ff

29. J S Werner, *The Primitive Methodist Connexion*, Wisconsin USA, 1984; R W Ambler, *Ranters, Revivalists and Reformers,* Hull 1989; D Valenze, *Prophetic Sons and Daughters*, Princeton USA, 1985; E D Graham, *Chosen by God*, WHS 1989; D C Dews (Ed), *From Mow Cop to Peake*, West Yorks, WHS Leeds 1982, ch by J M Turner pp 1-13

30. e.g. E A Rose, *The Methodist New Connexion 1797-1907*, PWHS vol 47 part 6 Oct 1990

31. esp. *The Protestant Evangelical Awakening*, CUP 1992

32. e.g. S J Kimbrough (Sn) and Oliver A Beckerlegge, *The Unpublished Poetry of Charles Wesley*, Vol 1 Abingdon, Nashville, USA, 1988, vol 2, 1990, PWHS Feb 1990, Feb 1991; J R Tyson, *Charles Wesley on Sanctification*, Marshall. Pickering 1986; ibid *Charles Wesley. A Reader*, OUP 1990

33. M Piette, *John Wesley on the Evolution of Protestantism*, 1925, ET 1938; G C Cell, *The Rediscovery of John Wesley*, NY, USA 1935; M Schmidt, *John Wesley – a Theological Biography*, ET 3 vols, Epworth 1962, 1971, 1973; A C Outler, *John Wesley*, OUP 1964; R Heitzenrater, *The Elusive Mr Wesley*, 2 vols, Nashville USA, 1984; ibid, *Mirror and Memory*, Reflections on early Methodism, Nashville, USA, 1989

34. J G Rule, *The Labouring Classes in Early Industrial England 1750-1850*, London 1986; ibid, *Albion's People. English Society 1714-1815*, Longmans 1992; L Colley, *In Defiance of Oligarchy*, CUP 1982; *Britons. Forging the Nation 1707-1737*, Yale USA 1992

35. HMGB vol 3, *The Nature of Methodism*, In W S F Pickering, Anglican-Methodist Relations, DLT 1961; R E Davies (Ed), *The Testing of the Churches 1932-1982*, ch 2, Epworth 1983

36. A Wilkinson, *Dissent or Conform?* SCM 1986, pp 3-82; A Hastings, *A History of English Christianity 1920-1985*, Collins 1986, ch 6, 15, 30, 35, 39

37. E R Norman, *Church and Society in England 1770-1970*, OUP 1976

38. cf J M Turner, *Herbert Butterfield – Christian Historian*, PWHS vol 46 Feb 1987; D & E Hawkins, *The World of Science – the Religious and Social Thought of C A Coulson*, Epworth 1989; L Griffiths, *Living in a Divided and Distinguished World*, A tribute to Basil Willey, Epworth Review vol 12 No 2 1985

39. A F Walls, *The Missionary Movement in Christian History*, T & T Clark 1996 etc

Chapter 9

Wesley and Early Methodism Studies1993-2003

A Review Article

Historians speak of the 'Long Eighteenth Century' from the Revolution of 1688-89 to the Acts of 1828-29 which appeared to end England's 'ancien régime' and the over-dominance of the Church of England, followed by the Reform Act of 1832. For a clear survey we have Frank O'Gorman, *The Long Eighteenth Century* (Arnold 1999). This is admirably fair and comprehensive. For the Church of England John Walsh, Colin Haydon and Stephen Taylor (Eds), *The Church of England c. 1689-1833* (CUP 1993) especially the long introductory chapter by Walsh and Taylor, dispels the convenient 'myth' of a totally moribund Church waiting for John Wesley. The European context is vital since the Evangelical Revival did not begin in Great Britain. W R Ward's *Faith and Faction* (Epworth 1993) and *Christianity under the Ancien Régime 1648-1798* (CUP 1999) make clear that Wesley cannot be understood without an analysis of Pietism and the Moravians, not to speak of emigrations, and the extraordinary 'networking' of trans-Atlantic spirituality which made both Whitefield and Wesley talk about their 'world parish'. He shows the peoples' need for 'primary religion', the 'religion of the heart' – Wesley's phrase – picked up by Ted Campbell in his survey *The Religion of the Heart* (university of South Carolina Press 1991). This phenomenon crossed both the Atlantic and the Catholic-Protestant divide.

On Wesley and Methodism the second edition of Henry Rack, *Reasonable Enthusiast – John Wesley and the Rise of Methodism* (Epworth 2002) is still the outstanding 'Life and Times' with regard taken of the latest research. This is essential for the serious student. A somewhat easier 'read', equally authoritative, is Richard Heitzenrater, *Wesley and the People called Methodists* (Abingdon Press 1995). Like Rack, Heitzenrater has no illusions, showing that Methodism grew slowly with several crises which could have ended the Connexion. He also affirms that Wesley was not the greatest preacher of the age, an opinion elaborated in a later essay in R Sykes (Ed), *Beyond the Boundaries, Preaching in the Wesleyan Tradition* (Applied Theology Press, Oxford 1998). Wesley, of course, preached often in the open air, 'a cross to me', he said as late as 1772, but 'Most of Wesley's own preaching was within four walls to the societies and classes'. On the effect of preaching, hymnody and literature there are new insights in J P Van Noppen, *Transforming Words, the Early Methodist Revival from a Discourse Perspective* (Peter Lang, Bern 1999). Was Wesley manipulative? 'Post-modernism' has altered our approach to documents making the 'reader' with her agenda as important as the writer or speaker. Clearly Wesley always had his own 'spin', but was not in any way an ally of power-mongers or early capitalists! This is an important new approach. A non-Methodist approach can be enlightening. Certainly Roy Hattersley's *A Brand from the Burning, the Life of John Wesley* (Little, Brown 2002) shows Wesley as a man who exercised autocratic power. While Hattersley perhaps too easily accepts the 'myth' of the dead Church, this is a good read (despite its errors), as was his life of William Booth. Kenneth J Collins, *A Real Christian, the Life of John Wesley* (Abingdon 1999) is another lively introduction.

Professor W R Ward naughtily wrote that Norman Sykes and his pupils sprinkled holy water over the 18th century church. This is hardly true of John Kent whose *Wesley and the Wesleyans, Religion in Eighteenth Century Britain* (CUP 2002) might, on the surface, seem to be an antidote to some of Hattersley's points. He sees the notion of the Evangelical Revival and Wesley and his followers as 'the instruments of this divine intervention saving the nation from the tempting freedoms of the French Revolution as a persistent myth'. After this iconoclasm, he shows Wesley tapping into people's' need for 'primary religion'. Wesley's doctrine of, and popular aspiration to, holiness became in a generation a 'national body with a common sub-culture', where the goal became not holiness but respectability, meaning 'genuine hard-won moral and financial stability'. Hattersley's conclusions are similar. While there was surely genuine revival, there Is provocative challenge in Kent's account. My own book, *John Wesley, the Evangelical Awakening and the Rise of Methodism in England* (Epworth 2002), has more on Wesley's thinking and tactics, his ability to hold together the religion of the heart and disciplined spirituality. The consequence was the 'many Methodisms' which retained the skeleton of Wesley's system.

For other surveys of a wide field, there are two notable contributions of John Walsh. In *John Wesley, a Bicentennial Tribute* (Dr Williams's Trust 1993), he shows how, in the pursuit of his objectives, Wesley revealed 'organisational skills of the highest rank. He was a good strategist and a brilliant tactician ... essentially a pragmatist and experimenter.' Wesley should be seen 'not so much as an either/or but as a both/and theologian, a mediator between the worlds of élite and popular culture'. Walsh's chapter, 'Methodism and the Origins of English Speaking Evangelicalism' in the important *Evangelicalism – Comparative Studies of Popular Protestantism in North America, the British Isles and Beyond 1700-1900* edited by Mark Noll, David Bebbington and George Rawlyk (OUP 1994), shows the vital role of the 'Connexion' idea – the motto 'only connect', epigraph of E M Forster's most famous novel, could stand as a motto for the Methodist movement scooping up 'innumerable rockpools of piety'. No recent books elaborate the essence of Methodism better than David Hempton, *The Religion of the People – Methodism and Popular Religion c 1750-1900* (Routledge 1996) followed by *Religion and Popular Culture in Britain and Ireland* (CUP 1996) which has a chapter on 'Methodist Revolution?' and a proper consideration of Irish religion, including the pervasive and anti-Catholic element in Methodism. By analysing Wesley's attitude to the law and to the Church of England, he shows that popular evangelicalism offered a religious culture which could operate outside the Establishment without seriously destabilising the English state. This was achieved partly by Methodism with its combination of 'passion and piety, zeal and order, faith and works, thrift and charity, Puritanism and decency, individualism and community and verve and vulgarity'.   The both/and denomination? But, of course, if fragmented, a 'lightning conductor' of social tension.

Wesley must never be seen in isolation from his supporters or his opponents, not only the Hanoverian moderates but the 'Calvinists of the heart', including Whitefield. So we are well served by Simon Ross Valentine with his *John Bennet and the Origins of Methodist Evangelical Revival in England* (Scarecrow Press 1997) followed by the primary source, *Mirror of the Soul, the Diary of an Early Methodist Preacher John Bennet 1714-1754* (MPH 2002). Bennet was much more than the man who married Grace Murray – Wesley's 'last love'. These books show what it was like to be an early itinerant and how much Methodism depended on them. Bennet can be followed up in the generation of itinerants in John C Bowmer and John Vickers, *The Letters of John Pawson, Methodist Itinerant 1762-1806* (3 vols. MPH 1994-5). Pawson gives a realistic view of Methodism at the grass roots.   Occasionally one can sympathise with its opponents, since, 'perfect love' seems rather rare. Pawson almost rejoices when Charles Wesley dies, and sees John Wesley's demise as providential. But he is soon grumbling about a church 'without a head'.   John Lenton's *My Sons in the Gospel – An Analysis of Wesley's Itinerant Preachers* (WHS 2002) shows that there were 800 itinerants before Wesley's death, many of them reverting to local preaching, with about 100 becoming, like Bennet, dissenting ministers or Anglican priests.   The local preachers of Wesley's days are analysed by Margaret Batty in G Milburn and M Batty (Eds) *Workaday Preachers, the Story of Methodist Local Preachers* (MPH 1995).   Methodist worship was soon impossible without them.   Its internal life was very much maintained by the 60 per cent of its members who were women. Paul Wesley Chilcote's *She Offered The Christ – the Legacy of Women Preachers in Early Methodism* (Abingdon 1993) fills out the earlier, underrated accounts by Leslie Church.

Wesley saw first William Grimshaw as a possible 'successor', then John Fletcher. Faith Cook's lively *William Grimshaw of Haworth* (The Banner of Truth and Trust 1997) is perceptive and accurate, while Patrick Streiff's *Reluctant Saint, A Theological Biography of Fletcher of Madeley* (Epworth 2001) is very important, showing how an Evangelical Arminian could dialogue with fellow evangelicals, while based in his Shropshire parish. 'Justification is a love look, and sanctification a love token' typifies Fletcher's spirituality, backed up in the end by his wife Mary Bosanquet. The theological seminary at Trevecca is a sad story, an attempt to conciliate. So we come to the Countess of Huntingdon.   Following Edwin Welch's pioneering work on primary documents, two contrasting books can be recommended.   Boyd Stanley Schlentler in *Queen of the Methodists, the Countess of Huntingdon and the Eighteenth Century Crisis of Church and Society* (Durham Academic Press 1997) writes as a critical historian, while Faith Cook in *Selina, Countess* *of Huntingdon. Her Pivotal Role in the 18th Century Evangelical Awakening* (Banner of Truth Trust 2001) is more sympathetic to Selina as a woman, but is not uncritical. There is more than a hint of jealousy at times in Wesley – 'Pope John' and 'Pope Joan' could not work together. After the '1770 Minutes' rumpus, John asked her to 'use her reason'. Selina called him papist and heretical! Again, here is the split between Arminians and 'Calvinists of the heart' which has soured relations between Methodists and Evangelical Anglicans, at times, to this day.

The Wesley family cannot be forgotten. Charles Isaac Wallace in *Susanna Wesley, the Complete Writings* (OUP 1997) brings together Susanna's Journals, letters and writings on educational and catechetical method – all after the rectory fire – showing her as a formidable woman in her own right with a command of spirituality revealed in John Newton's biography, *Susanna Wesley and the Puritan Tradition in Methodism* (Epworth 2002), now revised. The background of Susanna and Samuel Wesley can be explored in a revision by Robert C Monk of his *John Wesley – His Puritan Heritage* (Scarecrow Press 1999). If the Puritans were more significant for Wesley than often thought (look at the *Christian Library*) the relationship with the Moravians was crucial too, for a time. So Colin J Podmore's *The Moravian Church in England 1728-1760* (OUP 1998) is now significant for an understanding of the rift at Fetter Lane which alienated Methodist and Moravian – another theological divide which Reinhold Niebuhr saw as a fundamental difference between 'Reformers' and 'Evangelicals' although personalities came into it, too, I fear.

So what of Wesley the 'ecumenist' before his time? Does that 'myth' begin to evaporate? Eamon Duffy in a fascinating chapter on 'Wesley and the Counter Reformation' in Jane Garrett and Colin Matthew, *Revival and Religion since 1700* (Hambledon 1993) maintains that 'Wesley detested Roman Catholicism', even if he used Catholic spirituality as in Lopez and de Renty. David Butler's *Methodists and Papists. John Wesley and the Catholic Church in the Eighteenth Century* (DLT 1995) is authoritative here showing that, as so often, Wesley reflects a changing context – the Cork Riots of 1742 produced the oft-quoted eirenic 'Letter to a Roman Catholic' (appendix B). The sermon on 'the Catholic Spirit' has similar sentiments about essentials and 'adiaphora'. The 1778 Savile Act giving greater freedom to Catholics (numbering about 80000) showed Wesley unwilling to grant more freedom since Catholics do not keep faith with heretics. Drawing on many sources, he constantly quotes the Council of Constance (1415) which burned Jan Hus – a matter raised last year by the Czech government with the Pope. We must not conceal the anti-Catholic 'feel' of the 18th century which the Wesleys shared – Charles' anti-French poetry at the time of the Seven Years War is typical. Wesley and Bishop Richard Challoner exchanged polemics but never met.

Charles Wesley was no 'clone' of his brother. Kenneth Newport's critical edition of *The Sermons* (OUP 2001), shows him as a preacher – 23 sermons survive, some 'borrowed' from his brother, a matter not unknown then or now! Some of the sermons are pre-1738, but we have the two university sermons of 1739 and 1742, and one preached after the London earthquake of 1750, warning of doom to come. Later Charles preached extempore, John Pawson called him 'dry and lifeless' which he certainly wasn't in the 1740s! But it is the hymns that survive, on which J R Watson, *The English Hymn* (OUP 1997) is magisterial, though he fears that, sadly, we may be the last generation to sing them.

What now of the renaissance of American 'Wesleyan' scholarship? British readers need to be aware of the different contexts, with an attempt to find roots and continuity which sometimes results in a 'lining up' of Wesley with quite proper modern concerns, such as feminism and the environment, on which he had nothing significant to say. This misuse of Wesley makes historians wince. We can begin with the late Thomas Langford. His recent *Methodist Theology* in the 'Exploring Methodism' series (Epworth 1998) begins where Albert Outler left off, with his proper insistence that Wesley was a 'folk theologian', his ideas 'framed as he stood in the presence of God and among the people of God'. This is theology through sermon, hymn and practical spirituality. In two major volumes, *Practical Divinity* 2nd Ed, 2 vols (Abingdon 1998, 1999) he takes us from Wesley to Wainwright. Langford makes it clear that Wesley did not bequeath a theological system to his successors. 'Although Methodism cannot be understood apart from John Wesley, it also cannot be understood except as it has moved beyond Wesley.' Randy Maddox edited *Rethinking Wesley's Theology in Contemporary Methodism* (Abingdon 1998) including Brian Beck on Connexionalism. This does not offer much that is new. His *Responsible Grace – John Wesley's Practical Theology* (Abingdon 1994) is weighty, comprehensive and well argued, but occasionally lacking in context. Rather sharper is the German Manfred Marquart, *John Wesley's Social Ethics* (Abingdon 1992). This is still authoritative in the area where it is easy to forget that Wesley lived before the real rise of modern capitalism, not to speak of a world market. David Deeks has a very relevant chapter on Adam Smith and John Wesley in Philip R Meadows (Ed), *Windows on Wesley – Wesleyan Theology in Today's World* (Applied Theology Press 1997). Those who prefer a more conservative approach should find Kenneth Collins *The Scripture Way of Salvation, the Heart of John Wesley's Theology* (Abingdon 1997) and *A Faithful Witness – John Wesley's Homiletical Theology* (Wesley Heritage Press 1993) helpful introductions. Rather different in approach is the veteran 'Process Theologian' John R Cobb in *Grace and Responsibility – A Wesleyan Theology For Today* (Abingdon 1995). Cobb makes clear his agenda – 'This book approaches Wesley from the perspective of the problems and needs of United Methodism. It is a proposal for how this particular Wesleyan denomination can reclaim its past and move forward to its future.' He admits that Wesley is pre-Darwin. While this is a positive and interesting book, I am not sure that it solves Cobb's problem. The dilemma is driven home in Scott R Jones, *John Wesley's Conception and Use of Scripture* (Abingdon 1995). This is a careful and perceptive analysis of Wesley's assertion of the priority and primacy of Scripture. Jones makes clear that Wesley is correctly understood as conceiving religious authority for him to have five components: 'Scripture, reason, Christian antiquity, experience and the Church of England'. This is a modification of the 'Wesleyan Quadrilateral' which adds 'experience' to the historic Anglican triangle of scripture, tradition and reason. Jones would agree with G C Cell that scripture is the 'centre of gravity of his thinking', endorsed by tradition, including the Reformation, not contradicted by reason and confirmed by experience. But what now? That debate is still vital, underlined by James T MacCormack's *Thought from a Warmed Heart – A Commentary on John Wesley's Notes on the New Testament* (Colour Point, Newtownards, 2002). MacCormack, from an Irish standpoint, shows how 40 per cent of the *Notes* come from J A Bengel, the Pietist, Doddridge and others. Bengel was no fool, but was A S Peake exaggerating when he begged Methodists, approaching the union of 1932, to drop the *Notes* from their standards of preaching as the work of an 'outmoded exegete'? Can we still in any way sustain the kind of exegesis of the Book of Revelation? For Bengel, papal history all leads up to the Parousia in 1836! Wesley was embarrassed by this later, but retained it. For me, the key American book is Theodore Runyon's *New Creation. John Wesley's Theology Today* (Abingdon 1998). Jürgen Moltmann says this is *the* book on Wesley! The first five chapters give a clear survey of Wesley's theology, showing how 'generous orthodoxy' must be followed by 'orthopraxis' seen now, at last, free from Marxist overtones and *orthopathy* – a right balance between experience as transforming the individual, social, rational, sacramental and teleological, moving towards the goal of new creation in Christ and perfect love. This is well presented, particularly in the light of the charismatic movement. The means of grace are given proper emphasis and the social modes of spirituality, a matter stressed by Gordon Wakefield, *Methodist Spirituality* (Epworth 2000) and, from an American angle, Philip F Hardt, *The Soul of Methodism, the Class Meeting in Early New York Methodism* (University Press of America 2000). Runyon repeats his approach in the closing chapters of Richard Steele's *Heart Religion in the Methodist Tradition and Related Movements*, (Scarecrow Press 2001). Revival was a 'rope of sand' and still is, without the means of grace. Hardt sees the 'cell' as the modern 'class'.

What of Methodist worship? Karen B Westerfield Tucker's edited volume, *The Sunday Service of the Methodists* (Abingdon 1996), is unfortunately little known in Britain. Tucker analyses the styles of worship Wesley and his followers used, followed up by the late Raymond George, and representatives of the World Methodist community which must never be underrated.

What, then, finally do we *do* with tradition? The danger is to wallow in 'Wesleyolatry', or to indulge in nostalgia, 'if only we could get back'. But we move on. Do other Christians get tired of the Wesley industry? Geoffrey Wainwright has recently in *Methodists in Dialog* (Abingdon 1995) marked out six features of the tradition surveyed here, which can be shared ecumenically. The *scriptures* as the primary and abiding testimony to the redemptive work of God in Christ; the ministry of *evangelism* where the gospel was to be preached to every creature and needed only to be accepted in faith; thirdly a *generous orthodoxy*, wherein theological opinions might vary as long as they were consistent with the apostolic teaching; fourthly *sanctification* showing itself in moral earnestness and loving deeds; fifthly a *social concern* that was directed to the neediest of neighbours; sixthly the *Lord's Supper* as a sacramental sign of the fellowship graciously bestowed by the Triune God. These, says Wainwright, are 'the features which must be strengthened in contemporary Methodism if we are to maintain our historic identity, speak with a significant voice on the ecumenical scene and keep on a recognisably Christian track as the ways diverge'. I hope this decade of scholarship will help in that proper search for the source of the stream of tradition and for the future, which will be very different from John Wesley's world.

To Be Noted Now - 2008

Isabel Rivers, *Reason Grace and Sentiment - A Study of the Language of Religion and Ethics in England 1660-1780* Vol I (CUP 1991)

David M Chapman, *In Search of the Catholic Spirit - Methodists and Roman Catholics in Dialogue* (Epworth 2004)

Davis M Chapman *Born in Song – Methodist Worship in Britain* (Church in the Market Place Publications, Warrington, 2006)

David Hempton, *Methodism – Empire of the Spirit* (Yale 2005)

Alan P F Sell, *Protestant Nonconformist Texts* Vol 2 (Ashgate 2006)

B E Beck, *Exploring Methodism's Heritage – The Story of the Oxford Institute of Methodist Theological Studies* (Nashville Tennessee, 2004)

G Lloyd, *Charles Wesley and the Struggle for Methodist Identity* (OUP 2007)

Kenneth G C Newport and Ted H Campbell (Eds) *Charles Wesley – Life, Literature and Legacy* (Epworth 2007)

Richard P Heitzenrater (Ed), *The Poor and the People Called Methodists* (Abingdon 2002)

Bulletin of the John Rylands University Library of Manchester, Volume 85, Numbers 2 & 3, Summer and Autumn 2003. A feast of Essays on John Wesley etc as a Festschrift for Dr Henry Rack

A Bibliography of Methodist Historical Literature is produced each year by Dr Clive Field for the Wesley Historical Society

E Dorothy Graham, Saved to Serve. The Story of the Wesley Deaconess Order 1890-1978, MPH 2002

S T Kimbrough and Kenneth G C Newport (eds) The Journal of Charles Wesley, Abingdon 2007

Phyllis Mack, Heart Religion in the British Enlightenment. Gender and Emotion in Early Methodism, CUP 2008

Chapter 10

The Long Eighteenth Century, A Review Article, 1997

This curious phrase is often used of the period from the 'Glorious Revolution' of 1689 to the era of the French Revolution of 1789 or even extending to the end of the Napoleonic Wars or to Catholic Emancipation in 1829 when England ceased to be a confessional state. To attempt to review the enormous amount of research in eighteenth century histiography since I studied it under the late professor Norman Sykes and Sir John Plumb in 1952 would be ludicrous and we must be selective.[1] At that time Sir Lewis Namier was still a brooding presence about to launch the important History of Parliament project which continued his style of analysis of members of parliament with an apparent, but illusory, antipathy to any ideology.[2] Sir Herbert Butterfield's *George III and the Historians* (1957) is still in print giving a summary up till then of the long debate about the nature of the rule of George III.

We begin with Norman Sykes. He and his pupils have been accused of sprinkling holy water over the prelates of that age but his massive contribution to eighteenth-century studies cannot be gainsaid. The biography of *Edmund Gibson, Bishop of London* (OUP 1926) and *Church and State in the Eighteenth Century* (CUP 1934) showed the many positive features of the Hanoverian church countering the denigration of it by Evangelicals, Methodists and High Churchmen who had their own agendas. This is still an essential starting point but in the 1950s Sykes filled out the earlier picture. The mammoth biography of *William Wake, Archbishop of Canterbury* (2 vols CUP 1957) revealed much ecumenical activity involving the continental churches followed up in *Old Priest and New Presbyter* (CUP 1957) which pointed to the negotiations on ministry which marked the Anglican-Methodist conversations and very recently the 'PORVOO' agreement between the Church of England and the Scandinavian Lutheran churches. *From Sheldon to Secker, Aspects of English Church History 1600-1768* (CUP 1959) completed Sykes's work showing the falsity of the innuendo of R H Tawney that the Church of England had ceased to think about social ethics. Sykes had the great gift of pointing his pupils to areas which needed explanation without creating a 'school' or inhibiting new insights. His first pupil, Gordon Rupp, ended his career with a book covering the whole period: *Religion in England 1688-1791* (OUP 1986) which includes a fine summary of the Evangelical revival and Methodism (pp 326-490), even if some might find it rather old-fashioned now on the sociological side. It can be compared with the recent chapter by W R Ward in the *History of Religion in Britain* Ed S Gilley and W J Sheils (Blackwell 1994) entitled 'The Evangelical Revival in Eighteenth-Century Britain' pp 252-272.

The late G V Bennett whose suicide after the Crockford's Preface affair in 1987 robbed us of a fine historian, showed the continuing ideological basis of the Jacobites and the non-Jacobite Tories at the beginning of the century. *The Tory Crisis in Church and State 1688-1830: Francis Atterbury* (OUP 1976) analyses the working of minds in the Church of England like that of Samuel Wesley. In a rather different style Linda Colley shows the continuing ideological thread of Toryism in her *In Defiance of Oligarchy; the Tory Party 1714-1760* (OUP 1982) and more recently in *Britons, Forging the Nation* (Yale USA 1992) uncovers a continuing thread of patriotism and anti-Catholicism throughout the eighteenth century. John Foxe's *Book of Martyrs* and Bunyan's *Pilgrim's Progress* were still immensely popular. There is no doubt that much of this ethos rubbed off on John Wesley, whose Toryism was no mere show. Colin Haydon has recently convincingly shown how the Roman Catholic community was thought 'outlandish' and unpatriotic in his *Anti-Catholicism in Eighteenth Century England* (Manchester UP 1993). Wesley's ambivalent view of Catholicism has been seen in this context.

Professor Geoffrey Best's first major book *Temporal Pillars – Queen Anne's Bounty, the Ecclesiastical Commissioners and the Church of England* (CUP 1964) shows how the church used money in defining and establishing its mission especially after Blomfield's reforms but this is a much broader book than the title suggests, showing the breakdown of the old parish system, what Robert Southey called 'the little commonwealth'. The 'gentleman of the parish' was becoming too much dependent on the squire and the advancement of tithes and other agricultural changes were aiding nonconformity. This serves to illustrate the contrast between the cumbrous machinery of the Establishment and the various dissenting 'Connexions' especially Methodism. Deryck W Lovegrove's *Established Church, Sectarian People, Itinerancy and the Transformation of Establishment 1780-1830* (CUP 1988) depicts the old dissent copying the new to good effect leading to increased denominational awareness. Some of the possible complacency of Sykes's approach is compensated for in Peter Virgin's *The Church in an Age of Negligence. Ecclesiastical Structure and Problems of Church Reform 1700-1840* (James Clarke 1989). He analyses both the defects and increasing wealth, social standing and unpopularity of the clergy with a quarter of Justices of the Peace being clergymen in 1831. The more churchy professional clergy – Evangelical and Tractarian – were yet to come.

In recent years Dr John Walsh has done more than anyone to shift the whole emphasis of eighteenth-century church historical studies, making clear as had Sykes, that church history demands the same rigour as any other branch of history and that secular historians would do well not to ignore the heart of ecclesiastical life which is its spirituality and its motivation. In about twenty major chapters and articles he has shown both the varied nature of Evangelicalism and the varied influences which activated it and flowed into it. 'Simple chronology disposes of the stereotype of the whole revival a chain reaction from the Aldersgate Street experience and of John Wesley as a solitary Moses striking the rock of petrified Anglicanism to release a sudden stream of revival'.[3] Puritanism, Religious Societies, high church spirituality, Pietists and Herrnhuters all play their part and from it stem the groups cohering around Whitefield, Wesley and other 'Connexions'. Walsh shows why people were both attracted and repelled by Wesley[4] and Wesley's own development in social thinking from a yearning for a community of goods to this later thinking about rich and poor. He shows, too, the reasons why and where Methodism spread and among whom. The ever-recurring 'Halévy thesis' both in its earlier form concerning the 1740s and the more famous assertion that Methodism was the 'trigger' behind England's stability in the next century are tackled head on in some of Walsh's most significant essays.

John Walsh is a great stimulator of research students, the fruit of which can be seen in *The Church of England c. 1689-c 1833. From Toleration to Tractarianism* edited by John Walsh, Colin Haydon and Stephen Taylor (CUP 1993). This is now the best one-volume approach to the whole century, prefaced by a superb introduction which, without wasting a word, sets out new views of the long century and its main features. It is significant that it is the beginning and end of the period which are now prominent, typified by John Spurr's *The Restoration Church of England 1646-1689* (Yale University Press 1991) and J A C Champion's *The Pillars of Statecraft, the Church of England and its Enemies 1660-1730* (CUP 1992). At the other end of the century the late F C Mather[5] showed the strength of the high church typified by Horsley who incidentally saw Methodists at one time as the dupes of the French – dangerous English Jacobins! More recently Peter Nockles has opened up again the background of the Tractarians in *The Oxford Movement in Context. Anglican High Churchmanship 1760-1857* (CUP 1994). No longer is it possible to talk of a 'thin red line' of high churchmen linking the Non-Jurors to the Oxford Movement. The whole picture is far more complex and far more rich, as was the diversity of rational thinking at the beginning of the century.[6] Along with Nockles should be read Robert Hole's *Pulpit, Politics and Public Order in England 1700-1832*, (CUP 1989) which shows a secularization of political thought occurring in the churches and that religion was still used as a means of social control and to maintain public order and stability in a rapidly changing society – Hole includes Methodists like John Stephens and Adam Clarke in his analysis of the pulpit. The same period concerns A M C Waterman *Revolution, Economics and Religion. Christian Political Economy 1798-1883*, (CUP 1991). The contributions of Thomas Malthus, Copleston, Whateley, J B Sumner and Thomas Chalmers are shown to be weighty even if in the end their approach runs into the sand as was shown by Boyd Hilton in *The Age of Atonement, the Influence of Evangelicalism on Social and Economic Thought 1785-1865*, (OUP 1988). The parallelism of *laissez-faire* economics and the stress on the Atonement and the later parallelism of the corporate state and the doctrine of the Incarnation are made clear. There are limitations in Hilton's thesis – Methodists like Pope and Lofthouse and Lidgett and Congregationalists like Dale and Forsyth still stressed Atonement at the end of the nineteenth century and one must ask if the doctrine of the Incarnation and the Fatherhood of God, which clearly came to prevail, really came to influence politics and policy. These are complex and intriguing books well worth critical analysis.

One of the paradoxes of recent histiography has been the neglect of Protestant Dissent as distinct from Methodism. *The English Presbyterians* had some coverage in C G Bolam et al (Allen and Unwin 1968) and Michael Watts' *The Dissenters from the Reformation to the French Revolution* (OUP 1978) filled a need for an up to date summary but now James E Bradley's *Religion, Revolution and English Radicalism. Nonconformity in the Eighteenth Century* (CUP 1990) opens up new approaches using prosopography and psephology (to use the horrid jargon!). This means analysing *the people* who were the dissenters *and* their voting habits in centres of Dissent like Colchester. Bradley uses a 'Namierite' approach but shows that Namier's view that local affairs dominated politics is not the case. The American Revolution very much fuelled a combination of religion and radicalism in men like Caleb Evans of Bristol, who clashed with John Wesley on this issue. Far more dissenters had the vote than was perhaps thought to be the case. Dissent is shown as paving the way to radicalism. This is hardly a new idea, but it is presented with a wealth of statistical material difficult to refute. One might have hoped for more on the religious life of Dissent – I doubt if they were always discussing politics. But oh for a historian with the style of Bernard Manning!

What of politics in general? For general accounts one can recommend Speck and Christie.[7] Ian Christie's more specialized book *Stress and Stability in Late Eighteenth Century Britain. Reflections on the British Avoidance of Revolution* (OUP 1984) is significant in that the 'non-event' of an English revolution is shown to *be* a non-event! England was never really in such danger. Christie takes the line, taught by Kitson Clark in the 1950s, that England's social structure was quite different from that of France. I wonder! Lurking behind all that thinking on eighteenth-century history is Jonathan Clark. Three of Clark's books are germane here: *English Society 1688-1832. Ideology, Social Structure and Political Practice During the Ancien Regime* (CUP 1985), the shorter polemic *Revolution and Rebellion, State and Society in England in the Seventeenth and Eighteenth Centuries* (CUP 1986) and *The Language of Liberty 1660-1832. Political Discussion and Social Dynamics in the Anglo-American World* (CUP 1994). Behind all the amusing historians' infighting and constant pot shots at the 'old hat' Whigs and Liberals and the 'old guard' Marxists, Uncle Tom Cobleigh and all, Clark makes vital points. England, he claims, *was* still an *ancien régime*, the Church of England *was* still the dominant ideological force in the localities. There was a semblance of law and order and a ruling ideology more traditional than Lockean. This is to turn Namier on his head with a vengeance! Clark even sees Methodism as a sign of the vitality of the Church of England since it produced it, which is like saying that Martin Luther was a sign of the vitality of the late medieval church. Clark, too, attempts to show that England was still a confessional state and remained so until the legislation of 1828-9 ended the political isolation of Roman Catholics as well as Dissenters. The Church of England was then, even though it has never recognized it, one among many, a point I have made also.[8]   Clark's latest book shows indirectly the way in which Wesley reflected Tory opinion on the American Revolution though once it had occurred he accepted it since, as W R Ward points out, 'Methodism offered them a way of affirming their Englishness without being Anglican, the last thing that Clark's model permits'.[9]

If Clark is caviar for the general and the argument rages, a more sober approach is to be found in Paul Langford's *A Polite and Commercial People. England 1727-1783* (OUP 1992), the first of the New Oxford History of England series.   Langford stresses the stability of England in this period compared to the continent and the growth in commerce, industry and consumerism, taking up the argument of McKendrick and Plumb that England was going through a consumer boom which affected most of the population.[10] This is a change in life style remarked on frequently in Wesley's *Journal* and other writings with his rather obsessive comments on ladies' hats, finery, and silk dresses from Macclesfield. He might also have noticed the false bosoms and cork bottoms! Certainly the Methodists – largely artisans and many women, were increasingly prosperous. This is much more than just another 'rising bourgeoisie' theory and it clearly has weight. There is, of course, much more in Langford's elegant account, but it can be balanced by the late E P Thompson's *Customs in Common* (Merlin Press, 1991, Penguin 1993) who calls Langford's account 'patrician', while he is in no doubt 'plebeian'. The plebeian's living standards were very different from the aristocrats or the men of commerce. This is the world of food riots often led by women, of the 'crowd', of wife-selling and 'rough music' and the smugglers whom Wesley sought to tame. Thompson was very like William Cobbett with a hatred of the Industrial Revolution. Allowing for this romanticism, here is an essential read along with *Whigs and Hunters*, (Penguin 1977) and D Hay (Ed) *Albion's Fatal Tree* (Allen Lane, 1975).   Thompson has one last comment on Methodism. 'The church was profoundly Erastian; had it performed an effective, a psychologically compelling paternalist role, the Methodist movement would have been neither necessary nor possible.' (*Customs* p 49). Roy Porter's *English Society in the Eighteenth Century* (Penguin, 1982) is a good summary. He starkly depicts the life of the 'labouring classes' but asserts also, 'Theirs was not the expropriated hopeless begging-bowl destitution of parts of the present-day third world. The ordinary Georgian working family did not bask in a folksy golden age, but neither did it have one foot outside the refugee-camp', (p 160). Porter, who could harshly call John Wesley an 'egomaniacal authoritarian prophet' (p 194) is lively and readable on this period when Britain lost one Empire and gained another and when Methodism became one more part of God's strange people but, for the statistical and sociological analysis now needed, I would recommend John Rule's *Albion's People, English Society 1714-1815* (Longman 1982) with its companion volume *The Vital Century, England's Developing Economy 1714-1815* (Longman 1992).

The tale could continue loud and long. The endless fascination of sex and marriage can be explored with Lawrence Stone[11] – John Wesley's 'last love' and loveless marriage fits Stone's theory about the change to romantic love superbly! But two historians we dare not omit. The first is W R Ward.[12] Professor Ward's first book was on the *Land Tax in the Eighteenth Century* (1953). Recently alongside the editing of the *Journal* of John Wesley in the Bicentennial Edition has come a stream of books and articles showing the international character of the Evangelical Revival and the fascinating parallels between Europe, America and Great Britain. The other is David Hempton[13] who has opened the whole matter of the relationship of Methodism not only to Roman Catholicism but to Irish history, so easily neglected by the English. His survey article 'Religion in British Society 1740-1790' in J Black (Ed) *British Politics and Society from Walpole to Pitt 1742-1789* (Macmillan 1990) quite admirably summarizes the sheer variety of Georgian religion. If in 1750s Great Britain ninety per cent of church goers were 'Establishment', in 1851 half were nonconformists. In between is not only Methodism – 'an associational and voluntaryist form of religion which was a direct challenge to the confessional and territorial model of a state church' but also a vibrant traditional Evangelicalism which is now being explored by a new generation of historians led by David Bebbington and Mark Noll.[14] Whatever else this survey shows it is clear that eighteenth-century studies are alive and well. Finally, we can be thankful that we have in Henry Rack's *Reasonable Enthusiast* (Epworth 1989) a life of John Wesley and an account of the rise of Methodism which fits well into the new styles of histiography we have described.

References

1. cf L Stone, 'The New Eighteenth Century' in *The Past and the Present Revisited*, RKP 1987, pp 222-240; John Kent, *The Unacceptable Face*, SCM Press 1987, pp 74-131

2. L Colley, *Lewis Namier*, Weidenfeld and Nicholson, 1989

3. G V Bennett & J D Walsh (Eds) *Essays in Modern English Church History*, Black 1996, p 134. I note some of Walsh's *more recent* essays:
    i. 'Religious Societies Methodist and Evangelical 1738-1800' *Studies in Church History*, Blackwell 1986, pp 279-302
    ii. Methodism and the local community in the eighteenth century, Vie Ecclesiale University press 1989, pp 141-153
    iii. John Wesley and the Community of Goods in K Robbins (Ed) protestant evangelicalism... SCH Subsidia 7, Blackwell 1990, pp 25-50
    iv. '"Methodism" and the Origins of English Speaking Evangelicalism' in M A Noll et al (Eds) Evangelicalism OUP 1994, p 19-37
    v. 'Wesley versus Whitefield. The Conflict between the Two Giants of the Eighteenth Century Awakening' Christian History XII No. 2 1993, pp 34-37
    vi. 'The Church and Anglicanism in the "long" Eighteenth century' in John Walsh et al (Eds) *The Church of England 1689-1833* CUP 1993, pp 1-64

vii. *John Wesley 1703-1791* Dr Williams Trust, 1993
We await the publication of the Birkbeck Lectures

4. cf W S Gunter, *The Limits of Love Divine* Abingdon, Nashville 1989
5. F C Mather, *The High Church Prophet. Bishop Samuel Horsley 1733-1816 and the Caroline Tradition in the Late Georgian Church* OUP 1993. ibid 'Georgian Churchmanship Reconsidered. Some Variations in Anglican Public Worship 1714-1830' *JEH* 36, 1985, pp 255-283
6. cf D Pailin, 'Rational Religion in England from Herbert of Cherbury to William Paley' in S Gilley & W J Sheils (Eds) *A History of Religion in Britain*, Blackwell 1994, pp 211-233
7. W A Speck, *Stability and Strife. England 1714-60*, Arnold 1977; I R Christie *Wars and Revolution England 1760-1815*, Arnold 1982
8. J M Turner, *Conflict and Reconciliation*, Epworth 1985, ch 7
9. S Gilley etc. op cit p 268
10. cf N McKendrick, J Brewer, J H Plumb, *The Birth of a Consumer Society. The Commercialization of Eighteenth Century England*, London 1982
11. L Stone, *The Family, Sex and Marriage in England 1500-1800*, Penguin 1982; ibid, *The Road to Divorce 1530-1987*, OUP, 1995; ibid, *Uncertain Unions and Broken Lives. Marriage and Divorce in England 1660-1857* OUP, 1995
12. W R Ward, *The Protestant Evangelical Awakening*, CUP 1992; ibid, *Faith and Faction*, Epworth, 1993; ibid, 'The eighteenth-century Church: a European view.' In J Walsh et al (Eds) *The Church of England* op cit pp 285-298; ibid in S Gilley et al (Eds) op cit pp 252-274
13. 'Methodism and the Law 1740-1820.' *John Rylands Library Bulletin* 10 No. 3 1988, pp 93-107,; cf 'John Wesley and England's "Ancien Regime".' In S Mews (Ed) *Modern Religious Rebels*, Epworth 1993, pp 36-57; *Religion and Political Culture in Britain and Ireland,* CUP, 1996
14. D W Bebbington, *Evangelicalism in Modern Britain*, Unwin Hyman 1989; Mark A Noll, et al (Eds) *Evangelicalism. Comparative Studies of Popular Protestantism in North America, the British Isles and Beyond 1700-1990*, UOP 1994; Mark A Noll, *A History of Christianity in the United States and Canada*, Erdmans, 1992

We must add now:
B S Schlenther, *A Queen of the Methodists – The Countess of Huntingdon and the Eighteenth Century Crisis of Faith and Society,* Durham, 1991, p 136
M A Noll, *The Rise of Evangelicalism: The Age of Edwards, Whitefield and the Wesleys,* IUP 2004
S J Brown and T Tackett (Eds) *The Cambridge History of Christianity: Enlightenment, Reawakening and Revolution 1660-1815*, CUP, 2007
W Gibson and R G Ingram (Eds), *Religious Identities in Britain 1660-1832*, Ashgate 2005
W R Ward, *Christianity Under the Ancien Régime 1948-1789*, CUP, 1999
P Mack, *Heart Religion in the British Enlightenment*, CUP, 1999
A Harding, *Selina – Countess of Huntingdon*, Epworth, 2007
D B Hindmarsh, *The Evangelical Conversion Narrative*, OUP, 2005

Chapter 11

Robert Featherstone Wearmouth (1882-1963): Methodist Historian

This year marks the centenary of the birth of R F Wearmouth, who was one of the most notable of the products of the last phase of Primitive Methodism. Born into a mining family, he left school at the age of twelve to become first a pit-boy, then a soldier, acquiring a commission, then again a miner. He found meaning and purpose in life and proper ambition in the "little chapel by the wayside", as he always affectionately called it, at Oxhill in County Durham. He became one of the foremost historians of the religious side of working-class consciousness. But that was when he was middle-aged and elderly! Before that, on leave from the Army, he had been converted at a Christian Endeavour meeting by the warm-hearted chapel life of his village and the preaching of his beloved mentor John Clennell, who gave him the rudiments of a sound education. He was trained for the ministry at Hartley College – one of "Peake's men". He was a Primitive Methodist chaplain in the First World War – a story written up later in *Pages from a Padre's Diary* (1958). Serving as a minister in Grimsby, Oakham, Birmingham, Penzance, West Ham, Willesden Green, Leighton Buzzard, Berkhamsted and South Bank and Eston, he eked out time to complete his MA degree at Birmingham and his BSc and PhD at London University when G H D Cole, Harold J Laski and H L Beales were teaching. In the end he was an esteemed extra-mural teacher and a part-time history master at Berkhamsted School. This is a saga in itself of what Methodism was able to do for the underprivileged , for here was a man who could exercise not only a ministry *for* the poor but *with the* poor, for he was one of them.

This is the background of his pioneering work in chronicling the relationship of Methodism with the "common people". At a time when the religion of the people and "folk religion" are in vogue, typified by Hugh McLeod's *Religion and the People of Western Europe* (1981), it is salutary to consider just how much Wearmouth *was* a pioneer in what is now a far more sophisticated enterprise backed up by tools of sociological analysis not available to him. I want in this article to outline what Wearmouth wrote and to attempt a brief critique of his thesis, indicating some of the directions in which the argument has been taken since his work.

The mid-1930s saw the appearance of three significant books in the histiography of the "middle years" of Methodism – Maldwyn Edwards's *After Wesley, 1791-1849* (1935), Ernest R Taylor's *Methodism and Politics, 1791-1851* (1935), and R F Wearmouth's first and, in my estimation, his best book, *Methodism and the Working Class Movements in England, 1800-1850* (1937). Dr Wearmouth clearly accepted the general thesis of Dr Edwards and Mr Taylor, especially the familiar view that in Wesleyanism a 'dominant Toryism' made way for an 'underlying Liberalism'. Wearmouth's background was quite different from that of the Cambridge-trained pupil of Kitson Clark and of the erudite Welshman. He was one of the last of those Methodist autodidacts who wrote his books as a circuit minister and in retirement. This is history 'from below'. The first book, basically his doctoral thesis, shows the way in which Methodist *methods* and *techniques* – the class system, class meetings, quarterly meetings, camp meetings, 'the plan', and Conference – were picked up by the early working-class movements. Whilst the movements operated on parallel lines, there were also many Methodists deeply involved in the movement of working-class consciousness, especially Chartism and the early miners' unions. Wearmouth's case is clear, well argued, and influential. It is significant that a chapter in the Hammonds' study *The Town Labourer* was radically re-written in the light of Wearmouth's book. They speak, despite their strictures on its conservatism and quietism, of Methodism as 'an admirable school of democrats equipping working men for popular leadership'. The Methodist society gave opportunities to poor men to learn to speak in public, to organize common effort, and to take part in government and administration.

As a mere exercise in self government and social life, the chapel occupied a central place in the affections and thoughts of people who had little to do with the government of anything else.[1]

Wearmouth's point about the widespread borrowing of techniques has never been disputed. E P Thompson, whilst propounding his own version of Halévy's thesis about stability, acknowledges Wearmouth's pioneering work and pushes it further:

Those Wesleyan Annual Conferences with their 'platform', their caucus at work on the agendas and their careful management seem uncomfortably like another 'contribution' to the Labour movement of more recent times.[2]

A later book – *Some Working Class Movements of the Nineteenth Century* (1948) – contains a mine of information about the radical societies of 1816-23, the political unions of 1831-5, and the Chartists (1836-50), as well as the Luddites. Again there are parallels with Methodism. Sunday, 1st May 1842, was…

indeed a highday at Barnsley … at two o'clock in the afternoon there was a grand teetotal and anti-tobacco camp meeting on the Barebone; the preacher spun a long yarn about the 'grand principles of the charter' and as was expected all Hull, Hell and Halifax were there.[3]

From 1837 to 1850 five hundred such meetings, on the Primitive Methodist pattern, were organized by the Chartists, at most of which hymns were sung, prayers offered, and political sermons preached. Wearmouth now needs to be supplemented by those fine studies of Edward Royle, *Radical Politics, 1790-1900: Religion and Unbelief* (1971); *Victorian Infidels* (1974) and *The*

Infidel Tradition (1976). Royle is particularly good on the influence of Thomas Paine and Richard Carlile, the Zetetic Societies, and the generally anti-religious nature of many of the radical groups perhaps underestimated by Wearmouth. The well-known astute articles of E J Hobsbawm – "Methodism and the Threat of Revolution" in *Labouring Men* (1964) and the perceptive "Labour Sects" in *Primitive Rebels* (1959) – are also relevant here, especially the point about the relationship of Primitive Methodism to 'one-industry' areas such as the Durham coalfield and the relationship of religion to the early unions. Hobsbawm stresses the strength of the 'Primitives' in the semi-village (Durham, East Anglia and the 'miserable zone of petty and archaic industries in the West Midlands'). Hobsbawm also traces the infidel, rationalist element in English socialism, and is right to point to an 'apostolic succession' from the English Jacobins and Francis Place through anti-religious Owenites and Co-operators on to the free-thinking radicals who followed Holyoake and Bradlaugh, to the SDF and the Fabians with their dislike of 'tabernacle gas'. We might add the 'idealist stream', which takes up F D Maurice and the Christian Socialists, the Guild of St Matthew, the CSU, Scott Holland, Gore, Temple and Clement Attlee and the contribution of Methodism with its element of meliorism rather than revolution. No one stressed this more than Wearmouth, and it includes Tommy Hepburn, George Loveless, Joseph Arch, George Edwards, Thomas Burt, Arthur Henderson, Jack Lawson and Len Murray.

The next book takes us back to origins and roots: *Methodism and the Common People of the Eighteenth Century* (1943), published during the War. I would think this rather underrated by historians. It contains a very clear account of working class conditions, especially the food riots and deprivations and the role of the mob. John Walsh's articles "Methodism and the Mob" (*Studies in Church History* (Eds G J Cuming and D Baker) vol 8 (1972)) and "Elie Halévy and the Rise of Methodism" (Royal Historical Society, Fifth Series, vol 25 (1975)) and the writings of George Rudé, not to speak of E P Thompson's *Whigs and Hunters* (1975), fill out the picture now, but Wearmouth is by no means wholly dated, more especially since he shows how Methodism used people's talents, giving them scope in that strange combination of autocracy and democracy which became the Wesleyan system. Here was not, to use Thompson's phrase, 'the chiliasm of the defeated and the hopeless',[4] but a society which fuelled the *aspirations* of the artisans whose numbers were very high in early Methodism, pointing to that 'labour aristocracy' which features so much in recent writing and which was clearly influenced by Methodism and partly *produced* by it.[5]

Wearmouth's next book – *Methodism and the Struggle of the Working Classes, 1850-1900* (1954) – covered the later Victorian period. It illustrates his method – relentless and massive use of primary sources; no generalization without particularization! The contribution of Methodists to the unions in the North-East is established beyond a doubt, although at times Wearmouth overstates his case, attributing to Methodist influence what is true rather of some whom we may call 'lapsed' Methodists. No doubt they took some of their Methodism with them. It acted often as a stepping-stone either to secularism or to the Establishment.

More recent work by Pamela Horn, A R Griffin, G M Morris and Colin P Griffin tends to support Wearmouth's assertion of Methodist influence on moderate 'labour' politics, as does Nigel Scotland's recent *Methodism and the Revolt of the Field* (1981), which deals with East Anglian agricultural unionism, and James Obelkevich's outstanding *Religion and Rural Society: South Lindsey, 1825-75* (1976). Obelkevich shows Primitive Methodism appearing at a critical moment as the traditional culture was passing, 'but before the subsequent working class culture had developed to replace it'. Robert Moore's *Pitmen, Preachers and Politics* (1974) uses data from Wearmouth's own heartlands. Moore, however, shows that the conciliation style broke down in the 1920s with a breach between older styles of Methodist leadership and more abrasive styles of socialism, revealing weakness in Wearmouth's approach as lacking precise definition of socialism and the actual *policies* of the Methodists he lists.

The last large book was *The Social and Political Influence of Methodism in the Twentieth Century* (1958). This is Wearmouth's least convincing work. It begins with sections on the struggle of trade unions for full recognition, decent hours and living conditions, the birth of the Labour Party, and the development of the Welfare State. Then follows a section illustrating Methodist decline – due, Wearmouth believed, to lack of direct evangelism and revival and to Methodist Union itself, with its bureaucracy and large circuits. Union certainly led to further decline; but did Wearmouth really prefer a divided Methodism? Union in itself was hardly the *cause* of decline. The lack of any analysis of the secularization and de-Christianization of Western Europe is evident here. A D Gilbert's *Making of Post-Christian Britain* (1980) fills this gap to some extent. We then get the much more familiar Wearmouth style: details of Methodist involvement in local government typified by Wearmouth's friend Tom Benfold. The church was ready to service the 'New Leviathan' with responsible, incorruptible people. The early Labour Party owed much, claims Wearmouth, to people like Arthur Henderson, Jack Lawson, Ellen Wilkinson and William Whiteley (all North-Easterners), and at local level Peter Lee. The book ends with a rather scrappy section on Methodist social thinking – W F Lofthouse, S E Keeble and the rest – which can be supplemented by both Maldwyn and Michael Edwards's writings on the almost-forgotten Keeble. Contemporary history is difficult to write. Wearmouth didn't enhance his reputation by attempting it, though clearly his tributes to individuals will have evoked response with those who knew them.

The last two books were *Pages from a Padre's Diary* (1958), giving autobiographical insight into the war of 1914-18, which ties in with Alan Wilkinson's recent superb work on *The Church of England and the First World War* (1978), and *Methodism and the Trade Unions* (1959), a summary of the earlier books.

Wearmouth's books hammer home the thesis that Methodism – and more especially Primitive Methodism – made a vital contribution to the particular style which socialism assumed in the trade unions and the Labour Party. 'The Labour Party is more Methodist than Marxist,' said Morgan Phillips in 1951 in an oft-misquoted half-truth. At the level of ideology this is probably not the case; in idealism and personnel it was much more so. Wearmouth's thesis is supported, in the main, by the influential Harold Perkin in *The Origins of Modern English Society, 1780-1880* (1969). He shows how religion, especially Methodism, gave expression to emancipation from what he calls the 'dependency system' before it hardened into overt class-antagonism, provided models of class-organization, and gave forth examples of the benefits of non-violent organization influencing class-conflict in the direction of non-violence, and so 'administering an analgesic against the pains of labour'.

One last and vital point which more recent researches would suggest is the possibility of the explanation of the parallelism between Methodism and radical social movements being that both were dominated by the 'labour aristocracy'. Engineers, cobblers, carpenters, blacksmiths, cutlers, bricklayers, small shopkeepers, printers, saddlers and harness-makers and the like who were becoming marginally prosperous (or retaining a poverty-stricken independence like domestic textile workers) were those who brought political consciousness to the British working class. Were not these the very strata of the population to whom both the moderate Chartists and the Methodists would make their appeal? Certainly the classes who gained self-expression and self-consciousness in the chapels were also those who were likely to take a lead either in the struggle for popular radicalism or in the politics of the class-struggle. The fluid mass beneath – whom Engels and more recently E R Wickham (*Church and People in an Industrial City* (1957)) and Kitson Clark (*The Making of Victorian England* (1962), chapter VI, "The Religion of the People") describe as being outside the reach of the churches altogether – in all probability escaped the influence of the politician and, at least until the "new" unionism, of the trade union organization also. The respectability of the 'labour aristocracy' made a barrier between them and 'fustian jackets, unshaven chins and blistered hands' – a barrier made greater by the Temperance movement so well portrayed by Brian Harrison in *Drink and the Victorians, 1815-1872* (1971). The same style of thrifty worker would join a temperance group and a craft trade union. Dissatisfaction with one's position within the working class was in the nineteenth century more important politically than dissatisfaction with the position of the working class in society at large. The link between temperance , some forms of Dissent and liberal radicalism is clear enough. Temperance reformers were certainly straining towards a positive, collectivist view of the state which in T H Green's phrase was bound to remove 'obstacles to freedom'. Not for nothing were many radicals teetotallers and therefore frowned upon by Wesleyans who came later on the temperance scene. Dr Harrison is right to point to the temperance movement as one of several mid-Victorian agencies delaying the emergence of any distinctive and lasting working-class ideology. This is another piece of evidence suggesting that Victorian England has elements (the role of the Sunday-school is another) in its working-class movements not to be found on the Continent, preventing English working-class ideology from becoming totally Marxist.

But let a near-Marxist, Harold J Laski (certainly no friend of Methodism) have the last word:

Dr Wearmouth shows that the psychological influence of Methodism was to teach its votaries self-respect, self-confidence, the ability to organize and the ability to formulate their ideas, and his book [the first one] is an illuminating explanation of the foundations upon which some of the more characteristic of the features of the British Socialist Movement have been built.[6]

That, indeed, was Wearmouth's achievement as an historian.

Bibliography of R F Wearmouth's Writings

Books
1. *Methodism and the Working Class Movements in England, 1800-1850*, Epworth (1937)
2. *Methodism and the Common People of the Eighteenth Century*, Epworth (1943)
3. *Some Working Class Movements of the Nineteenth Century*, Epworth (1948)
4. *Methodism and the Struggle of the Working Classes, 1850-1900*, Backus, Leicester (1954)
5. *The Social and Political Influence of Methodism in the Twentieth Century*, Epworth (1958)
6. *Pages from a Padre's Diary*, Consett (1958)
7. *Methodism and the Trade Unions*, Epworth (1959)

Articles
"The First Methodist Conference, June 25-30, 1744" (*London Quarterly and Holborn Review*, 1944, pp 205-10)
"George Edwards – the Product and Leader of the Agricultural Labourers" (ibid, 1952, pp 40-3)
"The Background of Hugh Bourne's Achievement" (ibid, 1952, pp167-70)
"The Evolution of Primitive Methodism" (*Proceedings*, xxvii, pp 135-7) (Reprinted from *Daybreak*)
cf Ralph Lowery: *Robert Wearmouth of Oxhill – Social Historian*. Wesley Historical Society North-East Branch (1982)

References

1. J L and B Hammond, *The Town Labourer, 1760-1832*, II, Guild Books, 1949, p 108, 95
2. E P Thompson, *The Making of the English Working Class*, Pelican, 1963, p 47
3. R F Wearmouth, *Some Working Class Movements of the Nineteenth Century*, Epworth, 1948, p 148
4. E P Thompson, op cit p 419
5. cf C D Field *The Social Structure of English Methodism. Eighteenth to Twentieth Century;* British Journal of Sociology, Vol 28, No. 2 (1977), pp 199-225
6. See article on Wearmouth by J M Turner in New Dictionary of National Biography

Chapter 12

Methodism, Roman Catholicism and the Middle Ages: A Contextual Approach

The Eighteenth Century Context

'John Wesley detested Roman Catholicism,' claims Eamon Duffy.[1] Yet John Wesley wrote to the evangelical John Newton: 'Is not a papist a child of God? Is Thomas à Kempis, M de Renty, Gregory Lopez gone to hell? Believe it who can. The same is my brother and sister and mother'. He could also say: 'The same spirit works the same work of grace in men, upright of heart, of whatever denomination.'[2] Between these two poles of opinion lies a complex eighteenth century context which must embrace European as well as English and Irish History, the Seven Years War, and the Enlightenment, as well as the Evangelical revival.[3]

It can be argued that the Peace of Westphalia (1648) ended the Thirty Years War and a century of strife, that it was the end of religious wars as such. It did not seem like that to many Protestants. They could feel besieged in Catholic principalities with the possibility of further domination by Roman Catholicism. W R Ward is surely right in stating that the roots of eighteenth-century transatlantic revivalism can be found in the misplaced and persecuted Protestant minorities of Habsburg-dominated central Europe, in Silesia, Moravia and Bohemia, not to speak of the Huguenot 'diaspora', following the Revocation of the Edict of Nantes in 1685.[4] Even as late as the Seven Years War (1756-63), when England and Prussia were at war with France and Austria, the somewhat eccentric evangelical Howel Harris sought to create a 'Dad's Army' of volunteers to defend the east coast of England against the French: 'Lest our privileges and liberties should be taken from us, especially the liberty of the gospel which, should the Papists succeed, we should be robbed of'. Charles Wesley poured out patriotic poems long forgotten:

Rome with a new armada vow'd
To quench her thirst of British blood;
On vengeance and destruction bent,
They proudly hold their dire intent,
To keep with heretics their word,
And waste our isle with fire and sword.[5]

The whole history of Protestant religious renewal was deeply conditioned by the fear that confessional warfare was by no means at an end. The religious wars left a legacy of bitterness in Europe contributing to what the French historian Paul Hazard called 'the crisis of the European conscience' when France moved from believing with Bossuet (the great Catholic preacher) to doubting with Voltaire who wished to 'écraser l'infâme', that is to rid the world of Catholic and any other superstition. The Methodist historian Gordon Rupp[6] wrote of the 'great estrangement' when modern Europe bred a largely secular tradition, disentangled from religion and theology. This became true in great areas of politics, law, philosophy and science, even if much more than relics of the ancient regime remained.[7] The Churches had used up vital energy in their struggles.

We can point in England to a somewhat moderate religious fragmentation, paralleled on the continent, into the mystics, moralists and rationalists. The mystics in Europe included Roman Catholics and Jews as well as Protestants. 'Affectionate' religion or 'the religion of the heart' knew no denominational boundaries.[8] As a parallel development, Sir Herbert Butterfield, the Cambridge historian (who was a Methodist lay preacher), suggested that the scientific revolution of the seventeenth century was the most important event since the rise of Christianity, making Renaissance and Reformation seem like 'mere internal displacements within the system of medieval Christendom'.[9] Despite the 'rage of party' at the time of Queen Anne in Britain, Jacobitism, law, reliability and reason came to be stressed, not 'least in the higher echelons of society. There was a growth of deistic views and a rational style of piety, which contrasts with the intense religiosity of the previous century. But that could and did run underground, emerging again in the varieties of evangelicalism.'

Following G V Bennett, Professor Linda Colley[10] has revealed not only the underlying ideological thread of Toryism but a continuing mood of intense patriotism and anti-Catholicism throughout the century. Foxe's *Book of Martyrs* and Bunyan's *Pilgrim's Progress* were still immensely popular. Bunyan was much read in pietist circles on the continent as were other puritan writers in a fascinating 'networking' of literature and correspondence. There is no doubt that much of this ethos was part of Wesley's mind-set. His genuine Toryism was no mere shadow show. Colin Haydon[11] has shown how the Roman Catholic community in England – numbering about 80,000 in 1780 (more Catholics than Methodists) – was thought outlandish and unpatriotic. Wesley's strikingly ambivalent attitude to Roman Catholicism has to be seen in this context of mistrust. He could be eirenic to individuals – though he did not meet many Catholics, save in Ireland – as in the *Letter to a Roman Catholic* (1749). He had a willingness to explore Catholic spirituality, with reservations, but later showed a revulsion against what he believed was a Catholic inability to tolerate non-Catholics. Yet he was also totally opposed to any persecution or violence against them. Emancipation was a different matter. As Professor David Hempton has recently shown in detail: 'Wesley's anti-Catholicism was one of his profound and enduring legacies to the Wesleyan Connexion and the Connexion's rigorous anti-Catholicism, in which it genuinely reflected its following, was a most important determinant of Wesleyan political attitudes during the nineteenth century.'[12]

This, I fear, is more realistic than the anachronistic portrayal of John Wesley as a 'morning star' of the ecumenical movement. His theology and spirituality, especially his preaching of Christian perfection, is much more a portent of how Catholic and Protestant styles can be brought together. 'Heart can speak to heart.'

So we need to look at some paradoxical historical features of both Wesley and later Methodism, especially fostered and festered by Ireland and its complex history. Can Wesley be imagined as saying a loud 'Amen' to much of the recent Roman Catholic – Lutheran statement on Justification by Faith, while still rejecting papal magisterium?

'Withstanding Peter To The Face' – Methodism Roman Catholicism And The Middle Ages In The Eighteenth And Nineteenth Centuries

It needs to be made clear that there was a great deal of anti-Catholicism in the Church of England in the seventeenth and eighteenth centuries. It was manifested in the high-church tradition, in which John Wesley was nurtured, as much as in the more 'latitudinarian' and liberal elements in the Church. There was also a negative attitude to the Middle Ages – 'medieval' was often a word of abuse, as it is now, in the media. Ignorance and contempt for the Middle Ages was not compensated for by the high-church attention to the Fathers and to the primitive Church. Anglican rigorists like William Law knew little of the ' discretion' of St Benedict or the joy of creation of St Francis, while the great Bernadine tradition with its fine German inheritance through Hildegard of Bingen and the Sisters of Helfta, to say nothing of the great Victorines, was little known. There is in fact something faintly off-centre, exotic, about the mystic devotees at the beginning of the eighteenth century. They overvalued women like Antoinette de Bourignon (1618-80) and Mme. Guyon (1648-1717), and saintly ascetics like Gregory Lopez (1542-96) and M. de Renty (1611-49) counted far more than St John of the Cross or St Teresa.' Availability was one problem – the work of Pierre Poiret in providing texts is clearly important – but Bishop Lavington in his infamous *Enthusiasm of Methodists and Papists Compared* (1749-54) could talk of 'the most nasty, ridiculous, crack-brained, nay wicked saints, murtherers, traytors and rebels such as the Saints Francis, Dominic, Ignatius, Thomas à Becket, Hildebrand – this Hildebrand, one of the most wicked of mankind and most infamous of popes.' 'John Smith' (an anonymous Anglican scholar who had fascinating correspondence with Wesley) dismissed Augustine as a 'flighty, injudicious author'. St Bernard is likewise denigrated as 'somewhat enthusiastically given'. John Tillotson (1630-94) had earlier written of medieval schoolmen, while Edward Stillingfleet (1635-99), who influenced Wesley on episcopacy, in a *Discourse Concerning Idolatry Practised in the Church of Rome* (1672) poured scorn on the Catholic mystical tradition for its irrational fanaticism. He jeered at a new edition of the Revelations of Mother Julian of Norwich as a collection of 'fopperies' and 'blasphemous tittle tattle'. If, at times, Wesley's attacks on Popery seem exaggerated, we need to note that they were often not original but 'plagiarized' from Anglicans like Bishop John Williams, writing in the crisis period of Charles II and James I. As late as 1738, Bishop Edmund Gibson reprinted tracts from that period in three enormous volumes entitled *A Preservative Against Popery*. There is here formidable scholarship, not least from William Wake, later Archbishop of Canterbury, whom Norman Sykes portrayed as 'withstanding Peter to the face' in Paris but also seeking dialogue with French churchmen, Catholic as well as Protestant.[13]

So to Wesley. Following the Second Vatican Council, two of John Wesley's writings were featured, setting up one more Wesley 'myth'. They were *The Letter to a Roman Catholic* (1749) and the sermon on *The Catholic Spirit* (1750).[14] The context is the period after the second Jacobite Rebellion of 1745 and the Cork riots of 1749, which were one of the worst anti-Methodist riots of that decade. The letter, written from Dublin, defends Protestants in general, aiming at 'restoring at least some degree of love among our neighbours and countrymen'. Wesley then states an orthodox Protestant faith beginning with the Trinity, then Christ as prophet, priest and king (very like Calvin) and 'the blessed Virgin, who as well after as before she brought forth, continued a pure and unspotted virgin'. His own particular stance is articulated in Section 8:

I believe the infinite and eternal Spirit of God, equal with the Father and the Son, to be not only perfectly holy in himself but the immediate cause of all holiness in us: enlightening our understanding, rectifying our wills and affections, renewing our natures, uniting our persons to Christ, assuring us of the adoption of sons, leading us in our actions, purging and sanctifying our souls and bodies to a full and eternal enjoyment of God.

This is vintage Wesley, but he is also quite clear that 'common swearers, Sabbath breakers, whoremongers, liars, cheats, extortioners ... are no protestants ... they are the bane of society, the shame of mankind, the scum of the earth.'

The sermon on *The Catholic Spirit* (one of the 'standard' sermons) is very much in the Anglican tradition stemming back to Richard Hooker at the time of Elizabeth I, which clearly differentiates between the 'essentials' and the 'adiaphora' – those things on which Christians may differ, but need not quarrel. William Wake had similarly separated the 'necessary' and the 'accessory' and, indeed, anticipated a great deal of what Wesley said about the sacraments, especially transubstantiation, purgatory, prayers for the dead: 'The whole business of purgatory is but an error of the Latin church, not an article of the Catholick faith.' The difficulty – and Wesley had already faced it – is where the line is drawn between the 'essentials' and 'the rest'. What if 'the rest' seems unscriptural?

These two writings caused Cardinal Bea, when President of the Vatican Secretariat for Christian Unity, to declare: 'Because it is expressed so simply and effectively the main features of the ecumenical movement as recommended by church leaders today and, as far as Roman Catholics are concerned, the Second Vatican Council and Pope Paul VI, John Wesley's *Letter to a Roman Catholic* cannot but be a welcome source of inspiration and encouragement to all, both the ecumenically committed and the ecumenically indifferent.' Dr John Newton, from a Methodist angle, similarly stressed the importance of the 'ecumenical Wesley'.[15]

Wesley, however, in a letter to a Roman Catholic priest in the decade before, had set up ten errors of Rome, which were added to Holy Scripture: -
1. Seven sacraments not two;
2. Transubstantiation;
3. Communion in one kind only;
4. Purgatory and praying for the dead therein;
5. Praying to Saints;
6. Veneration of relics;
7. Worship of images;
8. Indulgences;
9. The priority and universality of the Roman Church;
10. The supremacy of the Bishop of Rome; to which he added 'monkery' in a letter to Dr Conyers Middleton in 1749.[16] He also complained that papists always added their own 'spin' to works of the Fathers and others they commended – a matter on which the pot could hardly call the kettle black, since Wesley did it quite ruthlessly in his *Christian Library*, 'eliminating' predestination from the Puritans. To shake up the Church of Ireland, he claimed that if the clergy really took their ministry seriously, there would be no more 'papists' in Ireland! He also saw the poverty of the Irish peasantry as a result of 'Popery', a common Protestant sneer, which continued for a century or more. Wesley produced a long document on the *Roman Catechism*, setting up a great deal of his often stated catalogue of criticisms from the canons of the Council of Trent, Bellarmine and other sources. Frankly, Wesley was not at his best in these documents. In one, he even thought Trent was in Germany! Much of it is lifted from Bishop John Williams and he would surely be aware of the 'Gibson' material. Some of it makes one sympathize with Mgr. Ronald Knox, who suggested that riding a horse is not a good recipe for reading, but we need to remember that Wesley was having to defend his movement from charges of popery. 'Peter' and 'Jack' could easily be mistaken for one another. Were not the 'confessions' of the 'Band' and 'Class' meetings of the Methodist Societies akin to confession to a priest, was one frequent charge.

Much more important was a controversy sparked off by the leading Catholic in England, Richard Challoner (1691-1781), at a time when Catholics and Methodists were competing for converts in parts of London, where embassies were centres of Catholicism, and the North of England, not to speak of Ireland, using strikingly similar methods of agreeing on a desperate concern for the poor. The use of itinerant preachers and priests is an interesting 'Catholic-Methodist' similarity. Each was given horses at the same time. Challoner and Wesley never met, though their spirituality had not a little in common. It was in 1760 that Challoner, anonymously, produced his 48-page *Caveat Against the Methodists.*[17] It was still in print in 1817. 'Methodists,' he said, 'are not the People of God. They are not true Gospel Christians; nor is their new-raised society the true Church of Christ or any part of it. The Methodist Teachers are not the true Ministers of Christ nor are they called or sent by him. The Methodist Rule of Faith is not the Rule of true Christianity. The Methodists' pretended assurance of their own justification and their eternal salvation is no true Christian Faith but a mere illusion and groundless presumption.'

Wesley answered the first two points in the *London Chronicle* in 1761, implying that Challoner is really attacking all Protestants. While agreeing that the Church has perpetuity, universality, unity, holiness and orthodoxy, he cannot attribute this to a succession of Ministry alone and uses a French Catholic, Pierre François de Courayer, to show that Anglican Orders are as valid as Roman Catholic orders. David Butler claims that 'Wesley is closer to Challoner than to Luther'. This is disputable, but both might have endorsed the 1987 Anglican/Roman Catholic International Commission document *Salvation and the Church*, which has passages closer to the thinking of Wesley on holiness.

All these documents – and Wesley wrote many – pale into insignificance compared with the controversies over moves for greater toleration of the Roman Catholic community still legally totally alienated, despite the power of Catholics in the higher echelons of society. For Wesley further emancipation was not desirable because of the sovereignty of the Pope. The Pope and Catholics must not be allowed to forget the Council of Constance of 1414-18. It had not only (with the Holy Roman Emperor's consent) burned Jan Hus at the stake, but made it clear that Catholics did not have to support heathen governments, a matter accentuated by the excommunication of Queen Elizabeth I. Wesley repeated his obsession with the Council of Constance frequently. This might be thought eccentric, but very recently the Czech Government at Prague has requested the Vatican to rescind the condemnation of Hus, exonerating him as a theologian. We shall return to this later. Wesley's stance on the Savile Act of 1778, granting limited toleration, was very unfortunate.[18] A Catholic Irish Capuchin Father Arthur O'Leary – with whom Wesley had breakfast later – claimed that Wesley supported the *Protestant Association* of Lord George Gordon, a controversy which lasted well into the next century, although Wesley was not the author of the pamphlet on which O'Leary pounced. Wesley had nothing to do with the Gordon Riots – one of the worst of eighteenth-century popular risings but did write an article in the *Freeman's Journal* in March 1780, responding to O'Leary, repeating again the history of the Council of Constance. As late as 1790, in a sermon *On The Wedding Garment*,[19] he returned yet again to the Council of Constance:

'But have the heads of the community [i.e. of the Church of Rome] as openly and explicitly renounced that capital doctrine of devils as they avowed it in the Council of Constance and practised it for many ages? Till they have done this, they will be chargeable with the blood of Jerome of Prague, basely murdered, and of many thousands both in the sight of God and man.'

In our day Gordon Rupp calls it 'one of the most shameful moments in the history of religion'.

Although he was unwise to pay a pastoral call on Gordon, Wesley was utterly opposed to any persecution of Roman Catholics and abhorred any violence, such as the Gordon Riots. He took the view of John Locke that full toleration could not be granted to those whose ultimate allegiance was to the Pope. This was to revert to a seventeenth century viewpoint, which had unfortunate and unforeseen consequences. Denial of full emancipation to Roman Catholics became part of the Methodist mind-set into the next century. It is not in my remit to outline what is a rather sad story of opposition to the negotiations which led to the Act of Emancipation of 1829.[20] After the union with Ireland of 1800, some kind of emancipation was becoming essential to both Catholics and other dissenters who gained new freedoms in 1828. it is interesting that the leading Wesleyan Methodist, Jabez Bunting (1779-1858) – seeing which way the cat would jump – accepted emancipation as a politically inevitable move, though he later bitterly opposed Prime Minister Peel on grants to the Maynooth Seminary in Ireland. He played a leading role (as did his son, William M Bunting) in the Evangelical Alliance, which had a strong anti-Catholic feel to it.

The situation in Ireland created a great deal of bitterness between Methodists and Catholics. Even so fine an evangelist as Gideon Ouseley joined the Orange Order. The notable Methodist leader William Arthur[21] who had been secretary of the Missionary Society and later Headmaster of Wesley College, Belfast, in *The Pope, the Kings and the People* (1876) launched a denunciation of the Vatican Council of 1870. It sought, he claimed, to make the Pope governor of the world, a reversion to the Middle Ages before Wyclif! Home Rule then divided Methodism, though, at first, many in England, being Liberals, supported W E Gladstone until the unfortunate divorce case of Parnell. The whole issue of Home Rule split the Liberal Party, the bitterness surviving into the twentieth century. Since the creation of Eire, after the First World War, Methodists have played some part in the Republic's politics. We need to note the conciliation of a later Headmaster of Wesley College, Stanley Worrall (1912-91). His stance was an outstanding piece of genuine ecumenism.[22]

A postscript here must be a reference to John Wesley's *Explanatory Notes Upon the New Testament*, published in 1755, which is important because it was to form, and still forms, part of the 'doctrinal standards' of first the Wesleyan Connexion and then the Methodist Church in Great Britain which was constituted in 1932. *The Notes* were, and are, intended for the use of preachers, but are hardly read now. *The Notes* are often based on the German Pietist J A Bengel (1687-1752).[23] His *Gnomon Novi Testamenti* was first published in German in 1742. Wesley used also the *Family Expositor* of Philip Doddridge and other contemporary writing while, as usual, giving his own particular 'spin'. Wesley here taps into a virile pietist tradition which certainly had its heroes in the Middle Ages – any who were 'real Christians', which did not include Popes! J A Bengel, at times, was astute and full of common sense anticipating modern biblical scholarship. He was amusingly paradoxical on Peter – he was not 'the rock', it was Christ himself, but he approved of Peter's approach to riches which was very different from some of his successors. The interpretation of the *Book of Revelation*, which Luther had once wished was not in the New Testament because of its exploitation by 'schwämerai' or crackpots, is bizarre to modern readers. Chiliasm or millenarianism was not a focal point of Wesley's theology though there was much of it around in pietist circles on the continent linking with fear of 'the Turk' as well as the Anti-Christ. For Bengel, the 'Beast' in *Revelation* is the Roman papacy. Revelation 13:1 is a key text, interpreted by Bengel and expanded by Wesley. The papal kingdom to them began in its present form with Gregory VII in 1073. a whole history is then traced:

- AD 1033 Benedict IX, a child of eleven years old, is Bishop of Rome and occasions 'grievous disorders for twenty years...'
- AD 1073 Hildebrand or Gregory VII comes to the throne...
- AD 1076 He deposes and excommunicates the Emperor...
- AD 1095 Urban II holds the first popish council at Clermont and gives rise to the crusades...
- AD 1123 The first Western General Council in the Lateran.
- The marriage of priests is forbidden...
- AD 1143 Celestine II is, by an important innovation, chosen to the Popedom without the suffrage of the people: the right of choosing the Pope is taken from the people, and afterwards from the clergy, and lodged in the cardinals alone. There follow crusades, Avignon, schism, the Reformation (1517), the Council of Trent, and in 1713 the constitution *Unigenitus*. So it continues until the Beast is finally to be slain, which will be in the year 1836.

It is interesting that Wesley adds to Bengel (Rev 13:7) the Albigensian Crusade as well as that against the Waldensians, who are now closely linked to the Methodists in Italy. We might today consider all this as the worst kind of 'eisegesis' but it was not uncommon in the seventeenth century, as Christopher Hill has recently shown in analysing Puritanism. Later it clearly embarrassed Wesley. In 1788 in a letter to Christopher Hopper, one of his leading Preachers, he makes clear that:

This date was that Bengelius had given as *his* opinion not that the world would end but that the millennial reign of Christ would *begin* in the year 1836. I have no opinion at all upon that head. I can determine nothing about it. These calculations are far above, out of my sight. I have only one thing to do, to save my own soul and those that hear me.'[24]

It is regrettable that Wesley did not add to this observation for the benefit of later readers.

In the 1920s, when the union between Wesleyan Methodists, the Primitive Methodists and the United Methodists was being negotiated, the biblical scholar Professor A S Peake of the University of Manchester, a Primitive Methodist layman, wished the *Notes* to be dropped from the proposed doctrinal clauses of the Deed of Union. It was, he claimed, the work of an 'outmoded exegete'.[25] 'It is obvious that Mr Wesley's exegesis of the NT, which was largely derived from Bengel, has frequently to be rejected. The whole exposition is radically unsound.' With hindsight it is a pity that Peake did not succeed in his wish. The *Notes* are still part of the 'doctrinal standards' though not to be used in any 'fundamentalist' manner. With the *Standard Sermons* they 'are not intended to impose a system of formal or speculative theology on Methodist preachers', but to set up 'standards of preaching and belief which should secure loyalty to the fundamental truths of the gospel of redemption and ensure the continued witness of the church to the realities of the Christian experience of salvation'. I would hazard a guess that few contemporary Methodists have ever read them! They are now part of a baggage from the eighteenth century. This may be solely a British problem.

We can leave Wesley and Popery by noting that he makes little reference to St Thomas Aquinas or Anselm and rarely mentions Bernard of Clairvaux or any of the great classic figures with whom he might have had some sympathy like St Francis or St Dominic. As we have seen, this is par for the eighteenth-century course. He does have one striking reference to St Augustine in a letter to John Fletcher:

I suppose you have read Dean Tucker's *Letters to Dr Kippis*. I read them on my journey from Gloucester hither and never before saw so clearly the rise and progress of Predestinarianism. Does not he show beyond all contradiction that it was hatched by Augustine in spite of Pelagius (who very probably held no other heresy than you and I do now); that it spread more and more in the Western Church till the eleventh century; that Peter Lombard then formed it into a complete system; that in the twelfth century Thomas Aquinas bestowed much pains in explaining and confirming it; that in the thirteenth century Duns Scotus did the same; that Ignatius Loyola and all the first Jesuits held it as all the Dominican and Augustine Friars (with the Jansenists) do to this day; that Bellermine was firm in it as were the bulk of the Romanists till the Council of Trent, when in furious opposition to Luther and Calvin disclaimed their ancient tenets.[26]

We must admit that Wesley was often bowled over by the latest book and that he had no pretensions to be a historian. His Christian friends in history are limited. Henry VIII, 'Bloody Mary' (he uses the phrase), and Charles II all meet Wesley's condemnation, together with Queen Elizabeth I who 'was as just and merciful as Nero and as good a Christian as Mahomet'.[27]

'Heart Speaks To Heart' – John Wesley's Use of Catholic Spirituality In His Doctrine of Perfect Love

It is often said that John Wesley's doctrine of Christian perfection or perfect love – 'faith working by love' – is truly Catholic. George Croft Cell's phrase is quoted: 'The Wesleyan reconstruction of the Christian ethic of life is an original and unique synthesis of the Protestant ethic of grace and the Catholic ethic of holiness.'[28] We must ask what influences from early traditions, the Middle Ages and Counter Reformation Catholicism fed into Wesley's theology.[29]

John Wesley saw scripture as the *primary* source of theology but took with great seriousness the traditions of the early Church. The Fathers were 'both nearest the foundation and eminently endued with the Spirit of whom all scripture is given'. So clergy were advised in1756 to read those who 'wrote before the Council of Nice' and then St Chrysostom, Basil, Jerome, Austin; and 'above all, the man of the broken heart, Ephrem Syrus'.[30] The Protestant Reformation, especially as stated in the formularies of the Church of England – the Thirty Nine Articles, the Homilies and the book of Common Prayer – is a vital part of 'tradition' for him too. There is no doubt he greatly valued the stress on poverty in the early Church and wished he could persuade his followers to practise Community of Goods.[31] He deplored, as did the Pietists, the wealth of the Church which followed Constantine's toleration of Christianity,[32] holding up Montanus as a good rather than a bad example.[33] A crucial early influence besides Ephrem Syrus (306-77), whom he read to his teenage lady friend in Georgia, was Macarius, 'the Egyptian', whom we believe to be a Syrian monk. He enabled Wesley to tap into the Cappadocian Fathers, Basil and the Gregorys. Macarius[34] sees perfection as a long struggle: There can be no brisk 'on with the new man, off with the old'. Macarius had an extremely high ideal of perfection. By grace we can attain this ideal in this life but what matters is that we should believe that God's commandments and promises are realistic even if perfection comes only after this life. Virtue and the fruits of the Spirit should be as perceptible as sin. Visions, and such phenomena, are valuable but only if they help us in our quest but 'we should run to grace as a chick runs to its mother'. If the Anglican Jeremy Taylor and William Law, the Non-Juror, were crucial for Wesley in his early development, so was Thomas à Kempis (1380-1471).[35] Here he became aware of that late medieval devotion so important for Catholic and Protestant alike – for Ignatius Loyola as much as for John Wesley, though Wesley was critical of Tauler and the more mystical tradition.[36] Wesley felt that, at times, Thomas à Kempis was too strict – 'holiness is happiness' is a Wesley phrase; but he issued an edition of à Kempis' *The Christian Pattern* as early as 1735. It was reprinted up to 1815. Wesley's mystical phase, which he later regretted, blaming William Law in an unpleasant correspondence, may have ended before 1738, but he still referred to à Kempis with his division of the approach to holiness – the spiritual life, the inward life, internal consolation, and Holy Communion.[37] His earlier mentors were more critically assessed but still quoted and commended. The French tradition deeply affected him even if he seems to have approached it almost in a 'pick and mix' fashion as did other Anglicans at the time. Jean Orcibal's analysis is essential reading at this point.

From his family came the reading of the Pensées[38] of Blaise Pascal, which he edited for *The Christian Library*, even including the familiar 'wager': - 'Heads or Tails? If you win, you gain everything, by choosing God. If you lose, you lose nothing but this finite life. Choice is unavoidable.' A prominent Methodist, Lord Soper, quoted Pascal at the end of his long life as a proper gamble for him! Reason cannot prove the existence of God – for 'it is the heart which perceives God not the reason' – yet all is of grace. 'You would not seek me if you did not possess me.' The teaching of the Quietists, Antoinette Bourignon and Mme. Guyon, and also Archbishop François Fénelon (1651-1715) whose *Discourse on Simplicity* he transcribed, haunt Wesley and they are all to be found in *The Christian Library*. 'We have not much to do with members of the Church of Rome (than with heathens, Mahometans and Jews) but we cannot doubt that many of them like the excellent Archbishop of Cambrai still retain (notwithstanding many mistakes) that "faith worketh by love".'[39] *That* was the crucial test even if the Oxford don in Wesley always seems to treat the writing of others as if they were undergraduate essays. Two other Catholics are constantly cited by Wesley.

The first is Gregory Lopez (1542-96),[40] a Spaniard who lived for years in Mexico as a hermit in a room with a Bible, a globe and a pair of compasses – 'a good and wise, though much mistaken man' Wesley called him, but felt him to be a saint only equalled later by John Fletcher. More important was an early reading of Edward Sheldon's translation of the life of Gaston Jean Baptiste de Renty (1611-49).[41] An abridged version duly appeared in 1741 with, says Wesley typically, the 'trash' removed. Wesley called him 'that perfect disciple of his Lord'. De Renty was a Parisian nobleman but seemed curiously detached from both wife and wealth – the parallel with Wesley is not to be missed! He founded a society of ladies who adored the sacrament, he cared for the poor, the aged, the exiled, gathering around him groups of devout Christians. Dr Henry Bett (of whom more later) was sure that de Renty's groups were the origin of the Methodist 'class meeting', more significant than even the Moravians in this respect. Be that as it may, Wesley constantly quotes him in his Journal and letters. He goes into *The Christian Library* to contribute to the five per cent of that collection which is from Roman Catholic sources.

It is striking that the Spanish tradition of spirituality (save for Lopez) does not appear. Wesley rejected the idea of 'the dark night of the soul' in his sermons even if he came near to one aspect of it at a time of depression:

And yet this is the mystery. I do not love God. I never did ... therefore I never believed in the Christian sense of the word. Therefore I am only an honest heathen ... and yet to be so employed of God! And so hedged in that I can neither get forward or backward! ... I am borne along I know not how that I can't stand still. I want all the world to come to – I know not what. Neither am I impelled to this by fear of any kind. I have no more fear than love.'

So wrote John Wesley to his brother Charles in 1766, partly in shorthand and Greek! Rowan Williams reckons this 'perhaps the most eloquent account in our language of justification by faith'. In the same letter, Wesley went on: 'O insist everywhere on *full* redemption receivable by *faith alone*! Consequently to be looked for *now*.'[42] This is no summons to cheap emotionalism, but the plea to preach complete trust in God in the midst of coldness, unhappiness, confusion, boredom. John of the Cross would have understood all that.

Wesley does not make as much use as one might expect of St François de Sales and the Salesian tradition of prayer, and de Caussade, now so much in vogue, was not available to him. Methodists like Neville Ward have much used it recently.[43] Francis and Dominic do not come into the picture. But who were more, unconsciously, in that tradition than the Methodist missionaries (and their brave, long-suffering wives) who went to West Africa, the Fiji islands and Tonga with total *disponibilité* or availability? They were examples of holiness, which Dietrich Bonhoeffer acknowledged, bowing in prayer before their memorial in the hall of Richmond College, London. Wesley was not a systematic theologian of the Augustine, Aquinas, Calvin style – his ceaseless activity made him rather a 'folk theologian' (Albert Outler's phrase)[44] whose *stance* and *balance* rather than the detail of his theology make him still relevant to the Church, even if the eighteenth century controversies are now for the historian.

We end this section with a summary of Wesley's relevance.[45]

Wesley's vision, program, and praxis were marked by the following six principal features. First, he looked to the *Scriptures* as the primary and abiding testimony to the redemptive work of Jesus Christ. Second, he was utterly committed to the ministry of *evangelism*, where the Gospel was to be preached to every creature and needed only to be accepted in faith. Third, he valued with respect to the Christian Tradition and the doctrine of the church a *generous orthodoxy*, wherein theological opinions might vary as long as they were consistent with apostolic teaching. Fourth, he expected *sanctification* to show itself in the moral earnestness and the loving deeds of the believers. Fifth, he manifested and encouraged *social concern* that was directed towards the neediest of neighbors. Sixth, he found in the *Lord's Supper* a sacramental sign of the fellowship graciously bestowed by the Triune God and the responsive sacrifice of praise and thanksgiving on the part of those who will glorify God and enjoy him for ever.'

Here 'heart can surely speak to heart'. That phrase comes, of course, from Cardinal John Henry Newman who, while highly critical of Wesley, could say in the Preface to the *Tracts for the Times*, written in his Anglican days: 'Methodism and Popery are in different ways the refuge of those whom the church (i.e. the Church of England) stints of the means of grace; they are the foster-mothers of abandoned children.'

'Ecumenism In Time' – Methodist Scholarship, Ecclesiology And The Middle Ages

Many have thought Dr John Scott Lidgett (1854-1953)[46] was the greatest Methodist since Wesley. His major works on the Atonement and the Fatherhood of God began to explore new avenues. When President of the Wesleyan Conference in 1908, he set an agenda for the twentieth century.

We must affirm our share in the great Catholic inheritance of the past ... Not a saint, a thinker, a hero or a martyr of the church but we claim our share in his character, influence and achievements by confessing the debt we owe to the great tradition which he has enriched by saintly consecration, true thought or noble conduct ... The unifying of Christendom for work in order to realize the Kingdom of God on earth is the primary object which faith sets before an enlightened Christian statesmanship. Where there are no differences, the watchword must be *union*; where they are comparatively short, *federation*; where they are more serious yet not destructive of the fundamental agreements of Christianity, *co-operation* in order to defend and promote the supreme interests and application of our common Christian life. The schismatic is always a traitor. Most of all he is such in the present day; Methodism, if true to its original spirit, will not look askance upon this great work or stand aloof from it.[47]

That agenda still stands at the beginning of another century. Our task is to look at how historical studies may help in relations between Methodism and Roman Catholicism.

Westminster College, London, a Methodist training college for teachers (now part of Oxford Brookes University), had as its Principal from 1868 to 1903, Dr James H Rigg (1821-1909).[48] While not a great thinker, Rigg, a 'liberal yet evangelical Protestant' as he called himself, expressed a strong Methodist claim to Catholicity. He supported the 'dual system' in English education, that is, both state-controlled and what are now called 'faith schools', sharing in education. In this, he supported Cardinal Manning, the great Catholic advocate of 'faith schools', and it needs to be remembered that in the late nineteenth century there were more Methodist than Roman Catholic schools. Most were taken over by Local Education Authorities after 1902. Rigg's principal theological works are on Wesley, F D Maurice and his supporters, and on Anglo-Catholicism, but his *Comparative View of Church Organisations, Primitive and Protestant* (1897, 3rd edition) is still germane. He took the view that the Early Church had variety in church order with no fixed forms. The key to ecclesiology is the provision of deep fellowship, what we now call *koinonia*. Roman Catholicism, he says, provided it later in monasticism and, with all its faults, the confessional. For Methodism, the 'class meeting is the germ-cell out of which the whole vital economy develops.' It is significant that Rigg was more critical of Independency than of other styles of ecclesiology because of its lack of effective 'magisterium'. Maybe Roman Catholics and Methodists could explore 'the balance of forces' which Rigg saw as the strength of Methodism, with the 'Conference', the 'District' and the 'Circuit' balanced by the local 'society' or church with its network of fellowship groups. Is the 'cell' the future for the local church in modern society?

Rigg was followed at Westminster College by Dr Herbert B Workman (1862-1951)[49] Principal from 1903 to 1930, he was a notable educationalist and a very productive historian, producing popular text books on the earlier and later Middle Ages, acclaimed by so astute an historian as Bishop Mandell Creighton whose *History of the Papacy from the Great Schism to the Sack of Rome* disturbed Lord Acton by failing to condemn wicked Popes out of hand, provoking the phrase about power tending to corrupt. In the *Place of Methodism in the Catholic Church* (1909, 2nd edition, 1921) Workman began with the view of Joachim of Fiore that the age of the Holy Spirit was coming:

The life of the church is a life of ceaseless growth ... Every communion of thinkers, every phase of faith has its place in and its relation to the great whole and plays some part, it may be *Protestant* and transient merely, it may be of more lasting constructive value, in the progress and development of the one Holy Catholic Church.'[50]

This is what later would be called a 'Whig' view of church history with the Reformation seen as a protest of individualism against the 'excessive solidarity of the medieval world'. The medieval world is, however, assessed in a far more positive manner than by any other Methodist up to that time. Workman made a constructive comparison between Wesley's tactics and those of the early friars with their stress on holiness rather than on apostolic succession or a mediating priesthood. They were basically lay as were the Benedictines, with, in the Rule of St Benedict, confession to the Abbot or the whole brotherhood, even if they were not priests. The stress on prayer – 'what the sword is to the huntsman, prayer is to the monk' (St Chrysostom) – fits too into the style of early Methodism. Even the Methodist Conference is shown to be similar to the organisation of the Franciscans. Workman has to admit that Wesley never made this comparison – indeed Wesley, quoting Mosheim, called Francis 'a well-meaning man though manifestly weak in the intellect'. It is strange that Workman's interesting comparisons make no notable mention of Dominic, who as a preacher and organiser is more akin to Wesley than Francis. Be that as it may, there is much here on what is now called 'the apostolate of the laity' in Catholicism and the 'priesthood of all believers' in Methodism.

Four other of Workman's books are germane to our concern.. He subtitled his *Persecution in the Early Church* (1906) a 'chapter in the history of renunciation', taking up that theme in the *Evolution of the Monastic Ideal from the Earliest Time to the Coming of the Friars* (1913) which he called 'a second chapter' in the history of Christian renunciation. This is a very sympathetic approach, dated now especially on St Francis, but in its day a welcome relief from the negative approach to the Middle Ages of earlier Methodists. As late as 1950, Professor David Knowles, in a lecture attended by the writer, recommended it to students as a noteworthy introduction from a Protestant. Workman could not resist claiming that the friars 'saw the world as their parish'. Making a significant statement:

In the striking phrase of St Ambrose, due provision is made for the 'soaring of the eagles' as well as 'the fluttering of the sparrows'. Protestantism on the other hand has too often driven out the eagles to save the sparrows or sought to exterminate the sparrows because of their inferiority to eagles. The Church of Rome would have used Wesley and Booth to found new orders within herself whose zeal and enthusiasm could have strengthened rather than weakened the church.[51]

Workman's most significant work, following up an earlier volume setting out *The Letter of John Hus*, was the two-volume *John Wyclif, A Study of the English Medieval Church* (OUP, 1926). As recently as 1985 Anthony Kenny, in his minor masterpiece on Wyclif, stated that Workman's book is still the standard biography, 'a mine of information about the circumstances of Wyclif's career and the chronology of his activities giving full details of anyone who ever crossed his path'. He admits that it is 'now quite inadequate as an account of Wyclif's philosophy or theology'. This may seem a little harsh, for Workman Is firmly contextual, avoiding too much stress on the popular 'Morning star of the Reformation' or 'Evening star of the Middle Ages' portrayal of Wyclif. He is seen as the prophetic conscience of his generation, influential in stimulating Bible translation, bible study and biblical (rather than anecdotal) preaching, fostering Lollards, and thus being a precursor of elements of early Nonconformity rather than of Luther, though he was clearly a definitive influence on Hus. Back to the 'great schism' and the 'Council of Constance'. This approach to Wyclif is taken up in the popular but slightly eccentric *John Wycliffe and the Beginnings of English Nonconformity* (1952) by K B McFarlane, a very different kind of historian. Let David Knowles sum Wyclif up. 'In his writings are to be found, collected together for the first time and pungently expressed almost all the popular charges against the Catholic Church of the later middle ages, and almost all the features of early Protestant opinion on such matters as the sole authority of Scripture, sacramental absolution, indulgences and church order.'[52] Recent work by Sir John Robson, Anne Hudson and others[53] has opened up a new positive view of the fourteenth and fifteenth centuries. The Medieval Church had been doing its work of civilising barbarians; it was now producing those who would rebel against its overall authority, a sign not of decay but of religious desire for reformation. Wyclif scholarship has been well summarised by another Methodist, Dr John Stacey.[54] Inevitably Protestants tend to take a hindsight approach but clearly Wyclif's criticism of Popes, priests and friars and his views on transubstantiation and poverty point to future thinking. Maybe a study of Wyclif could put again the role of 'heresy' and the matter of 'heart and 'circumference' back on the agenda. What do we make of the awkward heretic and radicals in our respective churches now? And Hus? Gordon Rupp claims that he initiated a 'movement a hundred times more powerful than Lollardy ... involving all classes of Bohemian people. Rooted in deep anti-clerical, anti-papal, and anti-Imperial sentiments which turned the Hussite movement into the most formidable schism and the most deeply-biting challenge to the authority of the Western Church before the Reformation.' It was centuries later that descendents of the Hussites – the *Unitas Fratrum* – sought refuge on the land of Count Zinzendorf. *Their* piety deeply influenced a young Anglican called John Wesley.

Broadly contemporary with Workman was Dr Henry Bett (1876-1952), tutor at Handsworth College, Birmingham from 1923 to 1940, when he became President of the Conference. Three medieval studies revealed a penetrating ability to expound the complexity of medieval theology and philosophy. Bett chose three figures who were hardly on the academic skyline in 1925 but have come into greater prominence since. The first was *Johannes Scotus Erigena* (CUP, 1925). Erigena's 'aphophatic' approach to God has recently been re-interpreted by John Macquarrie's *In Search of Deity* (1984). The ground of his approach can be found in Bett's clear, concise analysis of this Eastern-style scholar largely out of place in ninth-century Europe. *Joachim of Fiore* (Methuen, 1931) followed. In recent times there has been a renaissance of interest in Joachim (d. 1202), the later 'Spiritual Franciscans' and the whole medieval 'theological underworld'. The notion, for instance, of an Age of the Spirit following the Age of the Father and of the Son is with us again as the charismatic churches make huge headway in Asia, Africa and South America. The Holy Spirit is surely at the heart of authentic Methodist spirituality too. Bett's *Nicholas of Cusa* (Methuen, 1932) was also pioneering in its day for English scholarship. Recent scholarship has swept past Bett. His *Studies in Religion* (Epworth, 1929) include brief pieces on Meister Eckhart, mysticism and the doctrine of the Eucharist, where Bett reveals himself as a doughty Protestant, prepared to break a lance with 'realist' theories of the 'real presence', while oddly ignoring Bucer's and Calvin's links between the Eucharist and the Holy Spirit.

While Bett was teaching in Birmingham, Howard Watkin-Jones (1888-1953) was at Wesley College, Headingley, Leeds. When at Gonville and Caius College, Cambridge, he had been a pupil of H B Swete. He followed up his mentor's work with the *Holy Spirit in the Medieval Church* (Epworth, 1922) and *The Holy Spirit from Arminius to Wesley* (Epworth, 1929). These are massive and objective studies. No longer were the Middle Ages barren and barbarian before Renaissance and Reformation. Watkin-Jones is illuminating in his positive approach to the recurrent controversies over the *filioque* clause in the western version of the Nicene Creed, but his hints on links between the Holy Spirit and the presence of Christ in the Eucharist are also still relevant to discussions between Methodists and Catholics. Calvin, Watkin-Jones asserts, passes on to the church of later days the doctrine of the *Via Media* by which the Holy Spirit is set forth as the medium of Divine Grace at the Eucharist, incorporating with Christ those communicants who approach the Table of the Lord. If a Roman Catholic asks a Methodist about the Real Presence, the Methodist can quote Charles Wesley:

Come Holy Ghost, thine influence shed,
And realize the sign;
Thy life infuse into the bread,
Thy power into the wine.
Effectual let the tokens prove
And made, by heavenly art,
Fit channels to convey thy love
To every faithful heart.[55]

Is there a better *epiclesis*?

A Methodist willing to take Roman Catholic thinking with the utmost scholarly and ecumenical concern was Robert Newton Flew (1886-1962), Principal of Wesley House, Cambridge. His *The Idea of Perfection in Christian Theology* (OUP, 1934) did not touch greatly on the Middle Ages (pp 216-43). The age of vital interest in medieval feminine thought had not yet arrived. The influence of St Augustine and Dionysus the Areopagite is underlined. Flew takes up Ritschl's view that no one can have any understanding of Catholicism without knowledge of Bernard of Clairvaux's sermons on the *Song of Songs*. Bernard restored Jesus to the centre of piety - Jesus the man. Bernard's spirituality had four characteristics: the contemplative life is superior to the active, Christian perfection consists of love and may be attained in this life, God must be loved for his own sake, the full perfection of the soul can only be attained in the life beyond the grave. Aquinas, as a true Dominican, saw preaching and teachings as vital to a pure spirituality. Flew does not suggest a link with Wesley's views here though one can discern them, even if Aquinas was not remotely on Wesley's agenda. Flew's criticism of Aquinas is strongly Protestant, especially on the merit granted to those in Orders. He shows, too, that the homilies of Macarius were important to Wesley, anticipating the work of Albert Outler who may have exaggerated the point. Flew shows an eirenic spirit towards the post-Reformation spiritual traditions – St François de Sales, Quietism, Fénelon – though he claims that Wesley was not aware of Fénelon's later writings.

Newton Flew was eminently suitable to become chair of the *International Theological Commission on the Church* of the World Council of Churches. At Lund in 1952[56] important papers were presented to the Third World Conference on Faith and Order. Since the Church of Rome did not officially participate, Flew, on their behalf, wrote a statement on Roman Catholic ecclesiology. Flew had previously had a large part in producing a Methodist official statement, *The Nature of the Church According to the Teaching of the Methodists* (1937), which was normative until 1999 when it was officially replaced by the equally important *Called to Love and Praise*.[57] This is now the official British statement on the Church. The 1937 statement is quoted in the Lund document along with Flew's summary of Roman Catholic ecclesiology in the period prior to the Second Vatican Council. It is fascinating to compare the two and I commend that exercise! We then ask *how* and *where* and *why* have we progressed in relationships since 1952?

Three very different Methodists explored from different angles Roman Catholic spirituality. Dr W E Sangster (1900-1960), minister of the Central Hall Westminster during and after the Second World War, in his last major book *The Pure in Heart* (Epworth, 1954) finds Christian perfection and sanctity in many contexts and writes with penetrating but eirenic skill about Roman Catholic modes of establishing *who* is a saint. Neville Ward (1915-92), in a series of books on prayer, showed a fascinating combination of the philosophical theology of D Z Phillips and the spirituality of de Caussade. He helped many in all denominations to continue a life of prayer at a time of the dominance of 'secular' theology in the 1960s and 1970s. In one book, he uses the Rosary in a way totally familiar to a Catholic, who has maintained personal prayer, but quite new to most Methodist readers.

Then Dr Gordon S Wakefield (1921-2000), Principal of the Queen's College, Birmingham, which had close liaison with Oscott Seminary, having begun with studies of the spirituality of the Puritans and later John Bunyan, explored not only the spirituality of Methodism in all its forms, but the whole Christian tradition. His last important book[58] outlines Christian worship. The medieval tradition of the Mass is outlined clearly, with all its faults and excellencies. He uses modern Catholic scholarship, especially Eamon Duffy's *The Stripping of the Altars*,[59] which has rehabilitated to some extent the later years of Catholicism before the Reformation. It is even possible that the medieval 'prone', a service with sermon and prayers ('the bidding of the bedes') may have been an influence on Wesley's 'preaching service'.[60] A shorter, posthumous book[61] by Wakefield has a short exposition of medieval spirituality. There is now little trace, at least among historians, of the old anti-Catholic prejudices, but rather a realisation that what ultimately 'makes us tick' takes us beyond the barriers of ecclesiastical systems to a confession of the Lordship of Christ – as Wesley said in the sermon on *The Catholic Spirit*, when he, briefly, forgot the eighteenth century debates.

Catholicism, Methodism, The Middle Ages

I end with a personal note. In 1950 I attended lectures on the Middle Ages by the Benedictine David Knowles (1896-1974) and on the Reformation and Renaissance by Herbert Butterfield (1900-1979). For many years they were colleagues and friends at Peterhouse, Cambridge. Butterfield followed Knowles in the Regius Chair of History. In 1952 at the height of his powers, Butterfield published a short book *Christianity in European History*.[62] It is known now that Knowles 'vetted' it before publication. One could be tempted to quote Butterfield on the Middle Ages at length. He saw it as producing in the end 'the autonomy of the spiritual principle'. The Church was able to preserve the ancient culture then 'working for a thousand years as a leaven which leavened the whole lump until by the year AD 1500 the ancient classics had come to permeate the whole fabric of western civilization'. But, far more important, 'the real glory of the church was the multiplicity of saints and missionaries and the achievement of the friars in the field of scholarship was an incidental affair – their greater task was their religious work among the common people.' Later he says: 'Here is one of the reasons why it is well for us to hold fast to Christ and to spiritual things, while retaining great elasticity of mind about everything else.' To that, Knowles remarked that he found it 'altogether admirable'. Some years later, writing to Dr Geoffrey Nuttall, he said that we 'must recognise and rejoice at all real love and faith in God and our Lord Jesus Christ. Cor ad cor loquitur'.[63]

References

1. Eamon Duffy, 'Wesley and the Counter-Reformation' in Jane Garrett and Colin Matthews (Eds), *Revival and Religion Since 1700,* Hambledon Press, 1993, pp 1-21
2. John Wesley. *Letters*, J Telford (Ed), Epworth Press, 1931, vol 4, p 293 (to John Newton, 9 April 1765); and, for the second quotation, 'Preface to Clark's Lives of Eminent Persons', in John Wesley, *Works*, ed. Jackson, vol 14, p222
3. cf W R Ward, *The Protestant Evangelical Awakening*, CUP, 1992; idem, *Christianity Under the Ancien Regime*, CUP, 1999; John Bossy, *The English Catholic Community 1750-1850*, DLT, 1975
4. W R Ward, *Christianity etc.* ch 4
5. G Osborn, (Ed), *Poetic Works of John and Charles Wesley,* 1870, vol 6, p 181: W R Ward, 'The Protestant Frame of Mind', *History Today*, 40, Sept 1990, p 19
6. E G Rupp, *Religion in England 1688-1791*, OUP, 1986, pp 207ff
7. J C D Clark, *English Society 1688-1832*, CUP, 1985, esp. pp 199ff
8. Ted Campbell, *The Religion of the Heart,* University of South Carolina, 1981
9. H Butterfield, *The Origins of Modern Science 1300-1800*, Bell, 1949, p viii
10. G V Bennett, *The Tory Crisis of Church and State 1688-1730*, OUP, 1975; L Colley, *Britons – Forging the Nation 1707-1837*, Pimlico, 1992
11. C Haydon, *Anti-Catholicism in Eighteenth Century England 1714-1780*, Manchester UP, 1993
12. D Hempton, *Methodism and Politics in British Society 1750-1850*, Hutchinson, 1984, esp. pp 33ff; cf Eamon Duffy (Ed), *Challoner and his Church*, DLT, 1981, esp. pp 90-111
13. E G Rupp, *Religion in England 1688-1791*, OUP, 1986, p 207. I rely heavily on Rupp and on Norman Sykes, especially Sykes' lives of *Gibson*, (OUP, 1926) and *William Wake*, 2 vols (CUP, 1957). See J M

Turner, *Conflict and Reconciliation*, Epworth Press, 1985, ch 3, 'Methodism, Catholicism and Patterns of Dissent'; also H D Rack, *Reasonable Enthusiast: John Wesley and the Rise of Methodism*, Epworth Press, 2nd Edition, 2002

14. J Wesley, *Letters*, vol 3, pp 7ff (to a Roman Catholic, 18th July 1749); for the Cork riots see *Journal*, N Curnock (Ed), Epworth Press, 1938, vol 3, 409ff. The sermon 'Catholic Spirit' is found in J Wesley, *Standard Sermons*, E H Sugden (Ed), 1921, vol 2 pp 126ff, and in the *Works* (Bicentennial Edition), vol 2, Abingdon, 1985, pp 79ff

15. M Hurley (Ed), *John Wesley's Letter to a Roman Catholic*, 1968, p 16; J A Newton, 'Ecumenical Wesley', *Ecumenical Review*, 24, no. 2, April 1972; cf O A Beckerlegge (Ed), *John Wesley's Writings on Roman Catholicism*, Protestant Truth Society, n.d.; David Butler, *Methodists and Papists*, DLT, 1995; David Hempton, *Methodism and Politics in British Society 1750-1850*, Hutchinson, 1984

16. *Letters 1*, p 276 (to a Catholic priest, 1739; in the Bicentennial Edition, vol 25, p248, the date is given by Frank Baker as May 1735, not 1739 as in Telford's edition); Letters 2, p 319 (to Conyers Middleton, 4 January 1749)

17. Butler, *Methodists and Papists*, pp 70ff

18. Butler, pp 47ff

19. Sermon 127, Bicentennial Edition, vol 4, p 146. For the Council of Constance: W Ullmann, *A Short History of the Papacy in the Middle Ages*, Methuen, 1972, ch 12. See also E G Rupp, 'Christian Doctrine from 1350 to the Eve of the Reformation' in H Cunliffe-Jones and B Drewery (Eds), *A History of Christian Doctrine*, T & T Clark, 1978, p 294

20. For the later period: D Hempton, *Religion and Popular Culture in Britain and Ireland*, CUP, 1996; idem, *The Religion of the People. Methodism and Popular Religion 1750-1900*, Routledge, 1996; D Bowen, *The Protestant Crusade in Ireland 1800-1870*, Dublin, 1978

21. E R Norman, *Anti-Catholicism in Victorian England*, Allen and Unwin, 1968; N Taggart, *William Arthur*, Epworth Press, 1993, esp. pp 128ff

22. D L Cooney, *The Methodists in Ireland*, Colombia Press, 2001, p110; C Oldstone-Moore, *Hugh Price Hughes*, Cardiff, 1999; D W Bebbington, *The Nonconformist Conscience: Chapel and Politics 1870-1914*, Allen and Unwin, 1982, ch 5 'The Irish Question'

23. J Wesley, *Explanatory Notes on the New Testament*, 1755; modern edition, Epworth Press, 1924, pp 81, 100ff

24. *Letters* 8, p 63 (to Christopher Hopper, 3 June 1788)

25. J T Wilkinson, *Arthur Samuel Peake*, Epworth Press, 1971, p 107

26. *Letters* 6, pp 174-5

27. For the reference to King Charles II and 'Bloody Queen Mary', see *Journal 5*, p 248 (11 January 1768); to King Henry VIII and Oliver Cromwell, *Journal*, vol 5 p 522 (15 July 1773); to Queen Elizabeth I, *Journal 5*, p 257 (25 April 1768). Some references in Wesley to historical figures: *Letters* 2, p 60 (a positive quotation from St Augustine on the internal witness of the Spirit); *Letters* 2, p 101 (a

favourable reference to St Bernard in discussion of the internal witness of the Spirit); *Letters* 3, p332 ('Tauler, Behmen, and a whole army of mystic authors are with me nothing to St Paul'); *Journal* 2, p 467 (highly critical remarks on Luther's commentary on Galatians); *Journal* 3, p 409 (of Luther: 'Doubtless he was a man highly favoured of God, and a blessed instrument in His hand. But oh, what a pity he had no faithful friend ... [to] rebuke him plainly and sharply for his rough untractable spirit and bitter zeal for opinions, so greatly obstructive of the work of God'); *Journal* 4, p 480 ('I read the celebrated *Life of St Katharine of Genoa* ... I am sure this was a fool of a saint; that is, if it was not the folly of her historian, who has aggrandized her into a mere idiot. Indeed we seldom find a saint of God's making sainted by the Bishop of Rome')

28. G C Cell, *The Rediscovery of John Wesley*, NY 1935, p 347. But cf p 160, where Cell sees Wesley as a synthesis between Luther and Calvin. See also R E Davies et al (Eds), *A History of the Methodist Church in Great Britain*, I, 1965, ch 3 by Jean Orcibal

29. G S Wakefield, *Methodist Spirituality*, Epworth Press, 1999, pp 3ff; C Jones, G Wainwright, E Yarnold (Eds), *The Study of Spirituality,* SPCK, 1986; G S Wakefield (Ed), *A Dictionary of Spirituality*, SCM Press, 1983

30. J Wesley, *Works*, Ed Jackson, vol 10, p 465 (in the 1756 'Address to the Clergy')

31. J D Walsh, 'John Wesley and the Communion of Goods' in K Robbins (Ed), *Protestant Evangelicalism*, Blackwell, 1990, pp25-50

32. J Wesley, Sermon 61, on 'The Mystery of Iniquity', in *Works* (Bicentennial Edition) vol 2, Abingdon, 1984, pp 452-70 (in particular pp 462-464)

33. J Wesley, *Works*, Ed Jackson, vol 11, p 465f ('The Real Character of Montanus')

34. C Jones et al, pp 173ff

35. G S Wakefield (Ed), *Dictionary of Spirituality*, p 178

36. J Wesley, *Letters* 3, p 321 (to Dr Lavington, Bishop of Exeter, December 1751)

37. The correspondence with Law in 1738 is found in *Letters 1*, pp 238-244

38. C Jones et al, pp 406ff; Pascal: *Pensées*, J M Dent, 1947

39. For Fénelon and the Quietists, see *Letters* 5, p 193 (to Jane Catherine March, 6 July 1770); 6, p 39 (to Philothea Briggs, 8 September 1773)

40. G S Wakefield, *Methodist Spirituality*, p 4. See J Wesley, *Letters* 4 , p 265 (to Ann Foard, 29 September 1764) *Letters* 4, p 293 (to John Newton); *Letters* 5, p 283 (to Philothea Briggs, 16 October 1771) *Letters* 5, p 338 (to Philothea Briggs, 31 August 1772); *Letters* 7, p 127 (to Hester Ann Rowe, 25 June 1782); *Letters* 8 , p 171 (to nephew Samuel Wesley, 16 September 1789)

41. H Bett, "A French Marquis and the Class Meeting" in *Proceedings of the Wesley Historical Society*, 23, 1931, pp 43ff

42. J Wesley, *Letters* 5, pp 15ff (to Charles Wesley, 27 June 1766); cf Rowan Williams, *Open to Judgement*, DLT, 1994, 202ff

43. Neville Ward, *The Use of Praying*, Epworth Press, 1967; idem, *Five for Sorrow Ten for Joy*, Epworth Press, 1971

44. A Outler (Ed), *John Wesley*, OUP 1964, pp vii, xi

45. G Wainwright, *Methodists in Dialogue*, Abingdon, 1995, p 283f

46. J M Turner, 'Lidgett, John Scott' in T A Hart (Ed), *Dictionary of Historical Theology*, Eerdmans, 2000, pp 220-22; A Turberfield, *John Scott Lidgett*, Epworth, 2003

47. J S Lidgett, *Apostolic Ministry*, Culley, 1909, pp12ff

48. J T Smith, *Methodism and Education – J H Rigg, Romanism and Wesleyan Schools*, OUP, 1998; D Carter, *James H Rigg*, Foundery Press, 1994

49. cf H B Workman, *The Letters of John Hus*, C H Kelly, 1899; *The Dawn of the Reformation*, 2 vols, C H Kelly, 1901, 1902; *The Church of the West in the Middle Ages*, 2 vols, C H Kelly, 1903: *Persecution in the Early Church*, C H Kelly, 1906; *The History of Christian Thought to the Reformation*, Duckworth 1911; Methodism, CUP, 1912; *The Evolution of the Monastic Ideal,* Epworth Press, 1913; *The Place of Methodism in the Catholic Church*, 2nd edition, Epworth, 1921; *John Wyclif*, 2 vols. OUP, 1926

50. *Place of Methodism*, p 13, p 61f

51. Monastic Ideal*, pp 323-4*

52. D Knowles, *Saints and Scholars*, CUP, 1962, ch 19 on Wyclif; B L Manning, *The People's Faith in the Time of Wyclif*, CUP, 1919, 2nd edition, 1975

53. E Duffy, *Saints and Sinners. A History of the Popes*, Yale UP, USA, 1997, pp 87ff; A Kenny, *Wyclif*, OUP, 1985. See also *Studies in Church History. Subsidia 5*, from Ockham to Wyclif, A Hudson and M Wilkes (Eds), Blackwell, 1987; *Studies in Church History 7*, G J Cuming (Ed), CUP, 1971, chapter on the Council of Constance; *Library of Christian Classics*, vol 14: *From Wyclif to Erasmus*, M Spinks (Ed), SCM Press 1957

54. J Stacey, *John Wyclif and Reform*, Lutterworth, 1964. See also *Expository Times*, February 1982, February 1990; *Epworth Review*, January 1984, January 1990, January 1997. On Joachim see N Cohn, *The Pursuit of the Millennium*, Secker and Warburg, 1957

55. Hymns and Psalms 602

56. *The Nature of the Church*, SCM Press, 1952, R N Flew (Ed): sections on the Church of Rome and on Methodism; cf R N Flew, 'Methodism and the Catholic Tradition' in N P Williams (Ed), *Northern Catholicism*, SPCK, 1933, ch 17

57. *Called to Love and Praise*, Methodist Conference Statement, 1999

58. Gordon Wakefield, *An Outline of Christian Worship*, T and T Clark, 1998, ch 3

59. E Duffy, *The Stripping of the Altars. Traditional Religion in England 1400-1580*, Yale UP, 1992

60. N Wallwork, 'Wesley's Legacy in Worship' in J Stacey (Ed), *John Wesley: Contemporary Perspectives*, Epworth Press, 1988, ch 7

61. Gordon Wakefield, *Groundwork of Christian Spirituality*, Epworth Press, 2001, ch 3

62. H Butterfield, *Christianity in European History*, Collins, 1952, pp 15, 19, 20, 24, 38, 42

63. C Brooke et al, *David Knowles Remembered*, CUP, 1991, p 24, pp 101-2. See E G Rupp, *Just Men*, Epworth Press, 1977, ch 1 on Benedict, ch 2 on Francis, cf E G Rupp, 'Christian Doctrine from 1350 to the Eve of the Reformation' in H Cunliffe-Jones and B Drewery (Eds), *A History of Christian Doctrine*, T and Clark, 1978, pp 289-304, esp. pp 293-5.

Chapter 13

The Local Preacher in Methodism

Dr Benson Perkins was not given to extreme statements, but he referred to the 30,000 local preachers of 1950 as 'the greatest lay ministry in the world', conducting 16,000 services each Sunday. On the second Sunday in May 1995, out of 410 services of worship in the 305 Methodist churches in Cornwall, 247 were led by local preachers, 113 by ministers with 50 covered by other arrangements.[1] Without local preachers Methodist worship as we know it would not be possible. So it is astonishing that *Workaday Preachers*, so well edited by Geoffrey Milburn and Dr Margaret Batty, is the first major scholarly work about them.

The Methodist Constitution was not a great blueprint in John Wesley's mind, nor was the development of his mission. He was a pragmatic theologian. Conference itself developed from the four clerical friends of John and Charles Wesley who met with four laymen at the 'Foundery' in 1744 with that splendid agenda:

1. What to teach;
2. How to teach;
3. What to do – that is, how to regulate our doctrine, discipline and practice.

Conference was defined legally in 1784. Preachers are mentioned in the documents, but they were itinerant preachers stemming from men like Cennick, Humphreys and Maxfield whom Wesley called out as 'extraordinary messengers to provoke the regular clergy to jealousy', i.e. zeal. They were full-time itinerant lay preachers who developed into a Wesleyan presbyterate after Wesley's death. 'Acknowledge', said Gordon Rupp, 'that John Wesley did not aim to raise a troop of pale young curates, profound, distinguished and unintelligible – his Helpers, a few parsons, tradesmen, ex-soldiers were more like a gang of highwaymen conspiring together to go round England, calling the miners of Wales and Cornwall, the workers of the North, the soldiers of the Flemish camps, to stand and deliver to the Word'.[2] The purpose was 'to reform the nation by spreading scriptural holiness over the land'.

But many of these men and women had a more local role before being received by Wesley into itinerancy. They had little status. This was the case, too, with the 'exhorters' who acted as leaders of prayer in the societies, but were not supposed to 'take a text' (i.e. preach a formal sermon and expound Scripture).

Several points need to be made clear. Methodism began not as a denomination but as 'societies' closely linked as a 'Connexion' under Wesley. There were other connexions at the same time, like those linked with George

Whitefield and the Countess of Huntingdon. Worship in the full sense – what Wesley called the 'instituted means of grace' – was to be sought in the parish churches. In the very early stage there was no constitutional need for the local preacher in the technical sense, since class leaders, stewards, exhorters and itinerant preachers could perform all the tasks needed. Change came when 'preaching houses' were built. There were 40 in 1760, 120 in 1770, 470 at Wesley's death in 1791.[3] The number then rapidly escalated. Meetings were gradually elaborated – preaching services, watchnights, love feasts – becoming a substitute for the parish church. Local preachers were then needed, for there were more 'preaching services' than the itinerants could cope with. The latter tended to conduct services in the large urban places, a matter often resented by local preachers. Moreover, some itinerants did not possess the Herculean strength needed for that work – men like Dr Whitehead, Wesley's doctor, and Robert Carr Brackenbury, an alumnus of St Catharine's College, Cambridge, squire of Raithby Hall in Lincolnshire. The lack of constitutional provision for these local preachers and 'half-itinerants' is extraordinary.

A picture like this emerges. Local preachers were appointed by the 'assistant', the principal itinerant who later became the Superintendent. The Superintendent has always been finally responsible for the 'Preachers' Plan', the reason being a matter of human relations and pastoral care: 'local prejudices and partialities and animosities needed the fatherly hand of the Superintendent', said Jabez Bunting. Such can still be the case, though there is much more flexibility now. I remember nearly fifty years ago an old worthy complaining that he never preached at the Circuit church, a 'Morning Prayer' chapel. 'It's not cricket.' 'Indeed it's not cricket, it's making the Plan,' replied the redoubtable Superintendent Minister. Behind that story are many similar tales which blow much of the romanticism away.

There were early statements in 1746 and 1751 stressing the necessity of *gifts*, *graces* and *fruits*, but also ominous phrases about needing 'to clip their wings'. Local preachers had no recognised court for their own business. This was done by the Quarterly Meeting, though the Isle of Man had a proper local preachers' minute book in 1780. In 1796, five years after John Wesley's death, the Local Preachers' Meeting was recognised officially as part of the Methodist polity. The Superintendent was to meet the preachers each quarter. The preachers must meet in class and must not preach in other circuits without permission. The local preacher was trained like an apprentice – as many literally had been in secular employment – 'On Note', going with another preacher, 'On Trial' beginning to take wing, and finally 'On Full Plan', the master preacher able to preach anywhere in the Connexion, a matter which is still the case. All this style was taken up by the other Methodist groups which became independent of the Wesleyans. It is extraordinary how long this has survived despite all the changes in society and education.

Once Methodism was a 'church worshipping as well as a society meeting' (Duncan Coomer) local preachers were vital. A very mixed group they were –

shopkeepers, farmers, school teachers, skilled artisans, doctors like Hamilton and Whitehead, and formidable women like Mary Fletcher, widow of John Fletcher of Madeley, and Mary Barritt, though the Wesleyans did not normally use women in the early nineteenth century in the way that the Primitive Methodists and Bible Christians did. The sociology of the preachers became more middle class as the nineteenth century wore on, with in this century a great army of teachers in their ranks.

We cannot narrate all the divisions and schisms of the nineteenth century save to say that they were more about polity than about theology, and that local preachers were usually found on both sides of the conflict. Somehow Methodism never achieved the partnership of laity and ordained ministry which was desirable. The Wesleyan itinerancy in its immaturity tended to a hierarchical style which was deeply resented by some. A famous cartoon of the early nineteenth century is called 'Emblems of the Polity of Methodism'. It showed firstly a Wesleyan minister (dressed like Wesley!) sitting on a layman. 'Priestly tyranny'! On the opposite side of the cartoon two Primitive Methodist laymen were giving a minister 'the stick'. 'Lay despotism' the caption! In the middle, representing the Methodist New Connexion, was a top-hatted minister and a top-hatted layman arm in arm. Above their heads was the caption 'We be brethren' and underneath 'equal rights'. It was not until 1878 that laymen got equal rights in the Wesleyan Conference, with not a few local preachers entering it.

The Second Evangelical Revival, as it is often called now, produced the Frontier Tradition in the USA with its Camp Meetings, and in England Primitive Methodism. Hugh Bourne (1772-1852) and William Clowes (1789-1851), a carpenter and a potter, were expelled from Wesleyanism for 'not meeting in class', a nonsense really, and for insisting on Camp Meetings, which could be thought subversive at the time of the Napoleonic Wars. In Primitive Methodism, at least in the early days, the distinction between local and 'travelling' preachers was one of payment and administrative functions,. The local preachers could preside at the Lord's Supper at the Superintendent's behest, though the Lovefeast tended to be more popular.

In the early nineteenth century revival was in the air. Itinerant preaching and lay preaching was in no way a Methodist monopoly. Government became concerned at the danger of sectarianism. The Toleration Act itself was in danger. In 1811 Lord Sidmouth,[4] Home Secretary, noted that the list of persons taking out licences as preachers included 'blacksmiths, cobblers, tailors, chimney sweepers and what not' – carpenters were not mentioned! He sought to push through a Bill in which the provisions for licensing would have 'poleaxed' local preaching totally. The dissenting world acted responsibly with the Connexional solicitor, Thomas Allan, a local preacher, backed up by Thomas Thompson (1754-1828) MP, another local preacher who had the ear of William Wilberforce. Massive petitions were presented; the Wesleyans were successful. England was becoming a plural society in religious matters, with much of the repressive legislation disappearing in 1812 and later in 1828 and 1829. Allan was able to assure the government that 'we are not a political people, we simply wish to worship God and promote Christianity in the land by all means, and have been the steady friends of government.' Elie Halévy built his famous thesis about the influence of Methodism on sentiments like this, but government saw a new and ominous alliance of dissenting forces. Local preaching was now secure. The great Midlands revivals followed.

Primitive Methodism

Let's look briefly at Primitive Methodism. Here was a people's church with many preachers from the labouring groups and skilled workers whose influence on later unionism was rather greater than some left-wing historians believe, even if the Labour Party is not more Methodist than Marxist! But local preaching is our subject. Here is a circuit plan from Brandon of Lincolnshire in 1854. 'Beloved brethren, never disappoint a congregation if you can possibly attend. Go to your important work in the spirit of prayer. Choose the plainest text you can. In your discourse, aim at the glory of God and the conversion of sinners, do not allow, as some of you formerly have, slight bodily indisposition, a long journey, a dark night and inclement weather to deter you from your important duties … in the might of God grapple with the conversion of your hearers. Exhibit the cross … proclaim full redemption and pull sinners out of the fire.' There was another side, for the brother might be struck off the plan or 'sink down the plan' for pub-crawling or wife beating! Here was the self-disciplining, self-respecting, self-educated and self-absorbed element of the community increasingly forced to consider its own amelioration. It inevitably produced the 'labour aristocrat' and the union conciliator as well as a man like Joseph Capper (converted at Mow Cop) whose tongue was like the sledge hammer he used in his blacksmith's shop, arrested for subversion as a Chartist, or William Thornton of Ambler Thorn, near Halifax, who prayed at the great Chartist rally at Peep Green near Liversedge, on Whit Monday 1839. After the meeting, Feargus O'Connor, the Chartist leader, clapped his hand on Thornton's shoulder. 'Well done, Thornton, when we get the People's Charter, I will see that you are made Archbishop of York.' Thornton couldn't wait for the millennium and emigrated to America!

Later Primitive Methodists took part on the Revolt of the Field in Suffolk and Norfolk in the 1870s. Typical was George Edwards, who became a local preacher in 1872. He learned to read so that he could preach. His first job was as a human scarecrow. 'With my study of theology I began to realise that the social conditions of the people were not as God intended them to be. The gross injustice meted out to my parents and the terrible sufferings I had undergone as a boy had burned themselves into my soul like a hot iron. Many a time did I vow I would do something to better the conditions of my class.' That spirit took him from crow-scaring to parliament.[5] He has had many followers – the parliamentary local preacher is even now by no means a rare bird, and they sit on all sides of the house – Boyson, Beith and Boetang, to name but three.

Here is a final vignette[6] of the nineteenth century Primitives, a little romantic but vibrant with life. The year is 1886. 'It is to chapel we are going … It is a plain, unpretentious building, commodious enough but lacking both in beauty and comfort. In the pulpit is a tall, spare man with a face in which mysticism and intelligence are strangely blended. He is a miner from a neighbouring colliery … Never shall I forget the singing of that service. There was a little scraping and twanging of fiddle strings before all the stringed instruments – of which there were a dozen – were brought into accord with the organ, but then such a glorious outburst of music as could not fail to help the spirit of devotion. How these north folks sing … forgotten in the ecstatic bliss of mystic communion with Heaven were the bare unsightly walls , the hard seats, the dreary pit, perhaps beneath our very feet, in which men crawl like beasts for six days in the week, heaving coals, naked to the waist … After the first hymn came the prayer. Prayer is not for criticism. When a man is talking to his Maker, he should be safe from the attacks of fault finders. But there are men who have what the old Methodists called 'the gift of prayer' and the preacher had that gift … the pitman preacher talked with God with the familiarity which comes of frequent communion and yet withal with a reverence that moved even the restless youths sitting near the pulpit … a low rumbling of murmured responses broke forth in loud Amens. Suddenly one man sprang to his feet, and with a loud shout of 'Praise the Lord' jumped in the air. Few observed it or if they observed it took no notice, so absorbed were they in their own devotions. But the sermon – who shall describe it? It was a sermon to be heard not to be reported. What a mixture of humour, passionate appeal, thrilling exhortations and apposite illustrations it was … Laughter and tears this preacher commanded at will, and when he closed with heart searching appeals to the unconverted to fly to the cross for pardon, one almost wondered that men and women did not spring to their feet and rush somewhere, anywhere, exclaiming with Bunyan's Pilgrim; 'Life, life, eternal life.' The service was over and with the remembrance of that sermon as a lifelong legacy we retraced our steps homeward, stronger for having sat at the feet of this rugged Elijah of the coalpit, a hewer of coal for six days in the deep, dark mine and a very flame of fire on the seventh.'

I fear not all services were like that! Some Primitive Methodists could be almost Quaker-like in their quietness. People's church indeed. The reasons why Methodists failed to retain working men – and I underline *men* there – are complex. Revival tends in another generation to become earnest respectability.

The Wesleyans

But there are the Wesleyans – 'Don't forget the Wesleyans,' says a character in one of Disraeli's novels when an election was coming up! They had their local preaching characters, too, though local preachers had perhaps a lower profile than among the Primitives and the United Methodists. They were found on both sides of all the schisms and controversies. There were lay preaching supporters of Jabez Bunting like James Wood, first President of the Manchester Chamber of Commerce. There were also men like William Stephenson, a local preacher in North Shields who protested at the Peterloo Massacre in Manchester in 1819. He was told to hold his tongue, finally losing his job as a teacher in a colliery school and causing fourteen societies to break away. The price of protection under the law was silence on politics – or rather on radical politics – and not only in Wesleyanism either. Hugh Bourne disliked what he called 'speeching radicals'.

If there were influential men like Thomas Thompson, MP, Thomas Allan and scholars like Samuel Drew, who could take on Thomas Paine, there were rural characters like the physically handicapped Jonathan Saville of Halifax who stood in once for Jabez Bunting at a Luddite funeral and got stoned in the street by the mob! He once said, 'You can catch more flies with honey than with vinegar.' And of wandering thought in prayer, 'Nay ye cannot stop the birds flying over your 'ead but you can stop 'em building nests in yer 'air.' Sammy Hick the blacksmith preaching his famous sermon on sanctification in broad 'Yorkshire' many times. He was a great visionary and mystic and missionary advocate, as was Billy Dawson whom you could call an itinerant local preacher having modest private means. He made no bones about the bourgeois style of the famous Brunswick chapel in Leeds. What vexed him was the circular announcing the service at which he preached. 'The Trustees wishing to accommodate the respectable friends who may attend on this occasion, propose to reserve the entire gallery of the Brunswick chapel to their use. To facilitate this, silver will be taken at the foot of the stairs.' Dawson's less well-known local preaching friends rarely darkened the doors of the great chapel. Later, a local preacher of the calibre of Samuel Waddy, QC, said, 'Let there be fair play, equal work, equal rank, equal call in the sight of God almighty.' This was a different mood from Thomas Allan sixty years before who was content to 'officiate in the workhouses and small chapels, delighting mostly to address Gospel truth to the poor, the aged, the infirm, the friendless and the afflicted'.

The tensions between ardour and order, revivalism and education, clerical and lay, 'people's church' and bourgeoisie are an inevitable accompaniment of the evolution of Methodism from society to denomination and are not unknown to this day.

Some preachers were far from affluent. The Local Preachers' Mutual Aid Association – at first suspected by the Wesleyan hierarchy – was a typical Victorian Friendly Society, giving middle class Methodists an opportunity to identify with their own poor. Men like the Halifax historian and preacher, James Uriah Walker, recalled how as a Guardian of the Poor he and an Anglican had personally relieved a venerable local preacher. The Anglican was able to make Walker uncomfortable. Another example was John Turner of Cromford in Derbyshire who starved to death, reduced to a diet of turnips.[7] The early history of the LPMAA is a sad reflection of Methodist controversies, but by 1852 there were 2642 members and by 1854 it was able to give an annuity of four to eight shillings a week, enough to keep a man from the dreaded workhouse when the average wage was under a pound a week. This reminds us that the local preacher in Victorian days was found everywhere on the social scale from workhouse to Westminster. From small beginnings the LPMAA has grown to its present work with its Retirement Homes which are, of course, comparatively recent.

Twentieth Century

This century has been marked in the first place by a distinct change of style in the local preacher. Firstly in the resumption of local preaching by women, a matter of increasing significance when one considers the role of women like Dr Dorothy Farrar, who taught generations of deaconesses about the devotional life. She told me how she appeared at the circuit church in Halifax for the first time. 'Miss Farrar,' said the steward apologetically, 'you haven't got a hat on.' She lived nearby, slipped home, got out her academic gown and cap, and solved the poor steward's dilemma! One thinks of Dr Pauline Webb, Vice-President of the World Council of Churches, a superb communicator on radio, and the large number of women preachers from every strata of education. This century, too, has been notable for much more stress on proper training for local preachers, a nettle never really grasped by the Victorians. I think of a remarkable lady of Burton upon Trent – Ethel Hands. She had to retire as a headmistress at the age of 29, hardly able to walk. For years she trained the local preachers in the Bible and theology, and they often sat round her bed!

This is an area not without controversy, not just because of the great changes in theology but enormous changes in culture and in styles of worship, especially since the Second World War. I raise three issues here which especially impinge on local preachers and worship leadership, and the particular role of the laity in the teaching ministry of the church.

1. Firstly *preaching*, which I take in Bernard Lord Manning's classic phrase to be a 'manifestation of the incarnate Word from the Written Word by the spoken word'. It was as a layman – a Congregationalist Cambridge historian – that Manning wrote in 1931 bringing, as he put it, 'tidings from the back pew'[8]: 'If I go to church I want the preacher to preach, to look as if he was preaching and to talk as if he was preaching. I don't want any humbug about sermons being called 'addresses' or to be tempted by being told that there is going to be no text this morning … If you do not believe in preaching for the sake of the church and all who will hear you, do not preach.' Then he adds 'the first thing is very simple. It must be interesting. Do not fancy that your predecessors have reduced your congregation to its irreducible minimum … remember the probability, the extremely great probability that, unless you do

something about it, the sermon that you have prepared will merely bore people ... Have ever beside you to keep you humble and to spur you to fresh efforts, to raise you from satisfaction from your routine performance, the certainty that you are boring someone to death and the probability that you will bore him out of the Kingdom of God.' But he says too, 'effectual preaching means relentless study and personal contact of the most intimate kind across all social and political barriers. It is a great calling to deliver the authentic word of God to this age.' I chose to quote Manning because he was a *lay* preacher and a notable one. Since 1931 the 'boredom factor' has, I fear, not diminished. Educationalists have told us that preaching is a poor educational tool – they are right, for the aim of preaching is to kindle, articulate and strengthen faith, not primarily to impart information or satisfy curiosity. It is more like the vision of the artist or the poet or the musician than the teacher, which should be a challenge to all the teachers in the pulpit. A recent fine article on preaching by Richard Holloway, Primate of Scotland, rams that home.[9]

We denigrate now the authority figure six feet above controversy. The old oratorical style died the death about 1950. In the sixties every imaginable substitute was suggested – dialogue, discussion groups, drama. All have their proper place, and I too was in a 'Musical' this year!

But a change came in the seventies. In the Church of Rome it was made mandatory to preach at a Mass. An enormous amount of help has been given so that the homily may be Bible-based and relevant. The greater use of the lectionary has, perhaps, enabled us to escape from the preacher with bees in the bonnet, with the loss, on the other hand, of the 'character' from the pulpit. What now? We need much more variety in preaching. It does not always have to be a twenty minute exposition. It might be a short, sharp 'liturgical sermon' in the setting of Holy Communion, focusing on one Gospel point, or it might be an 'all age' occasion drawing on the congregation, as the sermon involves all. It might be a short sermon in the style of 'Thought for the Day'. It might be telling the Bible story. A college chaplain said to me not long ago, 'It's great, it's all new to them.' In *Workaday Preachers* Dr Donald English says the lay person is much nearer the 'real' world than the minister and can talk from it. Well! That 'real world' is likely to be the classroom rather than the boardroom or the shop floor. Many preachers are retired but we take the point, even if it is a little romantic.

But our preaching cannot bear all the weight of the church's ministry. We must not load one hour on Sunday with everything! In training for preaching we need to remember that we are part of the media, and while an overstress on the technique can be dangerous – we shan't win the world by technique! – we dare not ignore it. I am tired of being told 'It was great this morning. We could *hear* you.' Even with 'radio mikes' and an apparatus like a Nuremberg Rally some preachers are still inaudible *and* boring! So great variety is needed in preaching, matching the enormous variety of New Testament preaching. We need to hear this all over again. 'Good story telling controlled by good Christian theology.'

2. *Worship leadership*. I remember when I was a probationer minister my landlady, who was a devout Anglican, came to hear me preach. 'I'm not sure', she said, 'I like the preacher doing it all.' That was in 1956, and we did! The preacher prayed extempore, she read the lessons herself, preached and often gave out the notices. In some places my wife played the piano or harmonium as well! The people *sang* – and don't underestimate that in the North – and they listened. Don't underestimate the amazing receptivity of a congregation really listening to the Word preached well. That is genuine participation. Black congregations will accentuate this. But it *was* dominated by one voice, whether minister or local preacher. The change since 1956 has been immense – more responsive prayers, members of the congregation reading lessons, leading prayer. There is much more variety in styles of music, all-age worship; the Charismatic Movement, which has affected all churches including Rome, has made for much more participation. The liberation of all that has been immense. Preparation is or should be a corporate matter, but I sit in the pew and the leader – usually lay – does it all, and we are back to 1956. Some places never contact the preacher at all – it was so for me last week. This raises the whole business of the itinerant preacher. Is our style now irrelevant and outmoded? Should local preachers be more *local*? If so, what happens to churches which have no local preachers? If all worship is to be prepared corporately, does it mean it gets more time consuming and 'churchy'? Add to that the fact that many of our younger local preachers are often quite unaware of our traditions of prayer, our lore, why we have done what we have done, hymnody and varied prayer styles from the richness of sixty generations of Christian worship. We see then something of the enormous task in local preacher training now.

It is very different from the days when we had three basic text books – Ryder Smith's *What is the Old Testament?*, A M Hunter's *Introducing the New Testament* – still available, revised! – and Maldwyn Hughes' *Christian Foundations*. I read them and did the exams in a week! Actually those textbooks were first rate as text books by masters of the craft.

3. But there's that final point, the role of the lay preacher in the teaching ministry of the church – and I say 'teaching' here, not preaching. I think we must learn all over again the role of small groups in Christian spirituality. I have noted recently the enormous success of the 'Alpha' course in the Church of England and elsewhere. We need to catch up here. We need much more short courses on the faith to which those seeking meaning and faith can be invited. Lay preachers should be involved to the full. As we become a nation which 'believes but does not belong', this will become a vital part of our evangelistic strategy, as well as more evangelistic activity *during the week*. I notice that the parish churches are developing much more worship on weekdays at appropriate times. If we look at the early church the models there are interesting, though not of course entirely normative.

Many of our local preachers are retired – are they too Sunday oriented? Can there be ecumenical groups of teachers, doctors, health workers, social workers, trade unionists who can tackle the problems of the church in the world, or rather the problems of a post-Christian society? We were saying this in the sixties. I remember important initiatives in Sheffield, but it seemed to fade away. Westhill College, Birmingham, is now the centre of a growing network. Local preachers could – with their equivalents in the Church of England and other communions – play a role here, opening up topics and suggesting modes of action which are simply not possible or appropriate in a pulpit.

Many local preachers have, of course, been well known in public spheres and have been influential far beyond the boundaries of Methodism. Think of Arthur Henderson, administrative genius of the Labour Party; Isaac Foot, the epitome of the older Liberalism at the same time; George Tomlinson, Minister of Education in Atlee's cabinet; George Thomas, 'Mr Speaker' to millions in the 1970s; the academics varied in style like Cecil Pawson, T E Jessop, Victor Murray, Russell Hindmarsh, Morna Hooker, James Dunn, Charles Coulson, Herbert Butterfield; medics and business men; black leaders like Leon Murray, Sybil Phoenix and Ivan Weekes. There have been ten women Vice-Presidents in recent years of strikingly different styles and gifts.

Methodism has played a great part in the civic life of Great Britain after the Municipal Corporation Act of 1835, with that integrity and pride which was characteristic of the municipalities for a generation or so. Local preachers had their role here. I think of Alderman Brigg of Bolton (Labour), and Alderman Roberts of Grantham (National Liberal), whose preaching style is detectable in his daughter, just as Michael Foot sounded, even in his agnosticism, for all the world like his father. Perhaps that journalist of the *Independent* was right, we were at times 'too earnest'. Not all temperaments can survive in Methodism – read an Arnold Bennett Five Towns novel if you aren't sure what I mean, and compare it with George Eliot's portrayal of an earlier generation, not least her aunt, who is her character the preacher Dinah Morris in *Adam Bede*.

I end with three local preachers two of whom were of vital importance in the brief Christian renaissance after the Second World War. The first is Charles Coulson, scientist, Professor at London and Oxford, Chairman of Oxfam, Vice-President of Conference. Here is a typical Coulson sentence: 'It is my firm conviction that in proportion as we recover the sense and significance of the doctrine of the Holy Spirit, the agency of God's creative power within the universe, so we shall be able to appreciate the unity of science and faith.'[10]

Sir Herbert Butterfield has recently been linked with Sir Lewis Namier as the two most notable historical thinkers working in Britain. He died in 1979. In a book published that year he uttered prophecy dangerous for an historian, on matters which he brooded over for years. This is the world of the contemporary preacher. 'Secularism is very hostile to Christianity at the moment ... but it is fickle and flexible and amorphous, generally unhappy, always flitting like a lost soul in the world ... liable to sink in dark astrologies, weird theosophies and bleak superstitions. That, no doubt, is one of the reasons why Christianity found its opportunity in the ancient Roman Empire. I think that the spread of secularism offers Christianity not only its greatest test but also the greatest opportunity that it has ever had in history.'

He ends – and I would like to put these words over the entrance to what we must now call *Methodist Church House* – 'At any rate it is worth noting that in the present state of the world, it would be a tragic thing to be guided more by the fear of losing present church members than by the confidence that there are new ones to be won. There is a Providence in the historical process which makes it more profitable to be guided by one's faith and hopes than by one's fears.'[11] At least that is a change from the sociological determinists. After all, we believe in the optimism of grace. And for all preachers. I remember Pat Welch, another Vice-President and local preacher, ending a sermon dramatically: 'The steward opens the door for the preacher; the preacher opens the door for God.'

References

1. A Davis (Ed), *Called to Preach*, Cornwall District 1996, p 107
2. E G Rupp, *Is this a Christian Country*, Sheldon Press 1941, p 45
3. R E Davies, etc., *History of the Methodist Church in Great Britain* Vol I, 1965, p 228
4. G Milburn, M Batty, *Workaday Preachers*, pp 37ff. The nineteenth century material is a summary of my chapter pp 35-56. Primary references will be found there
5. Cf J M Turner, *People's Church*, Chapel Aid Lecture 1994
6. J Briggs and I Sellars, *Victorian Nonconformity*, Arnold 1973, p 35. PM Magazine 1896, pp 8, 30-31
7. J M Turner, Conference, Local Preachers and the LPMAA. In *Preachers All*, Essays to Commemorate the Silver Jubilee of the Yorkshire Branch of the WHS, pp 23ff
8. BL Manning, *A Layman in the Ministry*, Independent Press 1953, pp 135ff
9. Richard Holloway, *Limping Towards the Sunrise*, St Andrew 1996, pp 129ff
10. Charles Coulson, Commemoration Address 'Cassowary'. Handsworth College 1952, p 22
11. Herbert Butterfield, *Writings on Christianity and History*, Ed C T McIntire, OUP 1979, pp 248ff, cf *The Preachers' Quarterly* September 1953 Vol I, No. 1

This was a lecture given at Methodist Conference in 1996.

Chapter 14

After Thompson – Methodism and the English Working Class. An Essay in Historiography

If I may offer a text it is the first sentence of Hugh McLeod's *Religion and the Working Class in Nineteenth Century Britain.* 'There seems to be almost complete disagreement among historians about the role and significance of religion in British working-class life during the nineteenth century'. So a dose of healthy scepticism of all-embracing theses will not come amiss. But we begin with an approach which is still found in text books and in popular discussion.

'The Labour Party is more Methodist than Marxist', said Morgan Phillips, its General Secretary in 1951. I suppose half-truth is better than no truth at all. Phillips was echoing the famous thesis of the French historian, Elie Halévy, that in the vast work of social organisation which is one of the dominant characteristics of the nineteenth century England, it would be difficult to overestimate the part played by the Wesleyan revival ... we shall witness Methodism bringing under its influence first the dissenting sects, then the Establishment, finally secular opinion. We shall attempt to find here the key to the problem whose solution has hitherto escaped us, for we shall explain by this movement the extraordinary stability which English society was destined to enjoy throughout a period of revolutions and crises; what we shall truly term the miracle of modern England, anarchist but orderly, practical and businesslike but religious and even pietist'.[1] Halévy was neither original nor an expert on Methodism. His thesis had a long pre-history. Methodists made claims for themselves as exemplars of stability as early as the French wars.[2]

Frederick Denison Maurice, arguably the greatest Anglican theologian of his day, made the point long before Halévy. Maurice's son reports,

'As I have referred to the name of Wesley ... I will say that I have often heard my father speak of Wesley. It was always in the mode represented by the answer he once gave to the question:
'How do you account for the fact that England at the end of the eighteenth century escaped a revolution like that of France?'
'Oh!' he said at once, 'there is not the least doubt as to that. England escaped a political revolution because she had undergone a religious revolution.'
'You mean that brought by Wesley and Whitefield?'
'Of course!'
That was written in the Victorian 'Age of Equipoise'.
Ernst Troeltsch, the pioneer sociologist, made the same point.
'Methodism was one of the means by which the English world was rendered proof against the spirit of the French Revolution'.[3]

But is revolution to be avoided? Is to prevent it allowing religion to be the 'opium of the people'? William Cobbett, in 1820, suggested that 'Methodism beguiled man into the belief that to secure heaven hereafter you must be poor, ragged, almost die of hunger, that to be a child of grace, you must be an assemblage of skin and bones, distressing to the sight and offensive to the smell'.

The Hammonds suggested that it produced some democrats but that by and large, Methodism taught the workers submission and made them inhibited and intolerant[4] although the work of Dr R F Wearmouth caused a revision of the harsher judgement they had made. 'So Methodism, if it preached Toryism in its official declarations and a pietism that thought only of the next world in many of its chapels, was in fact an admirable school for democrats, equipping working men for popular leadership'. Halévy's point was really stood on its head by our modern Cobbett, E P Thompson, in *The Making of the English Working Class* which stands like a colossal boulder across the path of every subsequent historian and is without peer in its subject. Every history student delights to quote the passages in which he calls Methodism a 'psychic ordeal in which the character-structure of the rebellious pre-industrial labourer or artisan was violently recast into that of the submissive industrial worker. Energies in the week could go into work which was made easier by the Sabbath orgasms of feeling'. It was a 'ritualised form of psychic masturbation'. Methodism was the 'chiliasm of the defeated and the hopeless!' The 'box-like blackening chapels stood in the industrial districts like great traps for the human psyche ... the idea of a passionate Methodist lover in these days is ludicrous'.[5]

Perhaps Mr Thompson hadn't read the story of Samuel Bradburn and other itinerant preachers and their frequent pastoral calls to remote farm houses where there were attractive daughters! Their love affairs slightly dispel his critique, as does Dr Peter Gay's recent fascinating explorations of Victorian sexuality. Even Jabez Bunting hoped for a cold night on a coach ride so that , writing to his fiancée, 'we shall be obliged to squeeze together as close to each other as we can'.[6] Professor Kent,[7] one of Thompson's sternest and not always entirely fair critics, has shown, following Pollard, that the factory owners had other means of discipline besides Methodism and that 'chiliasm' or millenarianism was not characteristic of Methodism but that was not quite the point and we might note the antics of the Akroyds in Halifax and the brothers John and James Shutt at the Shaw Mills in Nidderdale. They found the Methodist virtues of honesty, sobriety and discipline doubly rewarding; in themselves they made for success in business, in their workers they helped to create an orderly labour force which would accept the new discipline of the factory.

This supports Thompson as does the scene in Manchester in 1821, two years after 'Peterloo'. John Stephens, superintendent minister (father of the Chartist Joseph Rayner Stephens) writes to Jabez Bunting:[8]

'The objects we have kept in view are: 1st to give the sound part of the society a decided ascendancy; 2nd to put down the opposition as to disable them from doing mischief; 3rd to cure those of them who are worth saving; 4th to take the rest one by one and crush them when they notoriously commit themselves ... they are growing tired of radicalism and as that dies religion will revive. Our congregations are good. Methodism stands high among the respectable people'.

This *is* Thompson's point and he claims, as does Halévy, a great deal for Methodism even if he casts it in the role of demon.

What can we say now, twenty five years after the publication of his seminal book? I would like to point to seven themes:
   (1) What was the social role and composition of Methodism in the eighteenth century?
   (2) Where now stands Halévy's 'myth' of Methodism and revolution?
   (3) Was Methodism really the religion of the Labour aristocracy?
   (4) Did Methodism cause or contribute to a schism between 'respectable' and 'unrespectable' poor?
   (5) What did Methodism and especially Primitive Methodism contribute to the working class and to the Labour Party?
   (6) Can Professor Perkins' thesis about the creation of a 'viable class society' be a modern substitute for Halévy's views?
   (7) What of a nonconformist conscience in Britain now?

   (1) Sociologically Methodism was a product of the sustained 'take off' of economic enterprise and the increase of population which accompanied it. In the eighteenth century the population of England and Wales increased from approximately five to nine million, reaching eighteen million by 1851[9] when half the population was urban. No change in human life since the beginning of civilization has been so profound as the coming of industrialization. If in 1700 the five most populous counties had been Middlesex, Somerset, Gloucester, Wiltshire and Northamptonshire, by 1800 they were Middlesex, Lancashire, the West Riding of Yorkshire, Staffordshire and Warwickshire. In the new urban areas which were beginning to grow in the pre-industrial period the church hardly touched the mass of population although even here it is possible to exaggerate. A good example is the pattern of settlement in the Shropshire coalfield which created great difficulties for the territorial parish. Mining and ore making villages grew up with complete disregard for established ecclesiastical boundaries and remote from parish churches.[10]

Throughout the expanding industrial North and Black Country, the Church of England's parochial machinery was totally inadequate. The much larger Northern parishes (there were only 70 parishes in Lancashire and 193 in the West Riding of Yorkshire compared with 731 in Norfolk and 510 in Suffolk) originating in Celtic Monasticism were to prove the seed beds of Methodism. Halifax parish is the classic case of the huge sprawling parish with inadequate chapelries to cope with the social changes in the Calder Valley.[11]

In pre-industrial England, religion provided the nearest approach to overt class attitudes with the social 'sandwich' – Anglican on top and bottom and Protestant dissenters in the middle. In the old society dissent flourished in precisely those groups which wished to and could afford to be somewhat independent of the paternal squirearchy. It was the middling groups of society who could afford the luxury of dissent. When 'dependency' in the parishes began to break down, dissent could be a possibility much lower in the social scale. It is now a kind of post-Thompson 'orthodoxy' that Methodism filled the gaps in the parish system. It was a movement from below and always seen as such by the dominant classes. It was, says Professor Kent, a 're-arrangement of the religious sub-culture', a creation of new institutions in the 'no-mans land between old Dissent and the Establishment'.[12] Methodism grew strong where the Church of England was weak and recruited from those sections of the population which were inadequately 'churched'.[13] Calderdale is a classic example but the same phenomenon is found in the Isle of Wight or Cornwall where parishes not only were large but parish churches were distant from centres of population. Circuits with over 1000 members at the end of the century were almost all to be found in grossly under-churched industrial areas of which Leeds, Bradford and Halifax can be taken as normative. The triangle formed by Halifax, Leeds and Sheffield was typical of the area of swift growth. Yorkshire, Staffordshire, Lancashire, Northumberland and Durham were strong centres of Methodism at the end of the eighteenth century. The southern counties except for Cornwall, Devon and Middlesex, continued to be a 'Methodist desert' well into the nineteenth century. Here often enough were the most effective parishes of the 'closed' type in which the squire was still dominant with all the sanctions that might evolve in a tight system of social control. Biographies and autobiographies show the preference of Methodist itinerants to be stationed in Halifax or Wakefield rather than, say, Hereford where James Dixon was working at the time Jabez Bunting was in Halifax.

'I believe that our circuit is the poorest circuit in all the Kingdom and that there is less religion in the County of Hereford than there is in any other County'.[14]

This was an area where the Establishment was far from weak, very different from the large West Riding parishes. As John Walsh puts it,

'Methodism was able to enlarge and articulate existing cells of godliness and weave into a connexional system all sorts of little marginal outcrops and expatriates. Converts often had a traditional religious background which rather dents the 'church decay' theory a little. The ideal conditions for a new society would that it be sited in a large freehold parish well stocked with artisans or industrial workers or statutory freeholders with a number of leaderless, disgruntled Nonconformists ready to be woven into the Connexional system with no parish clergymen (in 1743 out of 836 parishes in the diocese of York, 393 had non-resident incumbents and 315 were held by pluralists) or a non-resident or immoral clergyman, near to good roads, close to older settlements not far from the avuncular protection of a town society with an eloquent assistant preacher.'[15]

Yet even with all the circumstances ideally coinciding a society might not thrive or it might become bedevilled by divisions. Even without all the favourable predisposing factors, spiritual revival could still occur. In the city of York, as Dr Royle has shown, Methodism flourished alongside the Minster and a congeries of parishes, some Evangelical. Huddersfield was a like case, despite or because of Henry Venn. Likewise Alan Everitt revealed similar need for caution over interpretations of rural Lincolnshire.

The constituency seems basically artisan – neither 'lumpen proletariat' nor the middling groups characteristic of old Dissent. Dr Thompson's thesis that Methodism acted as a repressive element in creating a non-revolutionary working class consciousness hardly applies to *eighteenth* century Methodism. Here was a society or connexion developing into a denomination which enabled artisans to express their sense of belonging outside what Perkin called 'the dependency system'.[16] It can be argued, as by Bernard Semmel,[17] that the Wesley's 'Arminianism of the heart' was a religious equivalent of the contemporary belief in freedom and liberty. I am sceptical about this 'hijacking' of R R Palmer but clearly Methodism gave men and women a prodigious degree of importance before God – and this without any utopian sense of human perfectibility and a notable lack of millenarianism, when there was plenty of that around, typified by Joanna Southcott who was totally cold shouldered by the Wesleyans.[18] It can also be argued that with the partial breakdown of the old ruling order in some areas with increasing parochial conflict over enclosures or tithes, with growing status for the clergy (often on the Bench), Methodism provided a group system where new outsiders could gain status, a sense of identity and importance.[19] Recent attempts to suggest a sociological profile of early Methodism came to similar conclusions. There is clear evidence that the impact on the artisan group – masons, shoemakers, tailors, harness makers, saddlers, carpenters, croppers, stockingers and the like – was out of proportion to their numbers in the whole population.[20]

The parallels with Lollards and Puritans are illuminating. Those whom Dr Christopher Hill calls the 'industrious sort of people' were often drawn into the movement and many of the needy poor who were also attracted by Wesley and his preachers became industrious. But the coincidence with early industrialization is crucial. The representative townsman right up to the middle of the nineteenth century was the tradesman, craftsman, small master artisan – the 'little maisters' of Sheffield cutlery are typical. In the mill villages of Calderdale were the independent and threatened artisans and it is extraordinary that there appear to have been no Methodist members among the Luddites – though 'lapsed Methodists' are another matter as was Methodist parentage. These were the men who later can be called 'labour aristocrats' in contrast to the totally unskilled or semi-skilled labourers or the workers newly skilled in factory techniques. Angus Buchanan has underscored the point made long ago by W J Warner that this social group produced the leaders of many local Methodist societies in the first generation or two and also later recruits for the early trade unions who battled for their standards against the unskilled immigrants from the countryside or later 'Erin's root-fed hordes' from across the Irish sea.[21]

If you look at the youthful 'Dad's Army' of Wesley's early preachers,[22] you will find that with the exception of half a dozen who were soldiers, they (i.e. the itinerants) were nearly all from that social grade between middle and labouring classes – small tradesmen, small farmers, shopkeepers, clerks, schoolmasters and the like. Despite Wesley's dislike of the 'idle rich' and preference for the poor and despite his total rejection of any idea that the poor deserved their poverty, nevertheless as both Sir John Plumb[23] and E P Thompson showed, here was religion *for* the poor rather than *of* the poor. Clearly this is so of the leadership. So Alan Gilbert's assertion, which every history student now knows as well as his Thompson, is not wide of the mark that 'Evangelical nonconformity echoed the aspirations rather that the despair of the working classes'. It legitimated aspiration and improvement.[24]

Now this certainly could lead to social cleavage. John Wesley criticized the Methodists for any increase in affluence – an educated lady like Frances Mortimer of York, when she became Mrs John Pawson (Pawson was superintendent at Halifax in 1792 and President of the Conference), sold her beautiful silk dresses, becoming quakerly in her demeanour. But others clearly benefited from what has been called the birth of a consumer society in the eighteenth century.[25]

More importantly Methodism sought to change the styles of recreation of their convert and their community. Dr Thompson shows how the average English working man became more disciplined, more subject to the productive tempo of the 'clock', more reserved and methodical, less violent and less spontaneous. Traditional sports were displaced by more sedentary hobbies. 'the athletic exercises of quoits, wrestling, football, prison bars and shooting with the longbow are becoming obsolete – they are now pigeon-fanciers, canary-breeders and tulip growers'. That was in 1813 in Lancashire.[26] Later Edward Welbourne, writing of the Durham miners, states that they i.e. the Methodists, took away from 'the pitman, his dog, his fighting cock and his gun'. Prayer meetings would replace 'pay night frolics'. J G Rule dealing with Cornwall and Robert Colls on the North East has recently underlined the point but it is ambiguous. Methodism was able to link up with folk customs and 'folk religion' and remould it. Wesley's greatness was that he could straddle the world of the Age of Reason and the world of the London poor for whom he would tramp in the snow collecting money on a one-man Christian Aid campaign when over eighty. Can we see this as a 'civilizing influence on the poor' with Dr Walsh[27] or as an inhibiting factor as some contemporaries clearly did?

The Whig *Edinburgh Review* in 1808 had an article by R A Ingram lambasting the joylessness of Methodism –

'The Methodists hate pleasures and amusements, no theatre, no cards, no dancing, no Punchinello, no dancing dogs, no blind fiddlers ... for the learning, the moderation and the rational piety of the Establishment we most earnestly wish a decided victory over the nonsense, the melancholy and the madness of the tabernacle'.

Much of this pamphleteering was perverse. 'Methodism' often meant evangelical in a broader sense. Yet a candid friend observed to Frances Pawson that Methodists made 'monasteries for your mind' and her husband buried John Wesley's annotated copy of Shakespeare as 'useless lumber not tending to edification'. Robert Southey, in the rival Tory *Quarterly Review*, gives another side.

'Go to the collieries or the manufactories of Birmingham and Sheffield and inquire what are the political consequences of Methodism whenever it has spread amongst the poor – industry and sobriety, quiet and orderly habits and the comforts which result from them will be found its fruits. But the 'philistinism', if such it is, he observed too – 'on those who love poetry it acts upon them as a mildewing superstition, blasting all genius in the bud withering every flower of loveliness and of innocent enjoyment'.[28]

Dr Thompson hardly excels that!

The call of the Methodists of this post-Wesley period was for disciplined, simple pious lives, removed from worldly pleasures and centred on home, chapel and business. The duty of hard work, the evils of luxury and extravagance, the virtues of foresight and thrift, moderation and self-discipline were instilled into ordinary church members and provided an undergirding to the moral earnestness and desperate conscientiousness which was to characterize Victorian England. So Methodism did not so much displace the folk beliefs as translate them into a religious idiom.[29] The consequences we shall see later.

(2) What of Halévy's thesis about Methodism and revolution? The number of articles on this matter is extraordinary! In recent years Methodist historians have denigrated it. Professor John Kent has waged a running battle with it for years; Gordon Rupp bid us forget the thesis in his last great book.[30] Much more important was John Walsh's brilliant analysis of Halévy's first shots at an interpretation of Methodism, written in 1906, translated as late as 1971 by Bernard Semmel. Walsh shows convincingly that Methodism was not strong enough to effect great social change in the 1740s and that Halévy exaggerates its role in the discontents of 1739-40 in the West Country.

In two brilliant articles, anticipating Thompson, Eric Hobsbawm claims, like Walsh, that Methodism was never strong enough to be a decisive factor and that in any case revolution to be successful needs a crisis in the affairs of the ruling class and also a body of revolutionaries capable of leading and directing the movement.[31] Widespread violence was likely in 1811-12 – the time of the Luddite crises when Jabez Bunting feared to walk the streets of Halifax by night, again in 1816/8 but there was no unity among the disaffected. The other real crisis periods were in 1829/32 and 1839/48 but the forces of order were able, when concentrated, to deal with ease and sometimes with humanity with any disorder as the history of Chartism shows though earlier repression as under 'Black Acts' or in the Captain Swing riots was excessive and inhuman.[32] Revolution demands more than hungry men and a disaffected working class. It needs leadership and a method of seizing power in the army, the police and local magistracy. Hobsbawm points to gross discontent – woollen and worsted weavers' wages were forced down from 34/6d in 1814 to 21 shillings down to a miserable 12/6d in 1838. But this was not a presage of revolution. Hobsbawm shows, as did R F Wearmouth, that Methodism and radicalism grew side by side in areas like Huddersfield, Leeds, Birstall and Wakefield which were all, after Nottingham, centres of Luddism. But there is little evidence that Methodism prevented revolution! It can become nonsensical. The failure of England to produce a revolution in 1848 – the year of revolutions in Europe – has been successively attributed to Methodism by Maldwyn Edwards; by some historians to F D Maurice, J M Ludlow and their friends; by Sir Philip Magnus to the Anti-Corn Law League and a Catholic writer concludes that 'the coherence and strength of the Catholic church in England has been shown in the elimination of any anti-religious character from the trade union movement'. This is to steal Methodism's thunder with a vengeance, if there was any thunder to steal![33] Such 'myths' have little foundation.

Dare one say with Gordon Rupp that England had undergone its revolutions in the Wars of the Roses, at the time of Henry VIII and Thomas Cromwell, in the Civil War and 1689? What George Kitson Clark taught me in Cambridge in the 1950s has been underlined recently by I R Christie in his Ford Lectures.[34] English society cannot adequately be compared with that of the Ancie Régime. While Halévy remains a formidable interpreter of nineteenth century England, he is flawed in his view of Methodism not least in assuming that Evangelicalism was an offshoot and development of Methodism which it certainly was not, Methodism was not even the pioneer of revival.[35] Christie's right wing approach, if that is what it is, is not far from that of the subtle Marxist Hobsbawm, but he is really nearer to A D Gilbert. Far from being a tool of repression, the Methodist movement offered a religious and social package, highly attractive to tens of thousands of people. By legitimizing self improvement or economic endeavour, Methodism provided a guide for successfully meeting social changes of the Industrial Revolution and so at least for some may have averted a potentially dangerous build up of frustration and political discontent. There are still paradoxes here, and we shall see how Halévy's thesis reappears as a ghost of itself later.

(3) It was Halévy, indeed, who used the phrase 'élite of the working class' which, in recent histiography, has become 'the labour aristocracy'. It is, I think, crucial to an understanding of the relationship of Methodism to the working class. There is continuity between the style of person who became Methodist in the eighteenth century and the kind of person who not only became a Methodist later but might become a member of a radical group- that rich infidel tradition which Dr Royle has brought to life so well or, later, Chartism.[36] Clearly not a few Methodists were involved in early trade unions and Chartism, whatever Jabez Bunting may have wished. We must not exaggerate the authority of the Wesleyan hierarchy – West Riding men and women have rarely taken them with the seriousness with which they took themselves! The same group whom we have found influenced by Methodism in the eighteenth century, formed a majority of Methodist societies in the first half of the nineteenth century also. There is little doubt that a majority of Methodists were artisans. Currie, Gilbert and Horsley show 62.7% of Wesleyans with 9.5% being labourers and 7.6% colliers, miners etc. compared with 47.7% of Primitive Methodists with 16.1% labourers, 12.5% colliers and miners, revealing that the Primitive Methodists were more representative of the labouring poor.[37] Even a prestigious London church like Hinde Street[38] in the West End, which was rather more bourgeois than most, included in its 26 trustees, a 'gentleman', a Fleet Street bookseller, builders, two tailors, a boot maker, a shoe maker, a cordwainer, a haberdasher, a cabinet maker, an ironmonger, a cheesemonger, a silver plater, a turner, a medicine vendor. A look at trustees' occupations at South Parade WM or Salem MNC Halifax would show a similar pattern, though Ebenezer Primitive Methodist, also in Halifax, had no one with the vote after the Reform Act of 1832!

This group had its own modes of self-respect which are not to be equated entirely with middle class values and mid-Victorian norms.[39] If William Lovett, the Chartist, could appeal to the 'most intelligent and influential portion of the working class', so could the Methodists. They were not much in evidence among the 'unshorn chains, blistered hands and fustian jackets', save for the Primitive Methodists in large industrial villages. There were those whom Feargus O'Connor claimed to represent, yet Methodists were present at the famous Peep Green Chartist rally when Ben Wilson, the Halifax Methodist Chartist, estimated a crowd of 200,000 on Whit Monday, 1838. That was the occasion when a Primitive Methodist from Round Hill, Ambler Thorn, William Thornton prayed at the opening. O'Connor put his hands in Thornton's shoulder 'Well done, Thornton, when we get the People's Charter, I will see that you are made Archbishop of York'.[40] Thornton emigrated rather than wait for the revolution.

Most Methodists were not Chartists but many expressed self-help and the quest for self respect in other forms both individual and collective – Mutual Improvement Societies, Friendly Societies, Co-operative stores stemming from Rochdale and Calderdale in the 1840s. I can still smell the whiff of the coffee beans from our local 'Co-op' to which my mother walked a mile or so in the

1930s when the 'divi' was still important! 'Poor man's masonry' would include the secret oaths of the men of Tolpuddle in 1834 but also the Independent Order of Oddfellows, the Antedeluvian Order of Buffaloes and all the rest! Membership of the Friendly Societies was four million in 1872 – there's even a part of Sowerby Bridge called Friendly! At least you got a ham tea at your funeral and money from the 'box' when you were ill. Chapel membership and membership of these groups was intermingled – I remember my grandfather, as late as 1955, deploring the decline of 'Oddfellowship' among the young.[41]

Two basic styles of self suspect and improvement are found in the Sunday School and the Temperance Movement. It is too glib to see the Sunday School as a mere means of social control.[42] It was much more a means of self improvement dominated, certainly in the West Riding, by 'labour aristocrats' rather than mill owners. The numbers of children and adults involved were extraordinary – Mount Zion, Ogden and Heptonstall are good early Calderdale examples, each with hundreds of children involved at any one time. Clearly the Victorian Sunday School was to give a veneer of protestant religion to thousands of working people. It is easy to caricature the treat and bun fights and Whit Walks and the white dresses on the 'Anniversary' platform, the 'feast' of Victorian nonconformity countering what were thought less wholesome community activities but the Sunday Schools provided not only much impetus to elementary education, which working class parents wanted, but also much of what is now called 'invisible religion', the vague folk religion of the English working class so well depicted in the 1950s by Richard Hoggart in *Uses of Literacy*.[43] Sunday Schools, too, could be subject to gusts of radicalism and revivalism – hence Jabez Bunting's dislike of some of their activities. They were independent of hierarchy and parsons. Even now at Southowram, Halifax, the Sunday School building of the Methodist church is not Methodist property but controlled by independent trustees – all 'chapel' people no doubt but they elect their own chairman! If 'class meetings' reached their thousands, Sunday Schools reached their millions!

(4) Temperance (or, as some prefer, teetotalism) is another area where it is easy to set up mythology. The work of Brian Harrison and Billington[44] has recently opened up this area. Temperance was not a bourgeois prejudice but had more radical and plebeian roots. Francis Place and William Cobbett alike saw drunkenness as a lack of proper self-respect. Robert Colls, writing about Durham pitmen, comments that conversions 'resulted in the convert transforming his self-image and therefore his habits'. John Wilson, Primitive Methodist miners' leader, avows that his conversion led him to give up drinking and gambling and made him see his life in new terms as a gift and something to be stewarded. The famous sermon anecdote of the miner having 'the mickey' taken out of him over miracles, saying, 'Well, if Jesus could turn beer into furniture for his house wouldn't he be able to turn water into wine', was no joke but a reality in many a nineteenth century home. Alcohol became a symbol of all that is evil at a time when drunkenness spread like a pestilence over Europe. 'The pledge' almost became a kind of

substitute for evangelical conversion, a badge of self esteem and clearly of respectability with two effects. One was a cleavage made more evident between chapel and pub. Go up the main road from Wolverhampton to Sedgley in the Black Country and you will pass the Fighting Cocks Inn on one side and a Methodist chapel on the other side, representing two rival working class styles – though the pub supporters might well have sent the children to Sunday School. My grandfather told me that at the turn of the century he sometimes went to the Music Hall on Saturday night but, as grandma disapproved, he told her he had important business at chapel! I would hazard a guess that temperance – which the Wesleyans for long suspected because of radical associations – was the last nail in the coffin of any Methodist attempt to reach the 'unrespectable' poor. That was left to the Roman Catholics. Though even here Cardinal Manning advocated and practised total abstinence.

After 1870 temperance was a normal part of the Methodist mind-set. Hugh McLeod in a neat phrase says that the cult of temperance in late Victorian nonconformity symbolized the transition from a religion of faith to a religion of works. To its later nineteenth century advocates temperance meant prosperous and happy homes. It meant new priorities, better furniture, books. It meant healthy and wholesome sport like cricket and soccer rather than gambling, contests of brute force and sport involving fighting animals. It was attractive to women too. The drunkard became the Methodist equivalent of the idle aristocrat, the public house his palace.

The second influence of temperance was a shift to a somewhat more collectivist view of the state. If T H Green[45] thought that the state should remove 'hindrances to freedom', drink was one such hindrance. State legislation was seen as a tool of morality – that debate rumbles on to this day when the temperance card can be seen played in some Methodist circles. It all seems like a secularization of scriptural holiness. Idleness, irresponsibility, indiscipline, waste had become the enemies. Giving to the poor had become Christian stewardship. Methodism became the religion of lower middle class self-respect though if we could tell the whole story it would be a tale of intense responsibility for society often enough in civic and political and charitable endeavour and earnestness.

(5) This leads to the thesis propounded by Professor Harold Perkin.[46] He sees religion as the midwife of class consciousness' – the midwife not the mother or the child. Methodism was but one religion of the working class and was often as not the gate through which large numbers of working class men passed in to religious indifference or secularism, the ultimate spiritual state of the majority in the great towns of the industrial age – he sees religion as having three roles in the industrial revolution. It gave expression to emancipation from the dependency system before it hardened into overt class antagonism. Emancipation from paternal and religious discipline went hand-in-hand with urbanization. Here is the sharpest paradox of the nineteenth century – the emergence In the midst of the greatest revival of religious faith

since the Middle Ages of the agnosticism and indifference which was to be the dominant spiritual position in modern Britain. Both were part of the emancipation from the old paternal society and the existence of competing groups which was characteristic of England compared with the Continent, providing a series of stepping stones by which the emancipated individual could make his way from the church to any position of Christian belief or at last into the great desert of unbelief on the other side of Jordan. Perkin exaggerates the role of some of the smaller groups here and builds too much on people like Thomas Cooper and Joseph Barker – lapsed Methodists both – but the basic point is at least arguable.

Methodism in particular provided the means or at least the modes of class organization, the moral earnestness, the sense of calling, the tight-knit organization spilled over into secular groups. Trained in oratory, initiative and organization, lay preachers naturally gravitated to the leadership of any movement they joined. The Methodists and lapsed Methodists – Lovett, Cooper and Co – from whatever connexion brought great powers of charismatic leadership to the political societies and trade unions. The legacy was the training and organization, the instinct and the framework for non-violent conflict through negotiation and discussion which paradoxically the English working class were to teach to their employers and rulers.

So Perkin's third point follows. Not so much by passive teaching and patience but by active example of the benefit of non-violent organization, religion influenced class conflict in the direction of non-violence and so administered an 'analgesic against the pains of labour'. If you compare Robert Coll's picture of the Durham miner we move from those who prayed for the death of blacklegs to more conciliatory style portrayed a generation later by Robert Moore[47] in his *Pitmen, Preachers and Politics*, a style which owed much to Primitive Methodism and which was passing away by the time of the general strike of 1926. Maybe Perkin is a latter-day Halévy telling us Methodism saved England from a Russian revolution!

(6) Primitive Methodism illustrates all this far better that the Wesleyans who are so often taken as the norm, with others the deviants.[48] Primitive Methodism, stemming originally from revival in the Cheshire Plain and in the Potteries during the Napoleonic Wars, is the classic case of the conversionist sect to denomination development. Though really quite separate from Wesleyanism after the initial tension between 'order' and 'ardour' in the Potteries when Hugh Bourne and William Clowes were expelled, it yet had many similarities with Wesleyanism including a stress on salvation for all, the circuit system and small spirituality. R F Wearmouth's point that Chartism borrowed Primitive Methodist and indeed Wesleyan organization styles has never been refuted.[49] Here was a revivalist form of Quakerism – unlike Wesleyanism it was a religion *of* the poor, its founders not Oxford dons but a carpenter and a potter.

172

Beginning with Camp Meetings – sober and tame compared with the American style despite Lorenzo Dow, these religious 'pop festivals' enabled the Primitives to develop 'fasts and feasts' in deliberate rivalry with the 'wakes'. With 200 members in 1811, the great Midlands Revival bumped numbers up to 16,000 by 1821. The 'Ranters' (a good old seventeenth century nickname) stormed through the Midlands into Lincolnshire and into East Anglia and up to the East Riding, often enough spearheaded by women preachers like Sarah Kirkland. The Primitives offered a Gospel to folk outside the normal reach of parish church and Wesleyan chapel alike – farm labourers, miners, fishermen, the nailers of the Black Country. The small industrial village and the extractive industrial areas were the heartlands of Primitive Methodists.

E J Hobsbawm[50] was right to point to the way in which Primitive Methodists could quickly establish themselves in villages or semi-village areas – a pattern of living which was destined to disappear as the modern patterns of urbanization and factory industry develops. In the villages the Primitive Methodists spread into areas not covered by Wesleyanism and had an appeal to farm labourers. The chapel gave a sense of belonging at a time of social pressure, a high proportion of members, men and women, holding office. While a 'no politics' rule might restrain pulpit firebrands – Hugh Bourne disliked 'speeching radicals' almost as much as Bunting – there was much union activity. In Oxfordshire Pamela Horn[51] has shown all the officers of the Oxford Branch of the Agricultural Union were Methodists, mainly Primitives. Joseph Arch of Barford who founded the Agricultural Workers' Union of 1872 was a Primitive Methodist. Earlier the Chartists recruited not a few Primitive Methodists – colourful characters like Joseph Markham, a shoemaker of 'radical' Leicester and his ally, John Skevington – coldshouldered by Bourne – who avowed 'although a man may be a Chartist and not a Christian, a man cannot be a Christian and not a Chartist except through ignorance'. Joseph Capper, a Cheshire man, was converted at Mow Cop in 1807. As a prominent Staffordshire Chartist he was arrested in 1843 and tried for 'sedition, conspiracy and rioting', being sentenced to two years imprisonment. It is said of Capper that 'his tongue was like the sledge hammer he used in his shop'.[52]

The English Labour Movement may have received its ideology from the 'atomic fall out' of the French Revolution – London Jacobins and Francis Place, Owenites and Co-operators, free thinking radicals flocking to Holyoake and Bradlaugh, the Social Democratic Federation and the Fabians with their dislike of 'tabernacle gas'. There is also the economic idealism of William Morris and Henry George and the Anglican idealistic stream from Maurice to Temple and Attlee but there is, too, the contribution of Primitive Methodism, especially in the North East. Robert Colls in the *Colliers Rant* and *Pitman of the Northern Coalfield* clearly stresses the functional value of Primitive Methodism, intermeshed with the whole life of communities. When the Marquess of Londonderry sacked the miners of Durham in 1844, the circuit found two thirds of its members homeless. 'Blacklegs' were despised but negotiators like Tommy Hepburn, Burt, Fenwick, John Wilson and Peter Lee were tough but conciliatory. While it would be foolish to romanticize there is truth in Stephen Mayor's assertion that by '1914 the Labour Movement was one of the great national institutions which was not feeling immensely the draught of indifference and scepticism'.[53] In the 'Revolt of the Field', the Primitives too played their role also,[54] George Edwards who began work as a human scarecrow and ended knighted, in Parliament, states that 'With my study of theology I soon began to realize that the conditions of the people were not as God intended them to be. The gross injustice meted out to my parents and the terrible sufferings I have undergone in my boyhood burned themselves into my soul like a hot iron. Many a time did I vow I would do something to better the conditions of my class'.

Worship among the Primitive Methodists was charismatic, lively and entertaining. Office was open to all; women could preach and become itinerants, formidable pioneers some of them were too! Discipline was strict, a brother might be expelled for pub crawling or wife beating! Here, says Colls, was a self-disciplining, self-respecting, self-educating and self-absorbed element of a growing dislocated redefined community, increasingly forced to consider its own amelioration. In the end the Primitive Methodists produced the sober, hard working thrifty 'labour aristocrat' who could fight indeed for his place in the sun but who would tend to be a conciliator rather than a revolutionary and who would later be as opposed to the working class scapegrace as to the hard-line Marxist. Primitive Methodism created a religious counter-culture which offered an alternative to the established church, to village culture and working culture alike. As James Obelkevich put it in his fine study of rural Lincolnshire, 'It appeared at a critical moment as the traditional culture was passing but before the subsequent working class culture had developed to replace it'.[55] Yet I would hazard the opinion that even as an interim faith, it played a role as a midwife in the painful birth of English socialism out of all proportion to its size.

(7) My last point concerns the Nonconformist Conscience. David Bebbington's recent study has rather modified the harsh picture of power struggling given by Professor Kent.[56] With all that we are not concerned here, but rather with the renewed concern, albeit paternalist, for the poor, the 'underclass' revealed by the *Bitter Cry of Outcast London* (1883) and the researches of Charles Booth in London and Rowntree in York. In 1898 measles alone carried off 13,000 folk. Drunkenness was still a fearful social evil and for 6 shillings you could buy 36 pints of beer in 1901. A ministry was needed to offer Gospel to mind and body. The basis of the *Forward Movement* was to provide centres of evangelism and social amelioration, the sacrament and the soup-ladle hand in hand, with a minister at the head who could remain long enough to be a social and often political force in the neighbourhood. This was the basis of centres like St James' Hall in London and the Manchester, Bradford and Leeds Missions. The *Forward Movement* in Methodism was the last great attempt to reach those alienated from the churches. The recent analysis of the West London Mission by Professor Bagwell[57] reveals interesting social experiments – the Sisters of the People led

by Katherine Price Hughes, which like the earlier National Children's Home and the Wesley Deaconess Order (both founded by Thomas Bowman Stephenson) made a creative use of talented women, the crèche, the hospice for the dying. Here was a radical Methodism tinged with the need for corporate and collective social policy. The pattern can be paralleled in Manchester, Birmingham, Leeds, Bradford and most large towns – attempts to bridge the vast gulf between the churches and the bulk of the industrial workers in the large conurbations. In recent years the *Mission Alongside the Poor Programme* provides a new link in a chain going back to Wesley's concern for the London poor living around 'the Foundery'.

We have only attempted an outline of the work done in the area of Methodism and the working class since Thompson's book. There is the danger that the approach tends to be functionalist and tends to summarise side effects rather than the reality of the Methodist societies which was essentially religious. This is the danger of generalized theses from Halévy to Perkin but we run the risk, since religion cannot be seen in a vacuum. Religious ideas cannot be detached from social environment[58] and here Marx is often enough wiser than Max Weber! Methodism is inextricably bound up with the rise and development of industrial England and has proved to be the religion of the lower middle class whatever its founder may have wished or hoped.

References

1. H McLeod, *Religion and the Working Class in Nineteenth Century Britain*, Macmillan 1984, p9; E Halévy , *A History of the English People in 1815*, Book III, Pelican Edition , 1938, p 10 pp 47-8
2. W R Ward, *Religion and Society in England 1790-1850*, Batsford, 1972, p 89
3. F Maurice (Ed), *Life of F D Maurice, 1884*, vol I p ix; E Troeltsch, *Social Teaching of the Christian Churches*, London 1931, vol 2
4. cited in W B Pemberton, *William Cobbett*, Penguin 1949, p 125; J L & B Hammond, *The Town Labourer 1760-1832*, Longmans Green 1949 Ed, vol II Ch XIII pp 93-108; J M Turner, R F Wearmouth as Historian, *Proceedings of the Wesley Historical Society*, Sept 1982, pp 111-117
5. E P Thompson, *The Making of the English Working Class*, Pelican Ed, 1968, pp 28-58; 385-440; 916-923
6. W R Ward, *The Early Correspondence of Jabez Bunting 1820-9*, Royal Historical Society, 1972, p 17; P Gay, *The Bourgeois Experience*, London 1985
7. J H S Kent, *The Age of Disunity*, Epworth, 1966, pp x-xi; J H S Kent, *The Unacceptable Face*, SCM 1987, pp 114-116; A Pollard, Factory Discipline in Early Nineteenth Century, *Economic History Review*, December 1963

8. B Jennings (Ed), *A History of Nidderdale*, 1967, p 416. cf Thompson op cit pp 381-2; W R Ward, *The Early Correspondence of Jabez Bunting*, pp 61-2

9. E Royle, *Modern Britain. A Social History 1750-1985*, Arnold 1987 pp 40ff; P Mathias, *The First Industrial Nation*, Methuen 1969, pp 186ff

10. B Trinder, *The Industrial Revolution in Shropshire*, Phillimore, 1973, p 297

11. C R Turner, *Population Trends in the Upper Calder Valley and the Wool-Textile Trade*, Newcastle Polytechnic B A Thesis (unpublished); J A Hargreaves, *Political Attitudes and Activities of Methodists in the Parish of Halifax 1830-1848*, Huddersfield Polytechnic M A Thesis 1985 (unpublished)

12. J H S Kent, *The Unacceptable Face*, pp 74-131

13. R Currie, A Micro-Theory of Methodist Growth, Proceedings of the Wesley Historical Society, 1967, pp 65-73; cf A Everitt, *The Pattern of Rural Dissent*, Leicester 1972, p8; J D Gay, *The Geography of Religion in England*, Duckworth 1971, pp 144ff; D Sylvester, The Church and the Geographer. *Liverpool Essays in Geography*, Ed; R W Steel and R Lawton 1967; D Fraser (Ed), *A History of Modern Leeds*, MUP 1980; D G Wright and J A Jowitt, *Victorian Bradford*, 1982, pp 37-62

14. W R Ward, *The Early Correspondence of Jabez Bunting*, 1982, pp 37-62; R W Dixon, *Life of James Dixon*, 1874, pp 27ff; T Jackson, *Life of Robert Newton*, 1855, pp 22ff

15. J D Walsh, Methodism and the Common People, In R Samuel (Ed) *People's History and Socialist Theory*, 1981, pp 754ff; J D Walsh, in *Proceedings of the Royal Historical Society*, Vol. 25, 1975, pp 1-20; A D Gilbert, *Religion and Society in Industrial England*, Longman, 1976 p83; A Everitt, op cit p 8; E Royle, op cit, pp 297-8; E Royle, *Nonconformity in Nineteenth Century York*, 1985, pp 196-208; 340-364

16. H Perkin, *The Origin of Modern English Society 1780-1980*, RKP, 1969, pp 196-208; 340-364

17. B Semmel, *The Methodist Revolution*, Heinemann, 1973, pp 81-109; G F Nuttall, *The Puritan Spirit*, Epworth, 1967, pp 67ff; R R Palmer, *The Age of the Democratic Revolution*, Princeton, 1959

18. J F C Harrison, *The Second Coming. Popular Millenarianism 1780-1850*, RKP, 1979

19. W R Ward, Church and Society in the First Half of the Nineteenth Century, in Davies, George, Rupp (Eds), *History of Methodist Church in Great Britain*, vol 2, Epworth, 1978, pp 11-96

20. C D Field, Sociology of Methodism, *British Journal of Sociology*, July 1977, pp 199-225

21. R A Buchanan, Methodism and the Evangelical Revival, An Interpretation in W S F Pickering (Ed), *Anglican Methodist Relations Some Institutional Factors*, DLT, 1961, p 79; L F Church, *More About the Early Methodist People*, Epworth, 1949, pp1-56

22. H Bett, *The Early Methodist Preachers*, Epworth, 1935, p33

23. J H Plumb, *England in the Eighteenth Century*, Penguin 1950, pp 93-94; Thompson, op cit, p 41

24. A D Gilbert, op cit, p 83

25. J Sutcliffe, *Experiences of Mrs Frances Pawson*, 1834; N McKendrick, S Brewer & J H Plumb, *The Birth of a Consumer Society*, Hutchinson, 1983, pp 265-85; R Porter, *English Society in the Eighteenth Century*, Penguin, 1982, pp 201ff

26. Thompson, op cit, p 451

27. J G Rule, *The Labouring Class in Early Industrial England 1750-1850*, Longmans, 1986, pp 220ff; R Colls, *The Pitmen of the Northern Coalfield, Work, Culture and Protest 1790-1850*, Manchester 1987, pp 118ff; E Welbourne, *Methodism and Social Character, The Miners' Union of Northumberland and Durham*, CUP, 1923, p 57; J D Walsh in Davies, op cit, vol 1 pp 31ff

28. For a summary of this area see J M Turner in Davies op cit, vol II 1978, pp 97ff

29. H McLeod, *Religion and the People of Western Europe, 1789-1970*, OUP 1981, p39

30. E G Rupp, *Religion in England 1688-1791*, OUP 1986, pp449ff; J H S Kent, *The Unacceptable Face*, 1987, pp 111ff; M Hill, *A Sociology of Religion*, Heinemann, 1973, ch9; A Hartley, Elie Halévy and England Now, *Encounter*, XLIV pp 40-6; A Gilbert, Methodism, Dissent and Political Stability in Early Industrial England, *Journal of Religious History*, Vol 10, 1988, pp 381-99; S Piggin, A Marxist looks at Methodism, *World Methodist History Society*, 1981, pp 290-365; J D Walsh, *Proceedings of the Royal Historical Society*, Vol 25, 1975; B Semmel, *The Birth of Methodism*, Chicago, 1971, (This contains the English text of the 1907 articles by Halévy, *La Naissance du Methodism en Angleterre*)

31. E Hobsbawm, Methodism and the Threat of Revolution, in *Labouring Man*, Weidenfeld and Nicholson, 1964, ch 3; *Primitive Rebels*, Manchester 1959, ch 8; E Hobsbawm, *Worlds of Labour*, London, 1984, ch 3

32. E P Thompson, *Whigs and Hunters. The Origins of the Black Act*, Penguin, 1976; D Hay et al, *Albion's Fatal Tree. Crime and Society in Eighteenth Century England*, Allen Lane, 1975; E J Hobsbawm and G Rudé, *Captain Swing*, Lawrence and Wishart, 1969

33. M Edwards, *Methodism and England*, Epworth 1943, pp 36-48; P Magnus, *Gladstone*, 1963, p 80; K S Inglis, *The Church and the Working Class in Victorian England*, RKP, 1963, p 330

34. G K Clark, *The English Inheritance*, SCM, 1950, ch 8; G K Clark, *The Making of Victorian England*, Methuen 1965, ch 6; I Christie, *Stress and Stability in Late Eighteenth Century Britain. Reflections on the British Avoidance of Revolution*, OUP 1984; M T Thomis and P Holt, *The Threat of Revolution in Britain 1789-1848*, Macmillan, 1977

35. J D Walsh, The Origins of the Evangelicals in the Eighteenth Century. In M Simon, *Aspects de l'Anglicanisme*, 1974, pp 87-102; J M Turner, *Conflict and Reconciliation*, Epworth, 1985, ch 6

36. E Royle and J Walvin, *English Radicals and Reformers 1760-1848*, Harvester Press, 1982; E Royle, *The Infidel Tradition*, Macmillan, 1976;

cf J Foster, *Class Struggle and the Industrial Revolution*, Weidenfeld and Nicholson, 1974; R Q Gray, *The Labour Aristocracy in Victorian Edinburgh*, 1976; G Crossick, *An Artisan Elite in Victorian Society*, 1978; H McLeod, *Class and Religion in the late Victorian City*, London, 1974; H McLeod, White Collar Values and the Rôle of Religion in G Crossick (Ed), *The Lower Middle Class in Britain*, Croom Helm, 1977, pp 61-88; D Thompson, The Making of the English Religious Classes, *Historical Journal*, 22 1979, pp 477-491

37. R Currie, A D Gilbert and L Horsley, *Churches and Churchgoers*, OUP 1977

38. P S Bagwell, *Outcast London – a Christian Response*, Epworth, 1987, p 87

39. J F C Harrison, *The Common People*, Fontana, 1984

40. cited from Wilson in E P Thompson, *op cit*, p 438

41. P H Gosden, *Self Help. Voluntary Association in the Nineteenth Century*, 1973

42. M G Jones, *The Charity School Movement*, CUP 1938, p 146; T W Lacquer, *Religion and Respectability. Sunday Schools and Working Class Culture 1780-1850*, Yale 1976; W R Ward, *Religion and Society in England 1790-1850*, pp 12-16; H F Matthews, *Methodism and the Education of the People 1791-1851*, Epworth 1951

43. T Luckmann, *The Invisible Religion*, Macmillan, 1967; R Hoggart, *The Uses of Literacy*, Penguin 1958

44. B Harrison, Religion and Recreation in Nineteenth Century England, *Past and Present*, No 38, 1967; B Harrison, *Drink and the Victorians 1815-1872*, Faber 1971; L Billington, Popular Religion and Social Reform. A Study of Teetotalism and Revivalism 1830-50, *Journal of Religious History*, vol X, 1978-9; H McLeod, *Religion and the People of Western Europe 1789-1970*, Macmillan, 1981, pp 39ff

45. T H Green, *Lectures on the Principles of Political Obligation*, 1924 Ed, pp 206ff; O MacDonagh, *Early Victorian Government 1830-1870*, London 1977

46. H Perkin, *The Origins of Modern English Society 1780-1880*, 1969 RKP, pp 176ff; 340ff

47. R Moore, *Pitmen, Preachers and Politics. The Effects of Methodism in a Durham Mining Community*, CUP 1974

48. J Werner, *The Primitive Methodist Connexion*, Wisconsin, 1984; C Dews (Ed), *From Mow Cop to Peake*, Essay by J M Turner, gives an overview, 1982; D M Valenze, *Prophetic Sons and Daughters*, Princeton, 1985; J Obelkevich, *Religion and Rural Society, South Lindsey 1825-1875*, OUP 1976; R Colls, op cit; R Moore, op cit

49. R F Wearmouth, *Methodism and the Working Class Movement of England 1800-1850*, Epworth 1937

50. E J Hobsbawm, Primitive Rebels, Manchester, 1959

51. P Horn, *Labouring Life in the Victorian Countryside*, Macmillan, 1976; P Horn, Joseph Arch, Kineton, 1971

52. R F Wearmouth, op cit, p 213; A Briggs, *Chartist Studies*, Macmillan 1959, ch 4

53. S H Mayor, *The Church and the Labour Movement*, IP 1967, p 339
54. N Scotland, *Methodism and the Revolt of the Field*, Sutton, 1981; G Edwards, *From Crow Scaring to Parliament*, London 1957, p 36
55. J Obelkevich, op cit, p 258
56. D W Bebbington, *The Nonconformist Conscience, Chapel and Politics 1870-1914*, George Allen and Unwin, 1982; J H S Kent, Hugh Price Hughes and the Nonconformist Conscience, in G V Bennett and J D Walsh *op cit*, pp 181-205; J M Turner in Davies, George, Rupp, *op cit*, vol 3, pp 309ff
57. P S Bagwell, *Outcast in London. A Christian Response*, Epworth 1957
58. S Yeo, *Religion and Voluntary Organizations in Crisis*, Croom Helm, 1976; A D Gilbert, *The Making of Post-Christian Britain*, Longmans 1980. Both from different angles show the interaction of religion and society.

Note my recent article:
The Ghost of E P Thompson – 'Many Methodisms' and Social Change, in R Sykes (Ed) *God's Own Story – Some Trends in Methodist Histiography*, Oxford Brookes University, 2003, pp 13-21; and *John Wesley* (Epworth 2002), ch 7 *Did Methodism Prevent Revolution?*

Chapter 15

Preaching, Theology and Spirituality in Twentieth Century British Methodism

In recent years a surprising number of books on preaching have appeared, especially in America, across the theological spectrum. Very few, however, link theology's changing face with what actually happens in Christian pulpits or in the media. An exception was the work of Professor Horton Davies,[1] though he does not discuss preaching after 1965. So let us look at changes in theology or a few of the major ones and see how they affected preaching styles in Methodism. Was there anything distinctive in Methodism's ethos?

We begin with Liberal Protestantism. We would need a full analysis of Friedrich Schleiermacher who died in 1834 to get at the roots here. Much of his thinking was expressed in preaching trenchantly analysed by Karl Barth.[2] From Schleiermacher stems a stress on religious consciousness which can put human discovery on a par with God's revelation. Schleiermacher believed that besides *knowing* and *doing*, i.e. science and morality, there was another activity of the human spirit, the activity of *feeling*, the immediate self-consciousness, direct and self-authenticating. This is the source of religion. True religion is sense and taste for the infinite. We might compare Von Hügel's later division into the *institutional*, the *intellectual,* and the *mystical*. The influence of Schleiermacher on Methodism has clearly been pervasive rather than direct. Protestantism, perhaps especially Methodism, has stressed 'experience' in a particular sense, which parallels Bible, tradition and reason, the Anglican 'triad' going back to Richard Hooker. A Methodist historian of repute, Henry Bett, in the *Spirit of Methodism* tried to show that this position was impregnable to scientific undermining.[3] Bett's debt to Schleiermacher is clear enough, and also, I suspect, this was so of Herbert Workman who saw the essence of Methodism in the doctrine of assurance *not* Christian perfection, a position not generally accepted by Methodist scholars.[4]

Schleiermacher pushes all this further as a feeling of dependence – 'like a dog dependent on its master' sneered the philosopher Hegel – but Schleiermacher points to Jesus as showing the perfect God consciousness which was 'a veritable existence of God in him'. He is the one perfect revelation of God in the human race, his work as Redeemer consists in imparting to others the strength of his consciousness of God. The 'not yet' of imperfection really takes the place of original sin. He calls his stance the theology of pious self awareness and there is a lot of it about again in our post-modernist world.

Add to this the stress of Albrecht Ritschl on the Kingdom as 'the organization of humanity through action inspired by love' and the conviction of Adolf Harnack that the essence of Christianity is the Fatherhood of God and the infinite value of the human soul,[5] and you have the foundation for the so-called quest of the historical Jesus. For, says Ritschl, God's self-revelation in history is the starting point not the conclusion of dogmatic reflection. So get behind tradition – and Paul – to the 'real Jesus', 'the Jesus of Galilee or Jerusalem, the Jesus with the prophet's fire, who was so gentle to children and erring women and yet before whom canting hypocrites and truculent ecclesiastics slunk away abashed'.[6] So wrote R J Campbell of the City Temple, whom P T Forsyth called a theological quack!

Despite the devastating effect on all this of Albert Schweitzer in 1907, who showed the apocalyptic streak in Jesus,[7] this style of thinking became pervasive in Protestantism. Newton Flew once met T R Glover whose *Jesus of History* was so influential and said, 'I've been preaching your books'.[8] It can be shown that there was a shift from atonement to incarnation in the later nineteenth century. One recalls the meeting between John Scott Lidgett and his mentor, William Burt Pope. 'John Scott, I have fought a great battle this week and have won a great victory. You remember the first question and answer of the catechism. What is God? An infinite and eternal spirit. Well, I have got them to alter it now it is to be *Who is God? Our Father.*[9] Nevertheless Lidgett and Lofthouse wrote outstanding books on atonement.[10] There was more theological meat here than in the Congregationalist 'New Theology'. Pushing on a bit, at the time of Methodist union in 1932, Methodist scholars were much concerned with religious experience in the widest sense, evaluating it in the light of recent developments in psychology typified in writings like William James's *The Varieties of Religious Experience* with its famous division of people into the 'once born' and the 'twice born' Maldwyn Hughes's *The Theology of Religious Experience*, along with Ryder Smith's *The Christian Experience*, are typical of this mood with a fine final book in this genre from the lay educationalist and former Primitive Methodist, Victor Murray, *Personal Experience and the Historic Faith.* In this book, Murray showed how *feeling, knowing, choosing, doing* and *belonging* are essentials of full Christian experience. His fellow Primitive Methodist, J T Wilkinson would agree. 'I hold that the fundamental ground of religion is neither in the authority of the church nor in the authority of an infallible book but in the verdict that there is a good deal of Quaker strain in me.'[11]

Alongside and following the 'theology of experience' there was some renaissance of Methodist spirituality associated particularly with W R Maltby and the New Testament scholar, J A Findlay of Didsbury College. Bodies like the Fellowship of the Kingdom and the School of Fellowship exemplify this with a more catholic wing associated with T S Gregory, A E Whitham, and J E Rattenbury which created the Methodist Sacramental Fellowship in 1935. When the cry of 'Popery' went up, Rattenbury was able to show that the Fellowship was loyally Methodist with a long inheritance of styles of corporate prayer. Rattenbury combined this with a passion for evangelism,[12] which in various styles was never far below the surface in any of the Methodist groups, like those surrounding Samuel Chadwick at Cliff College who would not support any attempt to silence George Jackson whose *Preaching and the*

Modern Mind caused a flurry in 1913 when Jackson was appointed to Didsbury[13]. Chadwick recognized a fellow evangelist even if they differed.

But what of preaching? I asked my ninety year old Welsh grandfather in 1959 who the great Methodist preachers were in 1900. Like a shot, he said Hugh Price Hughes, Mark Guy Pearse and John Scott Lidgett. Guy Pearse did much of the work of the West London Mission, Scott Lidgett had been grandfather's minister in Wolverhampton so no surprise there, but what of the more conservative W L Watkinson and Dr Dinsdale Young who until 1936 maintained an unrepentant conservative evangelicalism laced with great humanity at Westminster Central Hall? He repeated his text so often that you never forgot it!

But change was coming. Let's enter the portals of Brunswick Chapel, Leeds in which the first sermon in 1825 had been preached by Jabez Bunting and alas the last one by me in 1969. No church illustrates the power of preaching better. Successively, Alfred E Whitham, Leslie Weatherhead and William E Sangster filled the church from 1920 to 1939.[14] Whitham had a delightful mixture of genuine folksiness with a deep sacramentalism and a rich conception of the incarnation. His deep spirituality cohered with a warm humanity. Weatherhead, whose *Discipleship* was still a classic in the 1940s, exploited all the discoveries of the new psychology not only to counsel and help people individually but in his preaching. He used every device to make Jesus real to contemporary people – and that is a characteristic of Methodist preaching at its best. His theology was Liberal Protestant with a deep sense of the historical Jesus not yet dimmed by the scepticism of the form critics. Weatherhead was not merely a dynamic personality, he had an almost hypnotic skill in blending worship and preaching to make Jesus a living force. After 1936 he was able to exercise his skill at the City Temple, seeing its rebuilding in 1958, an outstanding ministry of twenty-four years. He said that the aim of preaching was making God real and changing the lives of men and women. William Strawson sums up Weatherhead's message. 'Christianity is the acceptance of the gift of friendship of Jesus. The reality of this is known through *imagination* not rational argument. Despite its dangers – the experience is shown to be real in its effect – good impulses, victory over faults, a sense of beauty, deeper self-understanding and integration of the personality'. Weatherhead was no mean theologian – though his speculations made him suspect to some! Little books like *The Will of God* helped many to come to terms with Providence, evil and suffering in a war-torn world.

W E Sangster was a more conventional Evangelical – Methodist to the core though not a cradle Methodist. He had an immense knowledge of the saints and of ordinary human nature, with enormous skill in sermon construction and illustration. To some in Leeds he seemed more in touch with ordinary men and women than Weatherhead. Attendance at Holy Communion increased at Brunswick though only a tenth of the congregation were communicants. Sangster's last service at Brunswick was attended by 2000 people in August 1939 before he went to his great ministry at Central Hall,

Westminster. But it was a congregation swamping a smaller community. His successor, Garfield Lickes, a fine preacher had 200people a fortnight later on the day the Second World War began on 3rd September, 1939. Hereby hangs a grim premonition of the fate of the Methodist preaching tradition. But let's listen to Whitham!

'I must have dozed off for I thought I was treading the streets of the Holy City pottering about like a tourist. In my wandering I came across the museum of that city of our dreams. I went in and a courteous attendant conducted me round. There was some armour there much bruised with battle. Many things were conspicuous by their absence. I saw nothing of Alexander's nor Napoleon's. There was no Pope's ring nor even the inkwell Luther might have thrown at the Devil nor Wesley's seal and keys nor the first Minutes of the Conference nor the last (I was sorry about that because my name was in it). I saw a widow's mite and the feather of a little bird. I saw some swaddling clothes, a hammer and three nails and a few flowers – I saw a sponge that had been dipped in vinegar and a small piece of silver ... While I was turning over a common drinking cup which had a very honourable place I whispered to the attendant. Have you got a towel and a basin in your collection? No, he said, not here to see. They are in constant use.'[15]

It was easy in the 1950s to denigrate Liberal Protestantism, but it led many to the Lord who might have been alienated. The point is that it was always liberal *evangelism* personalized in preaching. Maldwyn Hughes, when Principal of Wesley College, Cambridge, could still end a sermon asking if his congregation had seen the light! Or whether they had the experience of the warmed heart. I heard J A Findlay once preach on the meeting of Jesus and the woman of Samaria in John 4. There was the woman, there was Jesus. There was Mount Zion, there was Mount Gerizim. We were *there*. The dialogue was analysed and applied to us as if it took place just as St John described it and as if we could cotton on to all the Johannine nuances. All this impinged on me as a teenager when in Wolverhampton our minister, H Mortimer Sinfield, a pupil of Findlay, gave us his theology tinged with the homiletical style of W E Sangster. He made Jesus real – human, master, example, Lord and Saviour and that 'strange man on the Cross', as George Tyrrell the Catholic modernist called him, had me for life! I recall my first Sunday as a student in Cambridge in October, 1949. In St Catharine's College chapel Professor Charles Raven preached on the text 'What think ye of the Christ. Whose Son is He?', a sermon he preached with passionate intensity to each new generation for decades! All of a piece with William Temple and Russell Maltby – and then there's Donald Soper![16]

Soper has been the best known Methodist preacher for decades now. He inherited the radical nonconformist tradition of the Forward Movement, Liberal Protestantism of a Ritschlian style, philosophical theology from F R Tennant at Cambridge, socialism, pacifism, sacramentalism of the Whitham style. Soper caught the imagination of many by his logical and debonair style and his superb skill at communication at every level, including radio, TV and the House of Lords. His principles are stated in *The Advocacy of the Gospel* especially the need for two pulpits – one in church, the other outside it. 'We are to communicate the love of Christ – *goodwill on fire*, indefatigable, undefeated ... the true preparation for the preaching of the Gospel is the possession of the golden secret of the love of God, a personal experience of forgiveness of sins and an overwhelming desire to communicate that experience to others that they may come to the saving grace of their Lord and ours'.[17] The Roman Catholic historian, Adrian Hastings, is right to state: 'Remove a few minor idiosyncrasies and Soper's Methodism, in its wide social and sacramental character, fits very much within the mainstream of modern English religion just as the evangelism of Billy Graham does not'.[18]

We have lingered long with the Liberal Protestant phase. But another had emerged long before. In Britain the Congregationalist, Peter Taylor Forsyth in *Positive Preaching and Modern Mind*, was reminting old words like cross, atonement, judgement and reconciliation. He was not afraid to speak of sin and its remedy. Karl Barth at Safenwil in Switzerland hearing the distant guns of the Western Front brooded over the horrible fact that all his old liberal teachers supported the Kaiser in World War One. It all seemed dust – he wrote his great commentary on Romans feeling like a boy stumbling into a dark church pulling a rope and setting the great bell ringing. He threw a bombshell into the playground on the theologians. This was all in the aftermath of the victorious generals who had nearly destroyed European civilization by the methods they employed to save it. Here was a theology of the Word of God. A snatch from the Barmen Declaration of 1934:

'Jesus Christ as he is attested to us in Holy Scripture is the one Word of God whom we have to hear and whom we have to trust and obey in life and death. We condemn the false doctrine that the church can and must recognize as gods or revelations, other events or powers forms and truths apart from and alongside this one Word of God'.[19]

That needs applying in its context of the Nazis and what the Nazis called 'German Christianity'. Did Barthianism impinge on Methodism? We were, I think, more influenced by the rather milder Emil Brunner who deeply influenced Percy Scott, the biblical theology of C H Dodd, T W Manson and the Methodists Vincent Taylor and Norman Snaith with Continentals like Oscar Cullmann and Joachim Jeremias, whose study of the Parables of Jesus seemed almost infallible in the 1950s.[20] When I was on holiday in Guernsey some years ago, the local minister gave us a short sermon that was so pure Jeremias that, clad in shirt and shorts, I couldn't resist saying, 'Thank you Dr Jeremias' as I left!

There was in the thirties also a rediscovery of the great Reformers led in England by a group of Methodist scholars who had studied in Germany or Sweden in the early days of the Third Reich led by Gordon Rupp, Philip Watson, Percy Scott, Stanley Frost (who later worked in Canada), Raymond George and Rupert Davies. They showed that to talk of the 'Catholicity of

Protestantism' was not to talk nonsense but to explore a wider church worship which led firmly to justification by faith and the Wesleyan 'Optimism of Grace' combined with a wider application of classical Protestantism.[21]

Gordon Rupp was the guru of the more theologically minded Methodists of the period after the Second World War.[22] As a preacher (or speaker) he was able remarkably to be *en rapport* with any congregation with a range of illustrations and metaphors from art and church history to the latest TV programme and detective stories old and new – how many spotted the reference to Edgar Wallace in his book title *Just Men*? He said that his one consistent vocation was that of a Methodist preacher. He believed, and here he was solidly Methodist, that a theology that could not be preached was not of great importance. These were the days of the rise and fall of Hitler, the German Church struggle, the Second World War and the division and reconstruction of Germany after it. History, theology preaching and current affairs are indivisible. Churchmanship for Rupp was always bound up with 'worldmanship' and what he called the 'priesthood of unbelievers', the challenge of an estranged world. Most of Rupp's sermons were never committed to paper – the sermon which led me to offer for the ordained ministry was one such and I never told the preacher of its effect for many years! But that is *precisely* what preaching is about! And remember Rupp caught his vision of ministry not in a church but hearing Donald Soper on Tower Hill in the later 1920s.

The Local Preachers' Department report of 1951 on *Doctrinal Preaching* was written by Rupp and has a quite different feel about it than the contemporary writings of W E Sangster. As I look at my own sermons no one has been more influential than Rupp, especially as seeing Church History as a huge 'internet' down which one travels and enjoys the 'ecumenism of time'. Here's a clip from a BBC talk in 1958:

Helmuth Gollwitzer has recently made an anthology of letters of men and women who in the last fifteen years have died for their faith. In it he has placed a photograph of a monastery garden in the city of Cologne. A monastery garden – that conjures up a peaceful scene of quiet retirement far away from the battles of the world. But this is as it looked the morning after the great blitz which dissolved that city in a sea of flame. It is full of great blocks of rubble, great boulders of charred wood. And there has fallen into it by accident, and upright, the stone figure of Christ the King. He stands buried in the debris which reaches up to his armpits but none the less he stands wearing his crown. Monarch of all he surveys even though it is the worst wicked men can do and he stands with is arms outstretched to save them – for king in the Bible is the Shepherd King, the King who serves, the Good Shepherd who lays down his life for the sheep, for the 'little flock' for his followers and for 'the others' for whose sake also he did not disdain to die.[23]

By 1960 preaching was in crisis. Adrian Hastings sharply states 'The mid 1950s can be dated precisely as the end of the age of preaching; people suddenly ceased to think it worthwhile to listen to a special preacher. Whether this was caused by the religious shift produced by the liturgical movement or by the spread of television or by some other alteration in human sensibility is not clear.'[24] Neville Ward twists the knife in the wound in 1967. 'Among Methodists this is particularly true in the contemporary decline of preaching, a decline so devastating that most Methodists now are reaching the exasperation long since reached by Anglicans and Roman Catholics in which one expects little from the sermon and often finds this expectation justified.'[25] When I became a tutor at Queen's College, Birmingham in 1970 preaching in its traditional form seemed in eclipse. Educationalists scorned it, oratory was at a discount, the authority figure was suspect, there were plenty of alternatives to the sheer slog of the craft and art of sermon making but not the slightest evidence that they attracted people to the churches. Our little book *Queen's Sermons* showed that all was not lost! By 1975 I detected a change – students actually wanted to learn the craft, the grumble now is at lack of role models. Mervyn Willshaw in 1982 could write of 'a decline and rise of preaching'. In the Church of Rome since the Second Vatican Council there has been a renewal of preaching. Not a few, too, have pointed to the need for variety in preaching.[26]

The radicalism of the 1960s did not suggest much of a role for the preacher but radicals really cannot exist without the institutions they profess to despise! I would single out Dr John Vincent. In the sixties he was Superintendent of the Rochdale Mission, and since 1970 leader of the Urban Theological Unit in Sheffield. Vincent called his theology 'radical Christology'. He had a deep belief on the validity of the quest for the historical Jesus setting out a christology and a theology of mission based almost entirely on the Synoptic Gospels. His *Christ and Methodism* rejected totally the old Wesleyan framework though he has picked up much of it again since, especially Wesley's desperate concern for the poor.[27] Here is a typical Vincent homiletic:

1. Christ is where his deeds are done, and the disciple is called to *service*.
2. Christ is where the ministry of healing and redemption is continued and the disciple is called to *healing*.
3. Christ Is being dealt with, ministered unto or rejected in the person of others – hidden within the secular and the disciple is called to *recognition*.
4. Christ is on the cross and the disciple is called to *suffering*.
5. Christ is ruling the universe both openly and secretly and the disciple is called to *indication*.[28]

While John Vincent was in Rochdale, Colin Morris was a missionary in what is now Zambia, radical in his interventions in politics, a supporter of violent means to bring down illegal and racist regimes such as the UDI 'Smith' government in Rhodesia, now Zimbabwe. For some in the sixties here was a new hero – the reverse side of the coin of the pacifist Donald Soper. But what were Morris's sources? He affirms that the theologians read most in Zambia were Reinhold Niebuhr and Karl Barth and if ever Colin Morris mentions preaching, and he has written two notable books on the craft,[29] the name that is inevitably quoted is Peter Taylor Forsyth. An interesting trio and all very different in theological style from the liberation theologians of South Africa like Gutiérrez and José Miguez Bonino, the latter of whom is an Argentinean Methodist.[30]

Thirteen years of preaching in Zambia was no sinecure! 'I entered a situation of racial tension and preached the odd sermon about human equality and the God given dignity of all men. They were not particularly good sermons but before I knew it my congregation was in uproar, my church desecrated, my manse under siege.' But what is it all for and here we hit again that central Methodist point 'When we have defined, dissected and analysed it ... the central function of preaching is to make Christians by confronting people with the claims of Jesus. The sermon may be an act of adoration, a method of teaching by exposition but at its heart must be a thrusting challenge, the articulation of God's imperious demands, the offer of his forgiveness and the gift of his grace.'[31] Methodism's 'optimism of grace', the idea that individuals and society can and shall be transformed. It is interesting that Colin Morris after long years in political activism and long spells in the BBC including a notable communication task in Ireland, still maintains his love of and belief in preaching and preaching in the classic style.

If the 1960s saw radical theologies eclipse the older 'biblical theology' in which many of us were reared, there was also the beginning of the Charismatic Movement and a renewal of Evangelicalism across the churches and especially in the Church of England. The characteristics of Evangelicalism – the centrality of the *Bible*, the *Cross*, *conversion* and *activism* came to the fore again. If in the 1950s and 1960s no great ecumenical assembly was without a rousement by Gordon Rupp, after 1970 his place was taken by Dr Donald English, Chair of the World Methodist Council. Rupp, Sangster and Soper all came from London: English, by contrast was involved for some years with the Inter-Varsity Fellowship and brought a different style. At first a modification of the familiar Evangelical 'Bible Reading' stemming back to the Keswick Convention. But there is again the typical Methodist apostolic optimism perhaps at first somewhat more pietist than Rupp – *The Meaning of the Warmed Heart* is a pointer to that.[32] Just occasionally he was inclined to toss in a sentimental illustration, but over the years he developed in style and in graphic illustration and, not least, penetrating to the needs of modern culture. His most recent book must be one of the most succinct and pungent projections of church life into the new millennium and as a preacher he was probably unequalled in contemporary Methodism.[33]

Our story is coming to a close. Our thesis is that there is a Methodist thread of apostolic optimism and of the centrality of Christ in devotion and evangelism. But pause! Most Methodist sermons have been and are preached not by ministers but by local preachers, men and women. It would be ridiculous and patronizing not to end with them. We could look at the philosopher, T E Jessop at Hull, or the long and brilliant persuasive preaching and writing of Dr Pauline Webb who can still show 'em how it's done on Radio 4! There was Charles Coulson who did so much to enable scientists and Christians to cease eyeing one another with suspicion. One might take educationalists like Dr Marjorie Lonsdale or Ernest R Taylor of my *Alma Mater*, Wolverhampton Grammar School. I well remember him preaching a fine sermon called 'A historian looks at the Resurrection', still badly needed when the media can go bananas over an ossuary!

But I go to Yorkshire where at the beginning of the century Dorothy Hincksman Farrar and Herbert Butterfield were born in different strata of the Methodist constituency. Dorothy Farrar became a notable leader of spirituality at the Deaconess Institute at Ilkley. Herbert Butterfield became Regius Professor on Modern History at Cambridge and Vice Chancellor. Both kept their names on the list of local preachers to the end. So I end with a quotation from Dr Farrar and then one from Sir Herbert, who could at times be naughty and even outrageous but whose influence was immense.

Men and women who have loved God have never been able to think of their communion with Him as ending with their death. On the contrary, they have longed for a deeper communion when they would see God more clearly and love Him more perfectly than is possible in this life. Their longing has a curious certainty about it as though they had some inner assurance from God Himself that their hopes would not be disappointed.[34]

And the historian? I heard Butterfield preach at Wesley, Cambridge in 1950. the sermon is to be found in his book *History and Human Relations*.

One of the most solemn facts in all history – one of the most significant for anybody who cares to ponder over it – is the fact that Jesus Christ was not merely murdered by hooligans on a country road; he was condemned by everything that was most respectable in that day, everything that pretended to be most righteous – the religious leaders of the time, the authority of the Roman government and even the democracy itself which shouted to save Barabbas rather than Christ … Our attitude to the crucifixion must be that of self-identification with the rest of human nature. WE must say we did it.

And what set of Cambridge Divinity School lectures ever ended more dramatically?

I have nothing to say at the finish except that if one wants a permanent rock in life and goes deep enough for it, it is difficult for historical events to shake it. There are times when we can never meet the future with sufficient elasticity of mind especially if we are locked in the contemporary systems of thought. We can do worse than remember a principle which both gives us a firm rock and leaves us the maximum elasticity for our minds, the principle Hold to Christ and for the rest be totally uncommitted.

At the end of his life in 1979 he bade us remember that secularization gives the church its greatest chance of offering its gospel for a millennium! 'There is a Providence in the historical process which makes it more profitable to be guided by one's hopes than by one's fears.'[35] There is the essential optimism of grace which is at the heart of Methodist spirituality, theology and preaching, or so I believe.

References

1. H Davies, *The Ecumenical Century: Worship and Preaching in England, 1900-1965* (OUP, 1965, new edition, Eerdmans, 1996), chs IV, V, VI
2. Karl Barth, *The Theology of Schleiermacher* (T&T Clark, 1983); *Protestant Theology in the Nineteenth Century* (SCM Press, 1972)
3. Henry Bett, *The Spirit of Methodism* (Epworth Press, 1937), 131ff
4. H B Workmann, *The Place of Methodism in the Catholic Church* (Epworth Press 1921)
5. H R Mackintosh, *Types of Modern Theology* (Nisbet, 1937); A Harnack, *What is Christianity?* (E T Benn, 1958), esp. 51-62; K W Clements, *Lovers of Discord: Twentieth Century Theological Controversies in England* (SPCK, 1988), esp. ch 2; P Hinchliff, *God and History: Aspects of British Theology 1875-1914* (OUP, 1992), esp. chs 9 and 10; R N Flew, *Jesus and His Church* (Epworth Press, 1938), 20
6. R J Campbell, *The New Theology* (Chapman and Hall, 1907) 80-81
7. A Schweitzer, *The Quest of the Historical Jesus* (E T Black, 1910)
8. Boyd Hilton, *The Age of Atonement* (OUP, 1988); G S Wakefield, *Robert Newton Flew* (Epworth Press, 1971), 90
9. R E Davies (Ed), *John Scott Lidgett* (Epworth Press, 1957), 84
10. J S Lidgett, *The Spiritual Principle of Atonement* (Kelly, 1897); W F Lofthouse, *Ethics and Atonement* (Methuen, 1906); *Altar, Cross and Community* (Epworth Press, 1921)
11. H Maldwyn Hughes, *The Theology of Experience* (Kelly, 1915); E S Waterhouse, *The Philosophy of Religious Experience* (Epworth Press, 1923); C Ryder Smith, *The Christian Experience* (Epworth Press, 1926); Victor Murray, *Personal Experience and the Historic Faith* (Epworth Press, 1939); A Wilkinson, *Dissent or Conform?* (SCM Press, 1986)
12. J E Rattenbury, *Evangelism, its Shame and Glory* (Epworth Press, 1932); *Evangelism in Pagan England* (Epworth Press, 1954); H B Rattenbury, *Rat-Rhyme* (Artprint, 1994), 15-20; P W Chilcote, *The Legacy of J E Rattenbury* (Doxology, 3, 1986, 11-28)
13. G Jackson, *The Preacher and the Modern Mind* (Kelly, 1912); D W Bebbington, 'The Persecution of George Jackson: A British Fundamentalist Controversy' (in W J Sheils, Ed, *Persecution and Toleration*, Blackwell, 1984, 421-432)

14. A E Whitham, *The Discipline and Culture of the Spiritual Life* (Hodder and Stoughton, 1938); *The Pastures of His Presence* (Hodder and Stoughton, 1939); *The Catholic Christ* (Hodder and Stoughton, 1940); Leslie D Weatherhead, *The Transforming Friendship* (Epworth Press, 1928); *Jesus and Ourselves* (Epworth Press, 1930); *Discipleship* (Epworth Press, 1934); S A Odom, Ed, *Steady and Unsteady World: Sermons of Weatherhead* (Judson Press, 1986); W Strawson, 'The Significance of L D Weatherhead as Preacher' (in *The Methodist Recorder*, 9 June 1977); W E Sangster, *Westminster Sermons*, 2 Vols (Epworth Press, 1960, 1961); Sangster's early works were devotional writings but his four books on preaching were much read in their day: *The Craft of Sermon Illustration* (1956); *The Craft of Sermon Construction* (1949); *The Approach to Preaching* (1951); *Power in Preaching* (1958), all published by Epworth Press; C Morris, *Raising the Dead* (Harper Collins, Fount, 1996), xiv

15. A E Whitham, op cit, pp 40-41

16. B Frost, *Goodwill on Fire: Donald Soper's Life and Mission* (Hodder and Stoughton, 1996)

17. D O Soper, *The Advocacy of the Gospel* (Hodder and Stoughton, 1961), 39, 115

18. A Hastings, *A History of English Christianity 1920-1985* (Collins, 1986), 462-464

19. 'Doctrinal Proclamation of the German Confessional Church at First Synod of Barmen, 29-30 May 1934' (in J H Leith, ed., *Creeds of the Churches*, John Knox Press, 1982, 517ff)

20. cf O Cullmann, *Christ and Time* (SCM Press, 1951); J Jeremias, *The Parables of Jesus* (SCM Press, 1954); *New Testament Theology* (SCM Press, 1971)

21. R N Flew and R E Davies, eds., *The Catholicity of Protestantism* (Lutterworth Press, 1950); E G Rupp, *The Righteousness of God: Luther Studies* (Hodder and Stoughton, 1953)

22. J M Turner, 'Gordon Rupp as Historian' (*Epworth Review,* 1991, 70-82); E G Rupp, *The Sixty Plus and Other Sermons* (Collins, 1978)

23. E G Rupp, *Worldmanship and Churchmanship* (Epworth Press, 1958), 29-30

24. A Hastings, op cit, 465

25. Neville Ward, *The Use of Praying* (Epworth Press, 1967) 15

26. M Willshaw, 'The Decline and Rise of Preaching' 9in R E Davies, Ed, *The Testing of the Churches 1932-1982* (Epworth Press, 1982); M J Townsend, 'Preaching – Twenty-Five Years of Ups and Downs' (*Expository Times*, 95, 1983-84, 132-135); J M Turner, 'Is Preaching Outmoded' (*Worship and Preaching*, April 1975, 4-8); 'Preaching' (in D Pickford, ed., *The Future of Methodism: Approaching End or New Beginning?* (NACCAN, 1985, 23-26)

27. J J Vincent, *Christ and Methodism* (Epworth Press, 1965); *OK! Let's Be Methodists* (Epworth Press, 1989)

28. J J Vincent, *Secular Christ* (Lutterworth Press, 1968), 218; Colin Morris, *Mankind My Church* (Hodder and Stoughton, 1971)

29. Colin Morris, *The Word and the Words* (Epworth Press, 1975); *Raising the Dead: The Art of the Preacher as Public Reformer* (Fount, 1996)

30. G Guttiérrez, *The Theology of Liberation* (SCM Press, 1975); J Miguez Bonino, *Doing Theology in a Revolutionary Situation* (Fortress Press, 1975)

31. C Morris, *The Word and the Words*, 58, 145; D W Bebbington, *Evangelicalism in Modern Britain* (Unwin Hyman, 1989)

32. Donald English, *The Meaning of the Warmed Heart* (Methodist Home Mission Department, 1984)

33. Donald English, *Into the Twenty-First Century* (Methodist Publishing House, 1995)

34. D H Farrar, 'The Preacher's Life of Prayer' (in G P Lewis, ed., *The Preacher's Handbook* No. 1, 1949, 1-6)

35. H Butterfield, *Christianity and History* (Bell, 1949); *History and Human Relations* (Collins, 1951), 37-65; *Writings on Christianity and History* (OUP, 1979), 248-260.

Chapter 16

Church, State and Society – 2003

Archbishop Rowan Williams, in his Dimbleby Lecture in December 2002, spoke of 'the end of the Nation state'. Can the state guarantee economic equilibrium? Could it ever? Is maximum choice enough? Roger Scruton in *The West and the Rest – Globalization and the Terrorist Threat*[1] asks whether we face a clash of civilizations and the end of the 'social contract' – the same point in effect. I remember the first sentence of a Cambridge lecture course on Political Thought given by Dr Christopher Morris, whose expertise was in Tudor political theory. 'What is the state? Why should I obey it?' As he took us from Plato to NATO, he never let us forget those *very* old questions.

What is the state? Is it bound up totally with the organism of society; is it a 'machine' of society, seeking the 'greatest happiness of the greatest number' – the utilitarian liberal concept; or is it in the end the instrument of the ruling class or clique or revolutionaries as Marx affirmed, and as Mugabe and Saddam Hussein have shown in Zimbabwe and Iraq? R M McIver, in his classic *The Modern State*[2] distinguishes 'state' from 'society'. The state orders life but does not create it. It is, as it were, the paved highway of life, bordered by fields and cities. All the business of life is rendered possible by its aid and all who live along it must contribute to its upkeep, be 'stakeholders' as we now say. The highway is for the sake of the life that is lived along it and beyond it. The state is an organization created by the community as an instrument to serve the purpose of its members. Clearly we need to distinguish also between the state and the government. This is the liberal democratic view. Liberal democracies see the state as an instrument of society. 'Why should I obey it? – because I am a stakeholder in it.' What if I don't feel like that, as some Muslims would put it, feeling alienated? If a Nation's Constitution is democratic, should all religions and other parts of the plurality of society be equal before the law? Is an 'established' or 'national' Church compatible with such equality? Would its absence create the 'moral vacuum' Dr Williams talks about? 'Established' means any Church whose doctrines, worship and discipline are supported in some way by civil law, 'National' signifies a Church, which is independent of ecclesiastical control from outside that Church – 'No control by the Pope', as Henry VIII put it. This dual relationship has long existed in some Eastern Orthodox Churches. The system began to occur in Western Europe with the rise of the Nation state and the Reformation.

The British Isles has four 'models' of Church-state relationship. In England, the Church of England is by 'law established', that is it has a recognised, civic primacy with the monarch as its 'Supreme Governor', its principal bishops as part of the legislature, being members of the House of Lords. Church law is incorporated in the law of the realm. Parliament has a final veto on doctrine and worship, though its power has been dramatically limited by the Worship and Doctrine Measure of 1974. Free Church people should remember that we needed the Methodist Church Union Act of 1929 to legalise the union of 1932, and the Methodist Church Act of 1976 to define the purposes of the Methodist Church, and to extend Conference's powers to amend the Deed of Union to include the doctrinal standards clause.

Apologists for establishment, like Dr John Habgood,[3] claim that establishment enables the Church of England to exercise pastoral care of the whole population, building on the 'folk religion' of the past which he claims – I fear, dubiously, in the North – to be basically Anglican, giving the church its role as a critical and befriending counterbalance to the state within rather than outside the corridors of power. One thinks of Bishop George Bell's 'creative dissent' during the Second World War. More recently David Jenkins (mischievously?) defended establishment, because it gave him a platform for his radicalism!

On the other hand, the non-established dissenting Churches have had to fight for their status, still suffering from 'the assumption of effortless superiority', which an establishment unconsciously displays, provoking dissenting cantankerousness. Many viewed the establishment of the largest of the fragments into which the Western Church divided at the Reformation to be an injustice both to other ecclesiastical bodies and to those who are not Christians. They assert that a nation's national character is a matter of how it understands its ecclesiastical calling and does not depend on the status, which the state gives or allows. Some Anglicans, like the late Valerie Pitt, made the point as strongly as any Free Church person in the last major report on *Church and State* way back now in 1970. This was sharper, indeed, than the Free Church Report of 1953 which said that 'the Church of England would be gravely prejudiced if the essential and constitutional Protestantism of the Church of England became a dead letter'.[4]

More radical Christians see establishment as morally indefensible, inhibiting prophetic utterance and action. Christianity is not a 'civic' or 'folk' religion but demands an active and total allegiance to Christ. Reunion negotiations, especially the Anglican-Methodist Scheme of 1958-72 deemed some form of drastic change necessary. It is certainly on the agenda again from various angles inside and outside the Churches. Richard Dawkins recently said that state-sponsored education was a form of child abuse!

But there are other parts of Great Britain where the pattern is quite different. In Scotland the Church of Scotland, whose polity is Presbyterian, is established but autonomous. 'As a national church representative of the Christian faith of the Scottish people, it acknowledges the distinctive call and duty to bring the ordinances of religion to the people of Scotland through territorial ministry (1921).' This national recognition is linked with spiritual independence. Nevertheless smaller Churches in Scotland did feel marginalised, like the Methodist Synod in Scotland when it rejected union –

though there is quite a different 'feel' now. Cultural and national factors loomed large also. I recall Dr John Habgood, when Principal of Queen's College, saying he was glad he had been the Anglican Rector of Jedburgh in Scotland for five years, because he knew what it was like to be a dissenter! It will be fascinating to see how all this works out with new styles of government in Scotland as well as striking new initiatives in Church unity, but also disappointment, so far, from the Church of Scotland, while the Episcopal Church has accepted the possibility of women bishops.

In Wales and Northern Ireland, the Anglican Churches were disestablished by Gladstone in the Irish case, and Asquith and Lloyd George in the former. They were clearly minority Churches. Ecumenism in Wales is expressed nationally by a Covenant between Anglican and most non-episcopal Churches concerning ministry, worship, mission and education, a position not yet achieved in England. The rejection by the Church in Wales of an 'ecumenical bishop' seemed a reverse, though maybe local bishops in one area is not the wisest way forward. The Anglican Church in Wales has become more closely involved with Welsh culture since its disestablishment, while the Welsh non-episcopal Churches have endured sharp decline associated with social and economic factors such as the collapse of the coal industry in the villages, where chapels had once multiplied, and population movement and decline.

On a world scale the post-Second World War concept of a neutral, pluralist state with no dominant religious ideology has clashed with more traditional ideas of a confessional state – Christian, increasingly Islamic, as in Pakistan or in India, Hindu. All rather different from the 'Western' ideology of Pandit Nehru. With the rise of Islamic states in many parts of the world, there is need again for the ecumenical movement to take up a serious study of secular and democratic options. Yet the last World Council of Churches General Assembly gave President Mugabe a standing ovation in Harare! I do not forget, when I was President of the Council of Churches in Halifax, commenting on the Salman Rushdie 'death threat'. A leading Muslim wrote in the *Halifax Evening Courier* that I was a typical, modern, liberal Christian, who would not die for my faith. The Muslim voice is more sympathetic to establishment and compulsory religious education than sometimes we realise. Some Muslims clearly feel that disestablishment would mean marginalisation of all faiths.

We cannot forget, too, the tremendous changes in the post 1989 world. Eric Hobsbawm's penetrating book[5] on last century calls the period 1914-1989 'the Short Twentieth Century'. In 10 years the Soviet Empire crumbled. In South Africa the famous 'Kairos Document' of 1985 asserted that all Church life must be politicised since 'the church cannot collaborate with tyranny'. And now? Can a post-Mandela regime create a new South Africa? What is the role of churches there or in Zimbabwe? In Russia the Methodist Church has been given a civil status only after quite a struggle. Its Bishop, Rüdiger Minor, can now freely order his Church – but not all Christian bodies can do so, and the Orthodox bitterly resent them as interlopers.

Let us earth all this in England now in areas where there is sharp controversy:

1   Education

We can hardly think ourselves back into the bitter controversies over Education in Victorian times. Since 1870 when the 'School Boards' (later after 1902 LEAs) came into existence, we have had the 'dual system' of state and Church schools. In 1880 there were more Wesleyan schools – 900 – than Roman Catholic ones – though 'Rome' soon caught up. J H Rigg,[6] the formidable Wesleyan Principal of Westminster College, London, wanted a strong 'dual system' with Methodism keeping its schools. He fought hard against the Congregationalist R W Dale who wanted a totally secular system in which the Churches should teach 'religion'. His was an optimistic view of the Churches' strength. That particular rift has continued. Can the demands of the 1944 and 1988 Acts about 'collective worship' continue? Is 'religion' part of our historical heritage that it cannot be ignored? Is worship in state schools a mockery? Is a teaching of all the religions in a phenomenological manner the sure road to secularism and pluralism? Or are we pluralist anyway, a matter which William Temple would not have contemplated when he said: 'Schools should offer both individual development and a sense of world fellowship. There is only one candidate for this double function, it is Christianity.' Temple and Spencer Leeson[7] did not anticipate how pluralist post-war Britain was to become. I recall as a teenager clear calls to vocation to teach given in the church, with our training colleges available – we need this again in all the churches.

2   The Parish System

Can the Anglican claim to minister to all, as distinct from 'gathered churches', be maintained? Anglican churches are very much 'gathered', representing often one particular style – Evangelical, charismatic, Catholic, Liberal. Are we not all part of a religious market economy? People pick a church for lively worship, warm fellowship and something good for the children. Roman Catholic and Methodist churches are as concerned for community as Anglicans. There is still enormous scope for genuine partnership even if Local Ecumenical Partnerships and local Covenants are not always possible. Could the plight of some rural churches be alleviated if Anglicans trusted Methodists with worship leadership? The 'scalded cat' priest scurrying from one Eucharist to another is little use to anyone. Let us hope that if the Covenant cuts ice it can lead to more creative mobilisation of Christian resources. In areas of the North West I am sure there are untapped political and theological resources still unshared despite the creative work of both Luther King House and the Northern Ordination Course. There are many 'lone workers' in congregations doing their own things, not always aware of the 'Networks' and opportunities available. The 'Hoddle Affair' – remember that? – made me realise that the Churches together face a tremendous apologetic task which our theological resource centres must undertake with rigour and vigour.

3   National Establishment

Some years ago Dr Wesley Carr of Westminster Abbey kicked off a new style *Theology* magazine with an interesting article on establishment.[8] His 'spin' seemed a curious mixture of 'management styles' and conservatism. Is that where we are stuck? The Chadwick Report of 1970 suggested a new style of second chamber, a debate still continuing. What will be the role of the Churches in an elected or nominated Second Chamber? The single excellent Free Church peer like the late Lord Soper or the Baroness Richardson is not the answer. But what is? It is fascinating now to read Free Church cries at the beginning of the 20th century about the awful nature of 'the Beerage' and all that, a mood as dead as the dodo after World War One. But have the churches any really positive ideas? And the Monarchy?

I can't get worked up about Camilla Parker Bowles, but what of Prince Charles' desire to be 'Defender of Faith' not of *the faith*? The whole history of that phrase, given to Henry VIII by the Pope for his attacks on Luther, suggests an anachronism to say the least, as is much else stemming from the wars of religion such as the *Act of Settlement* of 1701, but revocation is more complex than it might seem. What of a Coronation with proper involvement of all the Churches – and, question mark, religions? Is such a ceremony possible? Will a Eucharist still be central as Archbishop Williams foresees? I recall Professor Norman Sykes working very hard on the 1953 Coronation. Who is really thinking it out now? Ian Bradley's recent book gives a few clues.[9]

I recall Rupert Davies' last letter to the *Methodist Recorder* in 1994[10] advocating Disestablishment. He did so as a genuine ecumenist. It is easy to advocate, but not so easy to see what should take its place. The USA does not suggest a good example, where 'fundamentalism' can play an ominous role. It is interesting that Roman Catholic writers in this area, like Adrian Hastings, did not take this position but looked for other models of establishment like Scotland. Hastings clearly feared an apparent repudiation of Christianity and I think was right to fear it. Is an apparent tolerant, neutralist state pursuing in utilitarian terms 'the greatest happiness of the greatest number' really what we desire? D L Munby[11] (now forgotten) in 1963 traced his idea of a secular society, which was to be pluralist, tolerant, pragmatic with no ruling ideology or world view. Establishments were simply 'vestigial survivals of the past, of little practical value'. Is it unrealistic or old-fashioned to say 'No' to that kind of liberalism and 'political correctness', which can so easily mask a subtle kind of totalitarianism, where any dissenters had better hold their tongues or be sacked? World religions are far from declining.

I end with two quotations, which are still germane. One is from that great romantic, Samuel Coleridge.[12] He said that the Church Catholic is 'the sustaining, correcting, befriending opposite of the world, the compensating counterforce to the inherent and inevitable evils and defects of the state'. The other is from the Cambridge historian, Sir Herbert Butterfield.[13] It is from a book of essays published in the year of his death in 1979. He was strangely prophetic at that time, even fearing the re-emergence of a clash between Christianity and Islam. 'Secularism is very hostile to Christianity at the moment and partly for understandable reasons but it is fickle, flexible and amorphous ... liable to sink back into dark astrologies, weird theosophies and bleak superstitions.' That, no doubt, is one reason why Christianity found its opportunity in the ancient Roman Empire. 'I think that the spread of secularism offers Christianity not only the greatest test but the greatest opportunity it has ever had in history ... There is a providence in the historical process which makes it more profitable to be guided by one's faith and one's hopes than by one's fears.' Is that now too optimistic in a postmodern world where writers like Callum Brown wrote of the death of Christian Britain?

My own view is not dissimilar from that of the late Adrian Hastings – a revised Establishment, more like that of Scotland than England. Maybe an Archbishop of the calibre of Rowan Williams can point towards the possibilities? Total disestablishment could lead to a nation more secular and chaotic with no common values – and we haven't much time to waste.

References

1   Roger Scruton, *The West and the Rest – Globalization and the Terrorist Threat*, Continuum 2002

2   R M McIver, *The Modern State*, OUP 1926, p 4, pp 482ff

3   J S Habgood, *Church and Nation in a Secular Age*, DLT 1983

4   *Church and State*, CIO, 1970, esp. pp 68ff; *The Free Churches and the State*, FCFC 1953; P M H Bell, *Disestablishment in Ireland and Wales*, SPCK 1969

5   E J Hobsbawm, *Age of Extremes. The Short Twentieth Century 1914-1991*, Michael Joseph 1994

6   J T Smith, *Methodism and Education 1849-1902*, OUP 1998

7   S Leeson, *Christian Education*, Longmans Green 1947

8   Cf W Carr, *Say One for Me. The Church of England in the Next Decade*, SPCK 1992; ibid *The Priestlike Task*, SPCK 1985

9   I Bradley, *God Save the Queen. The Spiritual Dimension of Monarchy*, DLT 2002

10   R E Davies, *The Church of England Observed*, Epworth Press 1984; ibid *The Methodist Recorder* 19 March 1994

11   D L Munby, *The Idea of a Secular Society*, OUP 1963

12   S T Coleridge, *On The Constitution of Church and State*, Ed J Barrett, Dent 1972, p 98

13   H Butterfield, *Writings on Christianity and History*, Ed C T McIntire, OUP 1979, p 251, p 260; cf for different viewpoints: G Davie, *Religion in Britain. Believing Without Belonging*, Blackwell 1994; C G Brown, *The Death of Christian Britain*, Routledge 2001; J Moses, *A Broad and Living Way. Church and State, a Continuous Establishment*, Canterbury Press 1995; A Warren (Ed), *A church for the Nation*, Gracewing 1992

Study Questions

1   Is the Establishment of one church now outmoded? If so, why?

2   Does 'folk religion' play any role now in British life? Should this be expressed by a national Church?

3   Are non-established Churches more 'prophetic' than the Church of England or Scotland?

4   Are we right still to expect worship in state schools?

5   How should 'the Covenant' affect the parish system? Is the parish idea a help or a hindrance to the Church of England?

6   What roles should faith communities play in a second chamber?

7   Can the monarchy be 'Defender of *Faith*' rather than of '*The Faith*'?

Epilogue

The Effect of Historians and Theologians on Preaching 1950-2008

How do theologians and their writings affect the preacher? This epilogue is a kind of theological autobiography. Some theologians have greatly influenced how I have preached, and what has been the heart of the faith for me.

Let me begin as a schoolboy. My first real encounter with Jesus was when listening to Dorothy L Sayers' *The Man Born to be King* on the radio during the Second World War. Jesus was no longer just a pious name. At Wolverhampton Grammar School we were taught the outline of the Bible in RE, and at Assembly some of the great hymns and prayers. In the Sixth Form, the Head, Warren Derry, took us through William Temple's *Christian Faith and Life* – the sermons which had a great impact at Oxford in 1931. Very often I have used Temple's version of the fable of the Grand Inquisitor from Dostoevsky on the first Sunday in Lent. Only last week I quoted Temple's definition of worship:

Worship is the submission of all our nature to God. It is the quickening of conscience by his holiness; the nourishment of mind with his truth; the purifying of imagination by his beauty; the opening of the heart to his love; the surrender of will to his purpose – and all this gathered up in adoration, the most selfless emotion of which our nature is capable, and therefore the chief remedy for all self-centredness which is our original sin and the source of all acts of sin,[1]

I began to read C S Lewis at that time. Much later I realized his astute way of putting complex matters like the Trinity and the Atonement in ways which the ordinary layperson could grasp. Dr Richard Harries, while not uncritical, saw Lewis as stating 'mainstream Christianity' read by all kind of Christians still.[2] In 2008 *The Times* had a list of the fifty greatest writers since 1945. Lewis came eleventh. His friend J R R Tolkien (*The Lord of the Rings*) came sixteenth. I recall quoting Lewis to Warren Derry. 'A man who was merely a man and said the sort of things Jesus said wouldn't be a great moral teacher. He'd either be a lunatic – on a level with the man who says he's a poached egg – or else he'd be the Devil of Hell. You must make your choice. Either this man was and is the Son of God or else a madman or something worse'.[3] *That* is not good apologetic, think out *why*, was the reply. He then told us that he had dinner with C S Lewis the previous week at his college – Magdalen, Oxford! He thought him brilliant but odd! Maybe, but I couldn't resist him.

At that time, I was a member of the large 'Questors' Youth Club at Beckminster Methodist Church. I trained as a church member under the Rev'd H M Sinfield. At one evening service, he made one of his periodical appeals for commitment to Christ. I had a genuine conversion experience at the Holy Communion which followed. This put the Eucharist for me, with preaching, at the heart of faith and practice. I began to explore the life and teaching of John Wesley and was 'plugged' into the Methodist tradition, continuing that while a student as a member of the Cambridge Methodist Society.

At an entrance examination in German, I had to translate a passage from Karl Barth. I asked Warren Derry about Barth. He lent me H R Mackintosh's *Types of Modern Theology*[4] – studies of Hegel, Schleiermacher, Ritschl, Troeltsch, Kierkegaard and Barth! I wonder how many sixth formers were given *that* to read! I studied it again as a Probationer Minister in 1956.

In 1949, I went up to St Catharine's College, Cambridge to read History. An immediate great influence was Herbert Butterfield, Professor of Modern History. His *Christianity and History* I read in *The Listener* some months before. Who can forget its ending?

'If one wants a permanent rock in life and goes deep enough for it, it is difficult for historical events to shake it. There are times when we can never meet the future with sufficient elasticity of mind, especially if we are locked in the contemporary systems of thought. We can do worse than remember a principle which gives us a firm rock and leaves us the maximum elasticity for our minds; the principle: Hold to Christ and for the rest be totally uncommitted.'

I would rate this book as one of the dozen most significant books both on the meaning of history and theology since the Second World War. Butterfield's Augustinian view of humanity is realistic. 'It is essential not to have faith in human nature. Such faith is a recent heresy and a very disastrous one ... what history does is to uncover man's universal 'sin'. Dare we quote this when thinking of the era of violence? 'Sometimes God has only to withhold his protection and let events take their course: "I will hide my face from them and I will see what their end shall be" – and the penalty comes from his formidable non-intervention'. Even in 2008, President George Bush might note: 'When men used to talk about making the world safe for democracy, one suspected one heard half an echo of a satirical laugh a great distance away somewhere amongst the inter-planetary space'. Yet, later when predicting a new rise of Islam, he felt that 'the church had its best chance for centuries to offer its gospel, if it ceased to strive for power and prestige'.[5] It is interesting that Professor David Ford in his great study of modern theology puts Butterfield in the fold as a theologian along with another great Cambridge mentor of many of us, church historian Professor Norman Sykes, under whom I studied English church, state and society.[6] It was he who suggested that I researched Anglican-Methodist relations after John Wesley, which, in the end, resulted in my book *Conflict and Reconciliation* in 1985. This period saw me become a Methodist local preacher. The theological text book was Maldwyn Hughes' *Christian Foundations*, a fine if now dated summary of the heart of the matter from a Methodist but not sectarian angle.[7] Newton Flew's *Jesus and His Church*[8] came into the picture as did, when thinking of the meaning of the Incarnation, Donald Baillie's *God Was In Christ*.[9] I found his picture of Jesus showing God's grace, free love and spontaneous generosity, and faith, total trust in God the Father in which we can all share, fully believable. God means: 'The one who at the same time makes absolute demands upon us and freely offers to give us all that he demands. It means the one who requires of us unlimited obedience and then supplies the obedience himself'. Rudolf Bultmann was right to call this book the most important in our time on Christology.

This was the period of what is now called 'Biblical Theology'. Thinking of the end of things (eschatology) how many of us quoted Oscar Cullmann[10] and his analogy of D-Day and V-Day, or C H Dodd's subtle picture of 'realized eschatology'. I have quoted to this day, this passage from Dodd:

'Unlike his first coming, it is not an event *in* history. It is the point at which *all* history is taken up into the larger whole of God's eternal purpose. It is the point at which not only the latest achievements of the race find fulfilment, but its forgotten struggles, and even its failures. And the forgotten people, whose struggles never showed any success will find their fulfilment too ... We speak of it as His *Second* Coming and that should keep us in mind that there was a first. At that one point God in Christ made himself into a character in history ... Singly we must pass the last frontier when our time is up. In a real sense that is the moment when Christ comes again for each of us, but everywhere in the New Testament it is mankind corporately that is in view when Christ is contemplated coming in glory to judge the living and the dead'.[11]

Is Dodd dated? Bishop Tom Wright[12] has recently opened up in great detail the whole area of eschatology in terms not of the immorality of the soul, but of resurrection. Is it the case that we have to adopt the Jewish style of apocalyptic, modified by what happened to Jesus? Whatever may be the case, in the 1950s the biblical scholars like Vincent Taylor, C H Dodd, T W and W Manson, J Jeremias opened up the New Testament in a way which is not entirely dated. How many sermons on the parables of Jesus owe much to Jeremias? In a quite different area at Cambridge, I studied the Reformation from an historian's angle Butterfield's lectures on Renaissance and Reformation – alas, never published – were magisterial. This was the era of the revival of Reformation scholarship in Britain – with Methodists Philip S Watson, Rupert Davies and Gordon Rupp leading a renaissance of interest in Luther and Calvin. I read *The Catholicity of Protestantism* in 1951[13] and realized that Protestantism was a declaration of the gospel, not a negative protest and that the Reformers believed in the essence of the church's faith in creeds and sacraments. Who would have thought that the Church of Rome at the end of the century would affirm with the Lutheran the centrality of justification by faith?[14] For me, linked with the renewal of protestant belief was the work of Reinhold Niebuhr, especially *The Nature and Destiny of Man* and *Faith and History* which had many parallels with Butterfield, not least a realistic view of human sin – pride of power, pride of knowledge and pride of virtue.[15] His brother Richard Niebuhr's *Christ and Culture* enabled us to see how, in very varied contexts, the Christian church had to oppose contemporary culture, sometimes capitulating to it, or living in tension with it or seeking to transform it. Contemporary post-modernism still wrestles with the positions Niebuhr set out,[16] as Geoffrey Wainwright has repeatedly shown.[17] Emil Brunner comes into the picture. While by no means infallible, his *Christianity and Civilization*,[18] which I read in 1951, linked with the study of political thought from Plato to NATO.

When I was at Didsbury College, Bristol from 1953 to 1956, the Principal Dr Frederic Greeves taught Systematic and Pastoral Theology and the Philosophy of Religion. He would recommend notable books, also predicting what could happen in the churches during the next decade. He pointed to the value of Bishop Lesslie Newbigin in 1956, stressing not only the need for church union but also the need to note a renewal of beliefs in the Holy Spirit. I found that Newbigin remarkably reflected the contexts of a rapidly changing world almost up to the end of the century. He helped many of us to see what secularity and secularization meant in the difficult 'Death of God' decade, even if he changed his views later.[19] He always put the mission and the unity of the church together. I have never given up the belief in the need for union, even if it tragically failed in England, save for the creation of the United Reformed Church. He made clear, too, the absolute centrality of the Cross and Resurrection of Jesus. To some, he seemed too Calvinistic or Barthian, but Newbigin knew well enough the danger of too much stressing of the Kingdom and denying the value of the church especially the local church. As a historian I felt his later rather negative 'post-modernist' denigration of the Enlightenment not helpful. Butterfield and Gordon Rupp were more positive on the value, and indeed, the necessity of the Enlightenment after the churches had been tearing themselves to pieces in Europe and Great Britain in the seventeenth century.[20] Newbigin's last book at the end of the 1990s set out what has often been called 'the Wesley Quadrilateral' – scripture, tradition, reason and experience.[21]

Dr Greeves also put me on to Peter Taylor Forsyth,[22] without any doubt the greatest Free church theologian of the early years of the twentieth century who believed – unlike Newbigin – that federation was probably more realistic than union between the churches. His stance should have been taken more seriously in Methodist negotiations with the Church of England in the 1960s. Also, before he became well known, Greeves recommended reading the Anglican F W Dillistone,[23] whose books on the Atonement and symbolism I found penetrating. It has always surprised me that Anglican Evangelicals seem now, so often, to forget Dillistone, Max Warren, J V Taylor and J E Fison who reminded us that there was no Pentecost save on the yonder side of

Calvary.[24] Atonement doctrine became very much a Methodist concern with the great trilogy of Vincent Taylor, followed by Morna Hooker – with me a research student at the University of Bristol – Frances Young with Kenneth Grayston summing up New Testament emphases in *Dying We Live*.[25]

The Trinity comes into the picture too. Fred Greeves stressed its vital significance drawing upon Leonard Hodgson. For many years I have ended sermons on Trinity Sunday with Hodgson's sentence: 'The formula for the Christian life is seeking, finding and doing the Father's will in the Father's world with the companionship of the Son by the guidance and strength of the Spirit. That is the meaning of membership of the church.' Of course, Karl Barth begins his theology with 'God's three ways of being God'. There has been a recent paradox – a resurgence of the doctrine of the Trinity among theologians while in worship there has been what has been called 'the Jesus heresy' – the omission of the Father from prayers and ditties.[26]

Pointing to the future, Dr Greeves said: 'You must read Paul Tillich, Rudolf Bultmann and Dietrich Bonhoeffer. They will explode on the British scene soon'. So, he prepared us for the 'Honest to God' debate after 1963, enabling some of us to be constructively radical. I was Chaplain at Leeds University at the time of 'student revolt' but able to maintain a 'generous orthodoxy', to use Geoffrey Wainwright's phrase. We could avoid swimming at the shallow end to use Gordon Rupp's naughty gibe at the Renewal Group to which I belonged.[27] But Greeves was right to conjecture that there would be a renewal of Evangelicalism in line with Newbigin's thinking. The 'charismatic movement' began in the same year as Bishop J A T Robinson's *Honest to God*. Now Pentecostalism is second only to Roman Catholicism, with over half a billion adherents in the world.

When Kenneth Grayson, at that time, explored biblical theology, Fred Greeves taught us 'the real nature of the church'. How often have I quoted this:

'A community worshipping, thinking, working together, bound together by the fellowship of the Holy Spirit in a common love for God and for his Son, so that the stronger help the weaker and the older help the younger in the craft of Christian love – that is the true church and that (as many of us have reason to thank God), it sometimes begins to be. In such a church 'full salvation' is no mere pious phrase and holiness is no Utopian and somewhat frightening ideal. And when Christians learn to live with a love like Christ's other people more readily want to become Christians.'[28]

In the late 1960s 'Liberation Theology' was dominant in some quarters adding to Lesslie Newbigin's fears for the Ecumenical Movement's future after the World Council of Churches meeting at Uppsala[29] in 1968. Some of us were saved from secularism and uncritical support of 'freedom fighting' by the more recent German scholarship of Jürgen Moltmann and Wolfhart Pannenberg.[30] Moltmann's *Theology of Hope* and *The Crucified God* put the Christ of cross and resurrection at the heart of theology. Moltmann was more favourable, although not uncritical of 'Liberation Theology' then sweeping South America[31] with its Marxist economic bias. Pannenberg made clear that if the Resurrection of Christ was not an historical event, Christianity falls entirely.

'If Jesus had not been raised from the dead, it would be impossible to ascribe any saving meaning to his death, for that death could then only have meant the failure of his ministry and nothing else ... the historical claim that Jesus is risen, is a tenable one on objective examination, even in the context of our present experience of reality. The distance of the present world from the eschatological future of God does not exclude the real appearance of the future in our present world. And it is on this that the Christian faith has always insisted throughout history.'[32]

This fits in with Newbigin's view and could be seen as vintage Barth also.

Another decade after my eleven years teaching at the Queen's College (now the Queen's Foundation) Birmingham to Anglican, Methodist and United Reformed ordinands and deacons, the theologians who have rung bells with me have represented the dialectic in Anglicanism between 'Catholics', 'liberals' and 'evangelicals'. They are Rowan Williams,[33] now Archbishop of Canterbury, Keith Ward,[34] formerly Professor at Oxford and Alister McGrath,[35] also Professor at Oxford, now in London. Dr Williams' *Wound of Knowledge* and *Resurrection* were especially valuable, although everything he has written is worth reading, even if the media attacks him as an incomprehensible and irrelevant academic. The same goes for Keith Ward even if history is not his strong point. He has recently moved to a more radical stance, but seeks to 'defend a view of Christianity that is coherent and integrated well with modern scientific and historical knowledge'. But it is clear that;

'the foundation of the Christian faith is that in Jesus God personally encountered human beings. Jesus showed the nature of God's love as he healed, liberated, forgave and reconciled, as he mixed with social undesirables and was critical of religious status and hypocrisy. His disciples believed that he gave his life for them, that he was raised from death to live with God and that through him, God acted to deliver them from evil and unite them to God forever.'

With all the changes Ward outlines, he makes clear that with the first generation of disciples we believe still that 'God encounters humans in and through Jesus and unites them in divine life'. McGrath began as a biologist and an atheist, so is able to take on Richard Dawkins on his own field as well as to outline the history of Protestant Christianity, while avoiding the dangers of fundamentalism. In many ways Williams, Ward and McGrath, in very different styles, summarize the function of theology in recent years.

In preaching, the theologian's value is in enabling the preacher to present what is significant for today. I have found congregations very responsive to new thinking so long as it is in their context and not over their heads with jargon, a matter I learned quickly as a student when my great aunt Beatrice, a formidable former matron, told me I was over her head, like a lady in Boston who told the future Archbishop of Canterbury, Michael Ramsey, when he was a curate there, teaching at Lincoln Theological College. My first appointments were in rural Essex, working-class Burton upon Trent and the suburban and inner-belt Sheffield at the time of the 'Honest to God' controversies. In those three appointments we still had a considerable number of young people linked with the churches, some of whom became university students needing a faith which would withstand the attacks of those who thought religion irrelevant and contrary to science. In Methodism we were fortunate to have Charles Coulson and Russell Hindmarsh[36] who, at that time, showed that scientists could be Christian and not just concerned with 'the God of the gaps', a phrase associated with Coulson. John Habgood,[37] later to be Principal of Queens College, Bishop of Durham and Archbishop of York makes Richard Dawkins' irrational attacks on faiths of all kinds look rather ridiculous. John Polkinghorne[38] has taken up that positive stance from the angle of a scientist and theologian.

The future? Methodism needs to renew its theological heart as does the Anglican Communion which has sadly become obsessed with controversies over homosexuality. Can one agree that Scripture is still central, but illuminated by tradition and history – the living faith of the dead not the dead faith of the living – confirmed by the disciplined use of reason and verified in personal experience? Each generation has to find fresh expressions of being the church, while realizing that such enterprises have occurred in many periods of Christian History.

References

1. William Temple, *Christian Faith and Life*, SCM Press 1950; *Readings in St John's Gospel*, Macmillan 1952, pp 68ff
2. Richard Harries, *C S Lewis, the Man and his God*, Collins 1987
3. C S Lewis, *Broadcast Talks*, Bles 1946, p 50
4. H R Mackintosh, *Types of Modern Theology*, Nisbet 1937
5. H Butterfield, *Christianity and History*, Bell 1949; *Writings on Christianity and History*, Ed C T McIntire, OUP 1979, pp 259-60, cf C T McIntire, *Herbert Butterfield – Historian as Dissenter*, Yale 2004
6. David F Ford (Ed), *The Modern Theologians. An Introduction to Christian Theology in the Twentieth Century*, Volume 2 Blackwell 1989, pp 22-8 (S W Sykes)
7. H Maldwyn Hughes, *Christian Foundations – An Introduction to Christian Doctrine*, Epworth 1948
8. R Newton Flew, *Jesus and His Church*, Epworth 1938; cf A M Ramsey, *The Gospel and the Catholic Church*, Longmans, Green 1936

9. Donald Baillie, *God was in Christ*, Faber and Faber 1948, pp 114ff; cf H H Farmer, *The World and God*, Nisbet 1935, p 25

10. O Cullman, *Christ and Time*, ET SCM Press 1951

11. C H Dodd, *The Coming of Christ*, CUP 1951, pp 26ff

12. N T Wright, *Jesus and the Victory of God*, SPCK 1996

13. R N Flew and R E Davies (Eds), *The Catholicity of Protestantism*, Lutterworth Press 1950

14. *The Joint Declaration on the Doctrine of Justification Between the Roman Catholic Church and the Lutheran World Federation*, 31 October 1999, Origins 28/8, 16 July 1998, pp 120-27; G Wainwright, *A Methodist Point of View on the Agreement*, One in Christ, 37 (2003), pp 3-31

15. H R Niebuhr, *The Nature and Destiny of Man – A Christian Interpretation*, Volume 1, Nisbet 1941, p 200, Volume 2, Nisbet 1943; *Faith and History. A Comparison of Christian and Modern Views of History*, Nisbet 1949; cf Richard Harries, *Reinhold Niebuhr and the Issues of Our Time,* Mowbray 1986

16. H Richard Niebuhr, *Christ and Culture*, Faber and Faber 1952

17. G Wainwright, *Doxology – the Praise of God in Worship, Doctrine and Life*, Epworth 1960, pp 384-6, 389, 394; *Embracing Purpose - Essays on God, the World and the Church*, Epworth 2007, p 25

18. Emil Brunner, *Christianity and Civilization* - Part One, *Foundations*, Nisbet 1948, Part Two, *Specific Problems*, Nisbet 1948

19. Note especially: L Newbigin, *The Reunion of the Church, a Defence of the South India Scheme*, SCM Press 1948, Revised 1960; *The Household of God*, SCM Press 1953; *A Faith for This One World*, SCM Press 1961; *Honest Religion for Secular Man*, SCM Press 1966, *The Finality of Christ*, SCM Press 1989; *The Open Secret*, SPCK 1978; *Foolishness to the Greeks*, SPCK 1986; *The Gospel in a Pluralist Society*, SPCK 1987; *Proper Confidence, Faith, Doubt and Certainty in Christian Discipleship*, SPCK 1995; For a fine theological biography: G Wainwright, *Lesslie Newbigin, a Theological Life*, OUP 2000

20. Gordon Rupp, *Religion in England 1688-1791*, OUP 1986, esp. pp 207ff; H Butterfield, *The Origins of Modern Science 1300-1800*, Bell 1949; G Himmelfarb, *The Road to Modernity*, Vintage 2008

21. L Newbigin, *Truth, Authority and Modernity*, Gracewing 1996, pp 25-63

22. N B Trevor Hart (Ed), *Justice, the True and Only Mercy. Essays on the Life and Theology of Peter Taylor Forsyth*, T and T Clark 1995

23. F W Dillistone, *The Christian Understanding of Atonement*, Nisbet 1968; *Christianity and Symbolism*, SCM Press 1955; *The Power of Symbols*, SCM Press 1986

24. John V Taylor, *The Go-Between God*, SCM Press 1975; *The Christlike God*, SCM Press 1992; J E Fison, *The Blessing of the Holy Spirit*, Longmans Green, 1950; *Fire Upon the Earth*, Edinburgh House Press, 1958, pp 7, 83

25. Vincent Taylor, *Jesus and His Sacrifice*, Macmillan 1937; *The Atonement in New Testament Teaching*, Epworth 1940; *Forgiveness and Reconciliation*, Macmillan 1956; Morna Hooker, *Not Ashamed of*

the Gospel, Paternoster 1994; Frances Young, *Sacrifice and the Death of Christ*, SPCK 1975; Kenneth Grayston, *Dying We Live – A New Enquiry into the Death of Christ in the New Testament*, DLT 1990

26. Leonard Hodgson, *The Doctrine of the Trinity in Contemporary Methodism*, MSF 2004; cf G Wainwright, *Embracing Purpose*, Epworth Press 2007; Susan J White, *Whatever Happened to the Father?* MSF, 2002; Norman Wallwork, *The Forgotten Trinity in Contemporary Methodism*, MSF, 2004

27. Gordon Rupp, *The Old Reformation and the New*, Epworth 1967, Ch 5, Methodist Recorder, June 1968, July 1968

28. Frederic Greeves, *Theology and the Cure of Souls. An Introduction to Pastoral Theology*, Epworth 1960, pp 78-9

29. J M Turner, *The Theology of Liberation – An Appraisal and a Critique*, Worship and Preaching, April 1977, Volume 7 NO 2, pp 4-9

30. Jürgen Moltmann, *Theology of Hope*, ET Epworth 1967; *Crucified God*, SCM Press 1974; *Theology and Joy*, SCM Press 1973; *The Future of Creation*, SCM Press 1979; Wolfhart Pannenberg, *Jesus – God and Man*, SCM Press 1968; *The Apostles Creed in the Light of Today's Questions*, SCM Press 1972; *Christian Spirituality and Sacramental Community*, DLT 1984; *Christianity in a Secularized World*, SCM Press 1988

31. Gustavo Gutierrez, A *Theology of Liberation. History, Politics and Salvation*, SCM Press 1974

32. Wolfhart Pannenberg, *The Apostles' Creed*, op cit pp 97, 114-15

33. Rowan Williams, *The Wound of Knowledge*, DLT 1979; *Resurrection, Interpreting the Easter Gospel*, DLT 1982; *On Christian Theology*, Blackwell 2002; *Christ on Trial*, Harper 2002; *Why Study the Past?* DLT 2005; *Tokens of Trust*, Canterbury Press 2007

34. Keith Ward, *Divine Action*, Collins 1990; *A Vision to Pursue*, SCM Press 1991; *Religion and Creation*, OUP 1996; *God, Faith and the New Millennium*, One World 1998; *Religion and Community*, OUP 2002; *Christianity, A Short Introduction*, One World 2000; *Pascal's Fire*, One World 2006; *Is Religion Dangerous?* Lion 2006; *Rethinking Christianity*, One World 2007, p vii, 1

35. A McGrath, *Historical Theology, An Introduction to the History of Christian Thought*, Blackwell 1998; *Dawkins' God – Genes, Memes and the Meaning of Life*, Blackwell 2005, *Christianity's Dangerous Idea – the Protestant Revolution*, SPCK 2007; *The Christian Vision of God*, SPCK, 2008

36. C A Coulson, *Science and Christian Belief*, OUP 1955; *Science, Technology and Christian Belief*, Epworth 1960; W Russell Hindmarsh, *Science and Faith*, Epworth 1968; Philip Luscombe, *Groundwork of Science and Religion*, Epworth 2002

37. John Habgood, *Religion and Science*, Mills and Boon 1964; *A Working Faith*, DLT 1980; *Church and Nation in a Secular Age*, DLT 1983; *Confessions of a Conservative Liberal*, SPCK 1988; *Faith and Uncertainty*, DLT 1997; *Being a Person, Where Faith and Science Meet*,

Hodder and Stoughton 1998; *Varieties of Unbelief*, DLT 2000; *The Gospel of Nature*, DLT 2002

38. John Polkinghorne, *One World, the Interaction of Science and Theology*, SPCK 1986; *Reason and Reality, the Relationship Between Science and Theology*, SPCK 1991; *The Gospel of Hope and the End of the World*, SPCK 2002; *Exploring Reality*, SPCK, 2005.

Previous Publication of Articles and Chapters

Chapter 1   *Salvation and Church History*
             Insights into the Reformation
             In Donald English (Ed), *Windows on Salvation*, DLT 1994, pp
             56-73

Chapter 2   *John Neville Figgis (1866-1919)*
             Historian and Prophet
             Paper given at the Methodist Sacramental Fellowship
             Conference 1989

Chapter 3   *Theologian of Righteousness – Peter Taylor Forsyth (1848-1921)*
             Methodist Sacramental Fellowship Bulletin, No 119, 1989

Chapter 4   *John Wesley's Pragmatic Theology*
             In P R Meadows (Ed), *Windows on Wesley*
             Applied Theology Press, Westminster College, Oxford, 1997, pp
             1-18

Chapter 5   *The Last of the Wesleyans – Henry Bett (1876-1953)*
             Wesley Historical Society West Midlands Branch Silver Jubilee
             1990

Chapter 6   *The Christian and the Study of History – Sir Herbert Butterfield*
             (1900-1979)
             Proceedings of the Wesley Historical Society. Volume XLVI, No
             1, February 1987

Chapter 7   *Gordon Rupp (1910-1986) as Historian*
             Epworth Review, Volume 18, No 1, January 1991

Chapter 8   *British Methodist Historical Scholarship 1893-1993*
             Wesley Historical Society Centenary, Epworth Review, Volume
             20, No 3, September 1993

Chapter 9   *Wesley and Early Methodism Studies 1993-2003*
             Epworth Review, Volume 30, No 4, October 2003

Chapter 10   *The Long Eighteenth Century*
             Proceedings of the Wesley Historical Society, Volume LI, Part I,
             February 1997

Chapter 11   *Robert Featherstone Wearmouth 1882-1963.   Methodist*
             Historian,

Proceedings of the Wesley Historical Society. Volume XLIII, No 5, September 1982

Permission has been granted by all for the republishing for which I am most grateful.